"A WHITE HERON"

AND THE QUESTION OF

MINOR LITERATURE

LOUIS A. RENZA

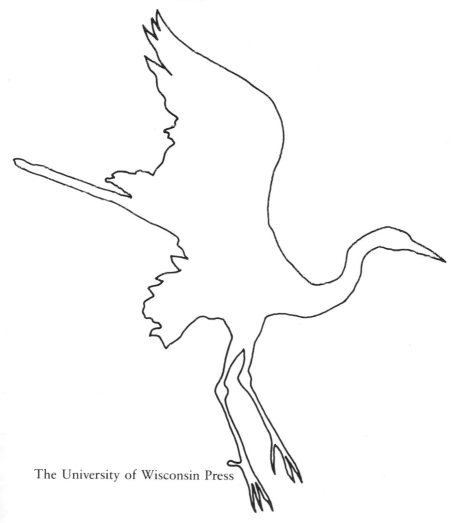

The University of Wisconsin Press

Published 1984

The University of Wisconsin Press
114 North Murray Street
Madison, Wisconsin 53715

The University of Wisconsin Press, Ltd.
1 Gower Street
London WC1E 6HA, England

First printing

Printed in the United States of America

For LC CIP information see the colophon

ISBN 0-299-09960-1

To Crista Jean

The question that he frames in all but words

Is what to make of a diminished thing.

—Robert Frost

CONTENTS

ACKNOWLEDGMENTS

Many people made this work literally possible: my parents, of course; Noel Perrin who innocently asked me to take his place at a conference where I first discussed Jewett's story; certain members of the Dartmouth English Department—I would like to cite Henry Terrie, James Heffernan, Alan Gaylord, and not least, Blanche Gelfant —whose interest in my project gave me the incentive to continue it.

Numerous scholars, not all of whom I can here enumerate, read and provided valuable recommendations for revising this work's much longer earlier drafts. Among these scholars, special thanks for their patience, dedication, and ideas must go to Paul Sherwin, Mary Kelley, John Brenkman, and Michael Denning. Leslie Brisman generously gave much appreciated advice for improving certain parts of the final manuscript after it had been submitted for publication at The University of Wisconsin Press. *Very* special thanks are due to my two colleagues at Dartmouth, James M. Cox and Donald Pease, who in their different ways not only gave me intellectually acute advice about various critical aspects of my subject, but showed continual faith in my project's value and in my ability to demonstrate it. And I am also indebted to Frank Lentricchia and Allen Fitchen for enthusiastically providing my work with a place in The Wisconsin Project on American Writers.

I could cite many other people, of course, who had an oblique but no less important influence on my writing this work. In this vein, let me mention here Marga Rahmann for her personal, practical, and intellectual encouragement; Bernard Bergen for his relevant theoretical detours; and others like Star Johnson, Anthony Rocchio, Robert C. S. Downs, Bruce Lewis, and especially John William Price, whose friendship through the years has variously constituted the milieu of my critical imagination.

But in the end, only my wife, Crista Rahmann Renza, has made possible the vision and performance of this work. Only she can read what Jewett called those unwritable things which this critical work holds in its heart.

A WHITE HERON

I   The woods were already filled with shadows one June evening, just before eight o'clock, though a bright sunset still glimmered
faintly among the trunks of the trees. A little girl was driving home
her cow, a plodding, dilatory, provoking creature in her behavior, but
a valued companion for all that. They were going away from the western light, and striking deep into the dark woods, but their feet were
familiar with the path, and it was no matter whether their eyes could
see it or not.

There was hardly a night the summer through when the old cow
could be found waiting at the pasture bars; on the contrary, it was
her greatest pleasure to hide herself away among the high huckleberry
bushes, and though she wore a loud bell she had made the discovery
that if one stood perfectly still it would not ring. So Sylvia had to
hunt for her until she found her, and call Co'! Co'! with never an an-
swering Moo, until her childish patience was quite spent. If the creature had not given good milk and plenty of it, the case would have
seemed very different to her owners. Besides, Sylvia had all the time
there was, and very little use to make of it. Sometimes in pleasant
weather it was a consolation to look upon the cow's pranks as an
intelligent attempt to play hide and seek, and as the child had no playmates she lent herself to this amusement with a good deal of zest.
Though this chase had been so long that the wary animal herself had
given an unusual signal of her whereabouts, Sylvia had only laughed
when she came upon Mistress Moolly at the swamp-side, and urged

her affectionately homeward with a twig of birch leaves. The old cow was not inclined to wander farther, she even turned in the right direction for once as they left the pasture, and stepped along the road at a good pace. She was quite ready to be milked now, and seldom stopped to browse. Sylvia wondered what her grandmother would say because they were so late. It was a great while since she had left home at half past five o'clock, but everybody knew the difficulty of making this errand a short one. Mrs. Tilley had chased the hornéd torment too many summer evenings herself to blame any one else for lingering, and was only thankful as she waited that she had Sylvia, nowadays, to give such valuable assistance. The good woman suspected that Sylvia loitered occasionally on her own account; there never was such a child for straying about out-of-doors since the world was made! Everybody said that it was a good change for a little maid who had tried to grow for eight years in a crowded manufacturing town, but, as for Sylvia herself, it seemed as if she never had been alive at all before she came to live at the farm. She thought often with wistful compassion of a wretched dry geranium that belonged to a town neighbor.

"'Afraid of folks,'" old Mrs. Tilley said to herself, with a smile, after she had made the unlikely choice of Sylvia from her daughter's houseful of children, and was returning to the farm. "'Afraid of folks,' they said! I guess she won't be troubled no great with 'em up to the old place!" When they reached the door of the lonely house and stopped to unlock it, and the cat came to purr loudly, and rub against them, a deserted pussy, indeed, but fat with young robins, Sylvia whispered that this was a beautiful place to live in, and she never should wish to go home.

The companions followed the shady woodroad, the cow taking slow steps, and the child very fast ones. The cow stopped long at the brook to drink, as if the pasture were not half a swamp, and Sylvia stood still and waited, letting her bare feet cool themselves in the shoal water, while the great twilight moths struck softly against her. She waded on through the brook as the cow moved away, and listened to the thrushes with a heart that beat fast with pleasure. There was a stirring in the great boughs overhead. They were full of little birds and beasts that seemed to be wide-awake, and going about their world, or else saying good-night to each other in sleepy twitters. Sylvia herself felt sleepy as she walked along. However, it was not much farther to the house, and the air was soft and sweet. She was not often in the woods so late as this, and it made her feel as if she were a part of the gray shadows and the moving leaves. She was just thinking how long it seemed since she first came to the farm a year ago, and wondering if everything went on in the noisy town just the same as when she was there; the thought of the great red-faced boy who used to chase and frighten her made her hurry along the path to escape from the shadow of the trees.

Suddenly this little woods-girl is horror-stricken to hear a clear whistle not very far away. Not a bird's whistle, which would have a sort of friendliness, but a boy's whistle, determined, and somewhat aggressive. Sylvia left the cow to whatever sad fate might await her, and stepped discreetly aside into the bushes, but she was just too late. The enemy had discovered her, and called out in a very cheerful and persuasive tone, "Halloa, little girl, how far is it to the road?" and trembling Sylvia answered almost inaudibly, "A good ways."

She did not dare to look boldly at the tall young man, who carried a gun over his shoulder, but she came out of her bush and again followed the cow, while he walked alongside.

"I have been hunting for some birds," the stranger said kindly, "and I have lost my way, and need a friend very much. Don't be afraid," he added gallantly. "Speak up and tell me what your name is, and whether you think I can spend the night at your house, and go out gunning early in the morning."

Sylvia was more alarmed than before. Would not her grandmother consider her much to blame? But who could have foreseen such an accident as this? It did not appear to be her fault, and she hung her head as if the stem of it were broken, but managed to answer "Sylvy," with much effort when her companion again asked her name.

Mrs. Tilley was standing in the doorway when the trio came into view. The cow gave a loud moo by way of explanation.

"Yes, you'd better speak up for yourself, you old trial! Where'd she tucked herself away this time, Sylvy?" Sylvia kept an awed silence; she knew by instinct that her grandmother did not comprehend the gravity of the situation. She must be mistaking the stranger for one of the farmer-lads of the region.

The young man stood his gun beside the door, and dropped a heavy game-bag beside it; then he bade Mrs. Tilley good-evening, and repeated his wayfarer's story, and asked if he could have a night's lodging.

"Put me anywhere you like," he said. "I must be off early in the morning, before day; but I am very hungry, indeed. You can give me some milk at any rate, that's plain."

"Dear sakes, yes," responded the hostess, whose long slumbering hospitality seemed to be easily awakened. "You might fare better if you went out on the main road a mile or so, but you're welcome to what we've got. I'll milk right off, and you make yourself at home. You can sleep on husks or feathers," she proffered graciously. "I raised them all myself. There's good pasturing for geese just below here towards the ma'sh. Now step round and set a plate for the gentleman, Sylvy!" And Sylvia promptly stepped. She was glad to have something to do, and she was hungry herself.

It was a surprise to find so clean and comfortable a little dwelling in this New England wilderness. The young man had known the horrors of its most primitive housekeeping, and the dreary squalor of that level of society which does not rebel at the companionship of hens. This was the best thrift of an old-fashioned farmstead, though on such a small scale that it seemed like a hermitage. He listened eagerly to the old woman's quaint talk, he watched Sylvia's pale face and shining gray eyes with ever growing enthusiasm, and insisted that this was the best supper he had eaten for a month; then, afterward, the new-made friends sat down in the doorway together while the moon came up.

Soon it would be berry-time, and Sylvia was a great help at picking. The cow was a good milker, though a plaguy thing to keep track of, the hostess gossiped frankly, adding presently that she had buried four children, so that Sylvia's mother, and a son (who might be dead) in California, were all the children she had left. "Dan, my boy, was a great hand to go gunning," she explained sadly. "I never wanted for pa'tridges or gray squer'ls while he was to home. He's been a great wand'rer, I expect, and he's no hand to write letters. There, I don't blame him, I'd ha' seen the world myself if it had been so I could.

"Sylvia takes after him," the grandmother continued affectionately, after a minute's pause. "There ain't a foot o'ground she don't know her way over, and the wild creatur's counts her one o' themselves. Squer'ls she'll tame to come an' feed right out o' her hands, and all sorts o' birds. Last winter she got the jay-birds to bangeing here, and I believe she'd 'a' scanted herself of her own meals to have plenty to throw out amongst 'em, if I had n't kep' watch. Anything but crows, I tell her, I'm willin' to help support,—though Dan he went an' tamed one o' them that did seem to have reason same as folks. It was round here a good spell after he went away. Dan an' his father they did n't hitch,—but he never held up his head ag'in after Dan had dared him an' gone off."

The guest did not notice this hint of family sorrows in his eager interest in something else.

"So Sylvy knows all about birds, does she?" he exclaimed, as he looked round at the little girl who sat, very demure but increasingly sleepy, in the moonlight. "I am making a collection of birds myself. I have been at it ever since I was a boy." (Mrs. Tilley smiled.) "There are two or three very rare ones I have been hunting for these five years. I mean to get them on my own ground if they can be found."

"Do you cage 'em up?" asked Mrs. Tilley doubtfully, in response to this enthusiastic announcement.

"Oh, no, they're stuffed and preserved, dozens and dozens of them," said the ornithologist, "and I have shot or snared every one myself. I caught a glimpse of a white heron three miles from here on Saturday, and I have followed it in this direction. They have never been found in this district at all. The little white heron, it is," and he turned again to look at Sylvia with the hope of discovering that the rare bird was one of her acquaintances.

But Sylvia was watching a hop-toad in the narrow footpath.

"You would know the heron if you saw it," the stranger continued eagerly. "A queer tall white bird with soft feathers and long thin legs. And it would have a nest perhaps in the top of a high tree, made of sticks, something like a hawk's nest."

Sylvia's heart gave a wild beat; she knew that strange white bird, and had once stolen softly near where it stood in some bright green swamp grass, away over at the other side of the woods. There was an open place where the sunshine always seemed strangely yellow and hot, where tall, nodding rushes grew, and her grandmother had warned her that she might sink in the soft black mud underneath and never be heard of more. Not far beyond were the salt marshes and beyond those was the sea, the sea which Sylvia wondered and dreamed about, but never had looked upon, though its great voice could often be heard above the noise of the woods on stormy nights.

"I can't think of anything I should like so much as to find that heron's nest," the handsome stranger was saying. "I would give ten dollars to anybody who could show it to me," he added desperately, "and I mean to spend my whole vacation hunting for it if need be. Perhaps it was only migrating, or had been chased out of its own region by some bird of prey."

Mrs. Tilley gave amazed attention to all this, but Sylvia still watched the toad, not divining, as she might have done at some calmer time, that the creature wished to get to its hole under the doorstep, and was much hindered by the unusual spectators at that hour of the evening. No amount of thought, that night, could decide how many wished-for treasures the ten dollars, so lightly spoken of, would buy.

The next day the young sportsman hovered about the woods, and Sylvia kept him company, having lost her first fear of the friendly lad, who proved to be most kind and sympathetic. He told her many things about the birds and what they knew and where they lived and what they did with themselves. And he gave her a jack-knife, which she thought as great a treasure as if she were a desert-islander. All day long he did not once make her troubled or afraid except when he brought down some unsuspecting singing creature from its bough. Sylvia would have liked him vastly better without his gun; she could not understand why he killed the very birds he seemed to like so much. But as the day waned, Sylvia still watched the young man with loving admiration. She had never seen anybody so charming and delightful; the woman's heart, asleep in the child, was vaguely thrilled by a dream of love. Some premonition of that great power stirred and swayed these young foresters who traversed the solemn woodlands with soft-footed silent care. They stopped to listen to a bird's song; they pressed forward again eagerly, parting the branches,—speaking to each other rarely and in whispers; the young man going first and Sylvia following, fascinated, a few steps behind, with her gray eyes dark with excitement.

She grieved because the longed-for white heron was elusive, but she did not lead the guest, she only followed, and there was no such thing as speaking first. The sound of her own unquestioned voice would have terrified her,— it was hard enough to answer yes or no when there was need of that. At last evening began to fall, and they drove the cow home together, and Sylvia smiled with pleasure when they came to the place where she heard the whistle and was afraid only the night before.

II   Half a mile from home, at the farther edge of the woods, where the land was highest, a great pine-tree stood, the last of its generation. Whether it was left for a boundary mark, or for what reason, no one could say; the woodchoppers who had felled its mates were dead and gone long ago, and a whole forest of sturdy trees, pines and oaks and maples, had grown again. But the stately head of this old pine towered above them all and made a landmark for sea and shore miles and miles away. Sylvia knew it well. She had always believed that whoever climbed to the top of it could see the ocean; and the little girl had often laid her hand on the great rough trunk and looked up wistfully at those dark boughs that the wind always stirred, no matter how hot and still the air might be below. Now she thought of the tree with a new excitement, for why, if one climbed it at break of day, could not one see all the world, and easily discover whence the white heron flew, and mark the place, and find the hidden nest?

What a spirit of adventure, what wild ambition! What fancied triumph and delight and glory for the later morning when she could make known the secret! It was almost too real and too great for the childish heart to bear.

All night the door of the little house stood open, and the whippoorwills came and sang upon the very step. The young sportsman and his old hostess were sound asleep, but Sylvia's great design kept her broad awake and watching. She forgot to think of sleep. The short summer night seemed as long as the winter darkness, and at last when the whippoorwills ceased, and she was afraid the morning would after all come too soon, she stole out of the house and followed the pasture path through the woods, hastening toward the open ground beyond, listening with a sense of comfort and companionship to the drowsy twitter of a half-awakened bird, whose perch she had jarred in passing. Alas, if the great wave of human interest which flooded for the first time this dull little life should sweep away the satisfactions of an existence heart to heart with nature and the dumb life of the forest!

There was the huge tree asleep yet in the paling moonlight, and small and hopeful Sylvia began with utmost bravery to mount to the top of it, with tingling, eager blood coursing the channels of her whole frame, with her bare feet and fingers, that pinched and held like bird's claws to the monstrous ladder reaching up, up, almost to the sky itself. First she must mount the white oak tree that grew alongside, where she was almost lost among the dark branches and the green leaves heavy and wet with dew; a bird fluttered off its nest, and a red squirrel ran to and fro and scolded pettishly at the harmless housebreaker. Sylvia felt her way easily. She had often climbed there, and knew that higher still one of the oak's upper branches chafed against the pine trunk, just where its lower boughs were set close together. There, when she made the dangerous pass from one tree to the other, the great enterprise would really begin.

She crept out along the swaying oak limb at last, and took the daring step across into the old pine-tree. The way was harder than she thought; she must reach far and hold fast, the sharp dry twigs caught and held her and scratched her like angry talons, the pitch made her thin little fingers clumsy and stiff as she went round and round the tree's great stem, higher and higher upward. The sparrows and robins in the woods below were beginning to wake and twitter to the dawn, yet it seemed much lighter there aloft in the pine-tree, and the child knew that she must hurry if her project were to be of any use.

The tree seemed to lengthen itself out as she went up, and to reach farther and farther upward. It was like a great main-mast to the voyaging earth; it must truly have been amazed that morning through all its ponderous frame as it felt this determined spark of human spirit creeping and climbing from higher branch to branch. Who knows how steadily the least twigs held themselves to advantage this light, weak creature on her way! The old pine must have loved his new dependent. More than all the hawks, and bats, and moths, and even the sweet-voiced thrushes, was the brave, beating heart of the solitary gray-eyed child. And the tree stood still and held away the winds that June morning while the dawn grew bright in the east.

Sylvia's face was like a pale star, if one had seen it from the ground, when the last thorny bough was past, and she stood trembling and tired but wholly triumphant, high in the tree-top. Yes, there was the sea with the dawning sun making a golden dazzle over it, and toward that glorious east flew two hawks with slow-moving pinions. How low they looked in the air from that height when before one had only seen them far up, and dark against the blue sky. Their gray feathers were as soft as moths; they seemed only a little way from the tree, and Sylvia felt as if she too could go flying away among the clouds. Westward, the woodlands and farms reached miles and miles into the distance; here and there were church steeples, and white villages; truly it was a vast and awesome world.

The birds sang louder and louder. At last the sun came up bewilderingly bright. Sylvia could see the white sails of ships out at sea, and the clouds that were purple and rose-colored and yellow at first began to fade away. Where was the white heron's nest in the sea of green branches, and was this wonderful sight and pageant of the world the only reward for having climbed to such a giddy height? Now look down again, Sylvia, where the green marsh is set among the shining birches and dark hemlocks; there where you saw the white heron once you will see him again; look, look! a white spot of him like a single floating feather comes up from the dead hemlock and grows larger, and rises, and comes close at last, and goes by the landmark pine with steady sweep of wing and outstretched slender neck and crested head. And wait! wait! do not move a foot or a finger, little girl, do not send an arrow of light and consciousness from your two eager eyes, for the heron has perched on a pine bough not far beyond yours, and cries back to his mate on the nest, and plumes his feathers for the new day!

The child gives a long sigh a minute later when a company of shouting cat-birds comes also to the tree, and vexed by their fluttering and lawlessness the solemn heron goes away. She knows his secret now, the wild, light, slender bird that floats and wavers, and goes back like an arrow presently to his home in the green world beneath. Then Sylvia, well satisfied, makes her perilous way down again, not daring to look far below the branch she stands on, ready to cry sometimes because her fingers ache and her lamed feet slip. Wondering over and over again what the stranger would say to her, and what he would think when she told him how to find his way straight to the heron's nest.

"Sylvy, Sylvy!" called the busy old grandmother again and again, but nobody answered, and the small husk bed was empty, and Sylvia had disappeared.

The guest waked from a dream, and remembering his day's pleasure hurried to dress himself that it might sooner begin. He was sure from the way the shy little girl looked once or twice yesterday that she had at least seen the white heron, and now she must really be persuaded to tell. Here she comes now, paler than ever, and her worn old frock is torn and tattered, and smeared with pine pitch. The grandmother and the sportsman stand in the door together and question her, and the splendid moment has come to speak of the dead hemlock-tree by the green marsh.

But Sylvia does not speak after all, though the old grandmother fretfully rebukes her, and the young man's kind appealing eyes are looking straight in her own. He can make them rich with money; he has promised it, and they are poor now. He is so well worth making happy, and he waits to hear the story she can tell.

[No, she must keep silence! What is it that suddenly forbids her and makes her dumb? Has she been nine years growing, and now, when the great world for the first time puts out a hand to her, must she thrust it aside for a bird's sake? The murmur of the pine's green branches is in her ears, she remembers how the white heron came flying through the golden air and how they watched the sea and the morning together, and Sylvia cannot speak; she cannot tell the heron's secret and give its life away.]

Dear loyalty, that suffered a sharp pang as the guest went away disappointed later in the day, that could have served and followed him and loved him as a dog loves! Many a night Sylvia heard the echo of his whistle haunting the pasture path as she came home with the loitering cow. She forgot even her sorrow at the sharp report of his gun and the piteous sight of thrushes and sparrows dropping silent to the ground, their songs hushed and their pretty feathers stained and wet with blood. Were the birds better friends than their hunter might have been,—who can tell? Whatever treasures were lost to her, woodlands and summer-time, remember! Bring your gifts and graces and tell your secrets to this lonely country child!

PROLOGUE

This work attempts to address the fact that, at least for writers of criticism or literature in nineteenth- and twentieth-century America, writing occurs precisely in terms of a specific canonical situation. Canon formations may be depicted as necessary instances of a culture's self-definition, particularly in the way they transmit "contrastive frameworks, exemplif[y] forms of imagination considered valuable in [that] culture, and provide[] figures of judgment for our actions."[1] On the other hand, canon-formations may come to seem arbitrary, self-imprisoning cultural standards or rigidified, politically oppressive criteria which belie the fact that it is contingent, transitory personal and/or social "circumstantial constraints" that determine the privilege accorded certain literary works at different times and for different reasons.[2] But in either case, one produces literature and criticism — even critiques of canonicity itself — in relation to certain operative canonical situations.

I encountered such a situation when I first began to write about "A White Heron." American literary history, after all, had consigned Sarah Orne Jewett's works to the ambiguous status of "minor literature." They seemed neither altogether neglected nor significant enough to merit sustained let alone sophisticated critical attention. In her own time, Jewett had not produced any unusually popular work like, for example, Susan Warner's *The Wide, Wide World*; nor had she produced a work with the contemporary ideological impact of Harriet Beecher Stowe's *Uncle Tom's Cabin*. And from our own contemporary critical perspectives, one could not easily argue that she had produced either esthetically innovative or ideologically provocative works—let alone "texts" in the most recent sense of poststructuralist criticism.

Largely on the basis of her most ambitious and successful literary narrative, *The Country of the Pointed Firs* (1896), even favorably disposed earlier critics like Charles Miner Thompson and F. O. Matthiessen had judged Jewett's works "delicate," organically styled efforts, but still limited in range by their New England and late-nineteenth-century "regionalist" topoi.[3] As for "A White Heron" (1886), critics seemed to damn it with faint praise. If it was not considered a contrived ideological "fantasy" (Warner Berthoff), it was considered at best a sentimental, "consoling parable" about a passing regionalist culture in American life (Jay Martin).[4] Even for a critic wishing to regard this "classic story" as a "complex and most moving expression" of the "rural-urban conflict," the story failed to resolve this conflict since its protagonist was "not quite believable" or seemed never "to understand entirely why she acts the way she does."[5]

The question that thus naturally arose was not only why write about a writer with tenuous canonical status, but why write about a work which, though possessing a certain appeal for me (and others, to judge from its frequent appearance in anthologies of American literature), seemed clearly limited in its esthetic density and ideological intimations. Such a question, of course, betrayed my own situation in the American academic institution of criticism, my need, namely, to write something important on something of literary importance. To be sure, there were ways to justify this critical enterprise. Given contemporary criticism's propensity to interrogate and revise works in terms of a "new literary history," the very devaluations of Jewett's works and especially "A White Heron" could easily provide a pretext for such *au current* revisionism.

Indeed, the story had already been treated in this light. One had only to apply a slight pressure to its apparently modest oppositional staging of the little country girl and the hunter to release "A White Heron" from its "regionalist" identity and significance into more "major" critical codifications. For example, one could view the story as a mini-*Bildungsroman*, that is, regard the girl's encounter with the hunter as an obstacle facilitating her "rite of initiation," her "journey to self-discovery and maturity," a quest symbolized and doubled by the heron as "the elusive meaning of existence."[6] And one could revise even this interpretation from a more contemporary feminist viewpoint. According to Annis Pratt, male quest heroes—Pratt employs James Joyce's Stephen Dedalus from *A Portrait of the Artist as a Young Man* as her main example—endure "initiatory adventures that consummate in the simultaneous discovery of woman and earth"; but in "A White Heron," the girl endures her adventure only to *re*-discover "the natural world, which [as a female, she] already possesses as an extension of herself." Unlike male quest heroes, in other words, Sylvia (and by extension, Jewett herself) does not seek and find "the elusive meaning of existence" through the heron *as symbol,* but instead gains the tautological vision that "a heron is a heron, valuable for its heronness, a vehicle only of its own contrast to canine servitude" to the hunter.[7] The story thus internalizes in order to reject the hero of masculine quest literature.

However, Pratt's provocative revision of Jewett's story also led me to recognize the latter's vulnerability to critical inflation, in this case—and in spite of her "tautological" insight into the story—Pratt's own critical symbolization of what was only a *short* work (as opposed to a canonical novel) concerning only a *little* girl protagonist and *simply* a heron. More was at stake than this particular critic's logocentric revision of "A White Heron" as a self-present expression of a self-present paradigm of feminine vision. The story's lyric simplicity clearly lent itself to such revisions; but this same simplicity also served to expose the critic's canonical predispositions as well as the transformative if viable maneuvers which justified them. It was as if "A White Heron" were a rebus that invited each reader to solve it in accordance with his own canonical bent, whether traditional or revisionary. Symptomatic of the story's "readable" appearance was the way more than one critic had miswritten its title (or the way one tends to refer to it in passing) by substituting the definite for the indefinite article, "*The*" for "*A* White Heron."[8]

Thus, to write about a minor writer and a minor or at least minimally complex narrative was not only to court the premature devaluation of my own critical project, but also to focus on the relation between "minor literature" in general and the tendency of variable critical codifications to reproduce it in terms of received *or* revised criteria of "major literature." In the case of Jewett's story, in fact, it was possible to argue that it was constructed in terms of potential "major" codifications of which it was aware and against which it seemed willing to define itself as a "minor" literary event. For example, when Mrs. Tilley tells the hunter in response to his request for lodging, "You might fare better if you went out on the main road a mile or so, but you're welcome to what we've got" (see above, p. xvi), her statement could be understood as the story's own self-defining canonical situation. At least if one were to define criticism as the explication of a possible thought in relation to a text, one could begin to discuss "A White Heron" as subliminally aware of its ability to entertain the *critical* hunter's quest for a "major" literary object (not to mention meaning) even as it was designating as its topos a theme lying some distance from mainstream literary events. Like its keynoting cow, "A White Heron" thus might seem to confront such a critical reader with certain provocative ambiguities, but in the end it "was not inclined to wander farther" (p. xiv, above).

Yet to consider Jewett's story as an exemplary crossroads of various potential critical responses, a text that led one to rethink the difference between major and minor literature, was again to produce a reading in accord with certain privileged codes of contemporary criticism as well as egregiously to violate the unselfconscious tenor of the story's narrative operations. In short, it was to make a major critical issue out of the actual and potential criticism of materials seemingly of minor importance in the academic and popular literary market-place. Was it possible to avoid this situation?

And so the question of how both my text and Jewett's were enmeshed in different but parallel canonical situations became the focal point of this present critical project. If, as I suspected, "A White Heron" exhibited a self-defining and even perverse process of *becoming* minor literature, its criticism would somehow have to avoid the pitfalls of any prevailing canonical criteria that would define the story's scene of writing. Only a critical perspective able to focus on minor literature *as* a question, thus momentarily suspending canonical judgments, could give an account of "A White Heron" in accord with this view of it as in the process of striving to elude such criteria in order to retain its "dull little life" (p. xx, above) or minor literary value. Such a criticism could invoke the service of other critical perspectives that allowed for the reconsideration of "minor literature" as a signifier of literary value within a changeable canon. But it would also have to remain alert to their sometimes explicit, sometimes subtle tendencies to impose paradigms reflecting literary and/or ideological ambitions of their own.

"A WHITE HERON"

AND THE QUESTION OF

MINOR LITERATURE

1   An undeconstructed critical category, "minor literature" serves
as a conservative justification for an established if variable concept
of "major literature." What gets termed minor literature may alter,
of course, like a "stock market in constant fluctuation" from period
to period, as T. S. Eliot argued in his famous essay "What is Minor
Poetry?"[1] But the category's structural support of a canonical major
literature remains invariable. True, one can try to open up the canon
and, if only for reasons of academic pedagogy, reinstate "neglected
literature" to a position within the bounds of "highbrow" canonicity.
But in trying to teach neglected literary works, whatever their writers' canonical reputations and the historical or ideological causes of
their reduction to, say, the critical limbo of representative anthologies or something like the *Twayne Series of United States Authors,*
one still considers such works in the context of "great books" and,
no less alert to the possibility of overpraising "minor works by minor
authors," essentially preserves rather than challenges the accepted
concept of canonical thinking.[2]
    The same issue arises if one adopts Leslie Fiedler's egalitarian
method of escaping "elitist" canonical ideas by making "*ekstasis* rather
than instruction and delight our chief evaluative criterion." Fiedler
requests us to employ "an eclectic, amateur, neo-Romantic" perspective on literary works "that will enable us to read what was once popular literature not as popular but as literature, even as it enables us

to read what was once High Literature not as high but as literature."[3] But Fiedler's "ecstatic" criterion substitutes an immediately accessible marketplace concept of canon formation for the "impersonal" academic criteria that he too easily seeks to deny by mere "populist" counterideological fiat. This criterion addresses a restricted American ideological situation comprising a democratic mythos and commercial ethos; it also restrictively privileges a "fundamentally antinomian" literature that resists "respectable pieties of any kind" and "aspires to return to the condition of pure myth."[4] Ironically, it would make minor the already academically minor aspect of a story like "A White Heron." Far from resisting "pieties," Jewett's story appears to embrace them, and in both a populist *and* traditional sense defines itself as a benign or less ambitious version of major American literature. What Denis Donoghue notes about certain contemporary American poems equally applies to the operations of Jewett's story: they seem to make "a pact with their readers to observe the continuity and decency of discourse"; and unlike the manifest but failed literary ambitions of some literary works (e.g., the poetry of Poe or the novels of Thomas Wolfe), they remain "content with a quiet life and exquisite perfections."[5]

But Fiedler's thesis at least points to the American ideological desire to demystify hierarchical notions of literary canonicity and to the record of institutional criticism in failing to conceive of even an honorifically understood minor literature apart from a privileged notion of major literature. The reason for this failure may lie in such criticism's ambivalently "motivated"relation to its subject. On the one hand, because it "no longer [seems] troubled by the question of form,"[6] minor literature provides the critic with an epistemological context that helps him understand and recognize the formal innovations defining major literary works, and by extension, the formal parameters of knowledge itself. Major and minor literary works actively constitute our cultural tradition; they comprise, in the words of the young and self-consciously canonical Eliot, "an ideal order . . . [constantly] modified by the introduction of the new (the *really* new) work of art."[7] On the other hand, because such criticism tends to consider minor literature as only relatively or quantitatively different from major literature, one has to ask whether it does not use an in fact *qualitatively* different minor literature as a rhetorical strategy to assuage its own sense of literary secondariness. In arguing for the epistemological as well as cultural value of minor literature, formalist criticism seems to enlist such writing as a compliant ally, if not a self-evident double, of its own cognitive activity.

At a less conscious level, minor literature isolates and reveals the forms and topoi that determine our discursive knowledge of the world, forms and topoi which major literature over- and underdetermines or popular literature simply exploits for marketplace rather than cognitive reasons. For a semiotician like Maria Corti, this function justifies our cultivating a greater "*pietas* toward minor writers." Their works reproduce in explicit ways the norms of literary expression; they "guarantee the constant validity of the genre" by which we register "major" generic innovations; they constitute "the connective tissue of literary institutions" and serve as "protagonists" of institutional "stability"; and they provide the critic with materials with which "to construct subgroups with a precise but not obvious physiognomy."[8] In short, treated with "pietas," minor literature here becomes a positive trope, a crucial "protagonist," in criticism's own narrative project to systematize all literature as a stable phenomenon that lends itself to value-free codifications.

In one sense, this conception of a systematic criticism clearly resembles Northrop Frye's more famous polemical position that "criticism is a structure of thought and knowledge existing in its own right, with some measure of independence from the art it deals with." Frye argues that criticism should concern itself solely with developing "a systematic structure of knowledge" about an otherwise "unorganized" field of literature rather than with the shifting "value-judgments informed by taste." But insofar as one could argue that even a minor literary work "manifests something . . . already latent in the order of words" and "shapes itself" rather than "is . . . shaped externally," major and minor literary works differ only in the degree to which they express the "latent" archetypes through which human experience becomes knowable and which literature "imitates" better than other discursive modes: "The real difference between the original and the imitative poet is simply that the former is more profoundly imitative." Indeed, not unlike Corti and Fiedler, Frye will occasionally suggest that the nonmasterpiece work can engage these archetypes, if not more "profoundly," then more explicitly than the so-called masterpiece: "Literature most deeply influenced by the archetypal phase of symbolism impresses us as primitive and popular."[9]

But Frye's epistemologically catholic and institutional inclusion of minor literature also occurs against the background of American New Criticism's ex-clusive formulation of it.[10] For the New Critic, Frye's institutional precursor, the rubric "minor literature" applies to those literary works which cannot sustain themselves as autonomous verbal or "contextualist" events. Short on irony, tension, paradox, and ambiguity, minor works by definition invite "the heresy of paraphrase" and, mutatis mutandis, expose the author's interference or "intention," drawing our attention away from the verbal operations of the works themselves. Renaming it "the fallacy of premature teleology" in a pre-*Anatomy* essay, Frye himself, at least to a certain extent, subscribes to the New Critical shibboleth of "the intentional fallacy."[11] Yet this renaming actually constitutes a revision of the New Criticism's location of this fallacy in the poet's faulty work or perhaps the critic's faulty method with regard to it. In effect reducing New Criticism to minor literary criticism through his therefore more major critical perspective, Frye goes beyond the New Criticism by assigning this fallacy to the critic's failure to regard the work as part of a whole. Whether or not its "intentional" seams show, each literary work belongs to a total "order of words," the *langue* of "Literature" whose particular examples are subject to infinite descriptive or critical variations. In short, this *langue* provides Frye's "new" critic with an "inexhaustible source of new critical discoveries," a situation that would continue "even if new works of literature ceased to be written."[12]

Thus, though Frye would agree with the New Critics that "literature" proper entails an "autonomous verbal structure" rather than uses language "instrumentally"[13] — a distinction he again re-names as "centripetal" versus "centrifugal" modes of discourse — he also argues that criticism should primarily focus not on the presence or absence of this autonomy but on "how the structure came to be what it was and what its nearest [literary] relatives are."[14] And since in different degrees any written work has centripetal as well as centrifugal tendencies, that is, refers to the existing body of "Literature" and to a world beyond its verbal operations, Frye can mitigate the difference between an autonomous or major New Critical poem and one whose "intention is still thought to be apparent in the poem itself," so that it "is being regarded as incomplete."[15] From Frye's redemptive critical perspective, the literary work that seems performatively incomplete turns out to be only provisionally incomplete. Not only can his systematic criticism reprocess a "contextually" flawed or minor work into essential information for criticism, the archetypes and genres critics should know and apply to particular literary works, it can transport this work into a totalized literary context which endows it with an "ideal" epistemological and cultural if not esthetic value. In this sense, Frye's critical perspective makes the New Criticism's discourse itself seem "incomplete."

But this transformation of minor literature at the expense of a rhetorically reduced New Criticism also points to Frye's desire to align his critical system with an honorifically major literary project. His epistemological redemption of minor literature both helps him distinguish his critical activity from and set it above other modes of criticism, and determines this activity as itself a rhetorically "autonomous structure." For Frye, major rather than minor literature ultimately fuels criticism's self-systematic and unique enterprise: "The study of mediocre works of art, however energetic, obstinately remains a random and peripheral form of critical experience, whereas the profound masterpiece seems to draw us to a point at which we can see an enormous number of converging patterns of significance."[16] Systematic criticism and major literature are mutually interdependent; the former ideally gives a metaversion of the latter—orders the formal as well as archetypal mutations of a literary work within its own critically self-reflective terms.

In other words, Frye's call for the critic to assume "a total coherence" of all literary events including minor literature inevitably pertains to his own critical enterprise.[17] Here again we can see how he differentiates his sense of criticism from that of the New Critics who clearly acknowledge the discrepancy between their propositional, that is, "centrifugal" critical medium, and the literary work's recalcitrant or "centripetal" use of language.[18] In contrast, Frye's systematic ideal of criticism entails a self-referential and constantly variable principle of narration that can convert minor literary works into materials which testify to *its own* "total coherence" and "converging" critical "patterns." The "literary" aspirations of Frye's criticism appear, of course, in the very title of his major critical work. The *Anatomy of Criticism* advertises itself as a literary genre along the lines of the Menippean satire which, to interpolate Frye's definition, "presents us with a vision of the [literary] world in terms of a single intellectual pattern."[19] His use of terms like "centripetal" and "centrifugal," along with his explicitly stated methodological separation of criticism from "taste," suggests that Frye here presents literature in terms of the "single intellectual pattern" of an ersatz science.

This use of science as a trope of his criticism or its metaphorical paradigm both serves to acknowledge the cultural privilege accorded to modern science as a discourse of knowledge and shows the latter's dependence on literature's discourse-constitutive imperatives. On the one hand, his tropological use of scientific methodology works to differentiate the immediate acts of writing and reading literature from his therefore more autonomous act of systematic criticism. The trope of science, that is, defines Frye's critical activity as a demystification and even democratization of the literary object as defined by the specialized concerns of the New Criticism and its de facto critical authority.[20] On the other hand, this tropological grafting of scientific and critical discourse serves to demystify the privileged discourse of science as such, a discourse that no less than the institutionally dominant New Criticism could make his systematic criticism seem "minor," in this case as regards its own and its literary subject's underprivileged status in modern society.

In short, Frye's systematic criticism seeks to become both a comprehensive scientific discourse of literature and an allegorical incarnation of literary discourse—and at the same time, neither one nor the other. And here we can begin to see the "motivated" bias that defines Frye's inclusion of "minor literature" as part of his critical system. As a "bastard" scientific project and as a "centripetal" literary event, his critical system has a vested interest in completing the "incomplete" or minor New Critically defined literary work. Desiring to regard literary works as data leading to a systematic "total coherence" and to define his criticism as part of the literary "order of words,"

Frye must deny the possible existence of any "incomplete" literary work lest his criticism appear scientifically invalid or literarily incomplete to itself. Conversely, his systematic "completion" as well as inclusion of minor literature both validates his critical system's explanatory powers and constitutes an allegorical re-production of such literature.

But more important, in becoming a veritable allegory of ostensibly incomplete or minor literary works, Frye's systematic criticism in effect neutralizes the potential competition between its own narrative status and "literature" proper. That is, it situates itself on the same spectrum as minor literature and, by actively transforming it (albeit in conceptual terms) into a complete literary event, more closely "imitates" the operations of major literature. Indeed, differentiating itself from less self-aware verbal narratives including those of other criticisms, it raises itself above even the Menippean satire or "anatomy," its own self-designated literary genre. Frye's critical practice takes place in terms not of "a *single* intellectual pattern," in which Menippean satire is a minor literary genre, but of an endlessly shifting mobile of intersubstitutive genres, myths, archetypes, and symbols. Even his critical style, as Geoffrey Hartman claims, "is a romance multiplication of recognitions; its symmetry, an allegorical layering of the levels of recognition."[21] Metaromance, not metasatire, defines the generic ambition of Frye's *Anatomy.* At the benign expense of a minor literary genre, his criticism moves to a higher plane and, we could argue, is "profoundly imitative" of Coleridge's trinitarian epistemological division of the poetic faculties. For Frye, minor literature resembles the function of Coleridge's fancy which, to interpolate Coleridge's definition, "must receive all its [literary] materials ready made from the law of [conventionally established] association"; in comparison, the allegorical power of criticism to organize an otherwise chaotic series of literary works resembles the Coleridgean secondary imagination that "co-existing with the conscious will, yet still [is] identical with the primary [imagination, i.e., major literature] in the *kind* of its agency, and differing only in *degree,* and in the *mode* of its operation. It dissolves, diffuses, dissipates . . . struggles to idealize and unify."[22]

Frye's attempt to develop a systematic criticism clearly entails this diffusion and struggle to "recreate" and "unify" literary phenomena by "conscious will" and in its own image and likeness. In doing this, his critical "essays," as he terms them, also betray criticism's romantic quest to become "primary" or major literature in the face of certain demonic obstacles testing its faith in "the ideal order" of words, the very ideal that would justify his inflation of criticism as "literature." Such obstacles include more than the nonliterary pretensions but academically powerful precedence of the New Criticism. Even if criticism were privileged over literary activity in modern society, historical realities would limit its hope to become an autonomous and comprehensive grammar of all human knowledge.[23] Or as Raymond Chandler suggested when expressing his disdain for "the long-drawn acrimonious struggle to make [literary works] important which we all know will be gone forever in a few years," the situation of bourgeois modernity carries with it the impression of literature's entropy, its loss of "total coherence"—and so that of any would be "primary" critical system as well.[24]

Given the wish to believe in the enduring institution of "literature" and its canonical emanations, we could say that minor literature itself paradoxically appears as the major obstacle to Frye's critical romance. Such literature, doing no more and even less than imitate the "patterns" one finds in "the profound masterpiece," can remind criticism of its own a posteriori position in relation to its always prior literary subject. Thus, just as Frye raises minor literature and his critical system in relation to the New Criticism's purely rhetorical criteria, so he transumes or lowers the value of minor literature in the service of his systematic criticism's quest to become secondary only in "degree" or "kind" to major literature.

But in conceptualizing or "completing" minor literature on his criticism's systematic terms and in the context of its own literary ambition, Frye also isolates another possible concept of minor literature. Demystified, that is, in the variable structural webs of the *Anatomy,* minor literature becomes more than the diminished secondary projects of the New Criticism. It becomes synonymous with a noncompetitive mode of literary production, one indeed "content with the quiet [literary] life and exquisite perfections." Without Frye's self-interested critical redemption of it, minor literature seems in the process of becoming more minor than the traditional canonical notions of it initially lead us to suppose. Or rather, *after* we regard minor literature from Frye's as well as less systematic formalist perspectives, we can begin to focus on its becoming a fixed secondary literary activity within the dynamic field of major critical as well as "literary" projects. This residual conception of minor literature at least suggests the possibility that certain literary texts can elude the competitive paradigms of canonicity defining formalist criticism. Like Frye's dream of a value-free criticism that we have found to be nevertheless haunted with "masterpiece" desires, such *literature* perhaps tries to appear "in its own right, with some measure of independence from the [major literary and critical contexts] it deals with."

2   Once we recognize that "objective" critical formulations of minor literature tend to refashion it in the displaced image and motivated "unlikeness" of their various projects, we need to inquire whether other critical perspectives can account for a minor literature's *becoming* minor in relation to such formulations. Harold Bloom's "anxiety of influence" paradigm, for example, would explain this "becoming minor" as a textual trope. Each literary text necessarily entails an unconscious misprision of a major precursor text having the equivalent status of a castrating father figure.

Bloom's oedipal paradigm for intertextual relations generates the distinction between major and minor literature in terms of how each writer manifestly if unsuccessfully tries to "wrestle" with a precursor text written by one of the "strong poets" who together "make [literary history] by misreading one another, so as to clear imaginative space for themselves." The "weaker" or minor writers merely idealize their precursors; they accept a godlike figure synonymous with "cultural history, the dead poets, the embarrassments of a tradition grown too wealthy to need anything more"— in short, Eliot's and Frye's notion of a tradition-bound "ideal order" of words. "Strong" writers or texts "cannot accept substitutions" but rather strive to become discontinuous from or to "repress" their precursors by means of tropes that Bloom calls "revisionary ratios." Conversely, "weaker" writers, among whom Bloom includes Eliot himself, write with the assumption "that one poet's poems influence the poems of the other"; that is, they assume a "shared generosity. . . . Where generosity is involved, the poets influenced are minor."[25]

Since for Bloom all writing takes place in the war zone of this oedipalized conflict, minor literature at best can only reveal its diffident self-concealment from its own literary ambitions and the anxiety that attends them. Bloom thus reserves a place for a kind of transitional minor/major literary praxis. His version of this incipiently major writer, one "who never quite made it" but who still resists defining his poetic identity in terms of an idealized tradition of poets "other than the self," occurs in his critical-allegorical depiction of the relation between Beelzebub and Satan in *Paradise Lost*. Here, Satan represents the major modern poet who perversely struggles to deny his literary belatedness so as to realize an illusory ex nihilo or radical poetic status. Beelzebub's continuing support of Satan after their fall from a benign heavenly tradition suggests that even the mediocre writer tends to transfer if not eradicate his poetic ambition; in effect, he uses a *major writer's* mode of writing or poetic repression precisely to repress "the anxiety of influence" he experiences with "cultural history, the dead poets," an influence he therefore has neither repressed himself nor perhaps desires to repress.

One could argue that the same inadequate strategy of repression defines the intertextual scene of writing for the writer who, without apparent equivocation, seems to accept the principle that a received literary tradition of major literary texts comprises a continuous or benign series of literary relations dependent on "shared generosity." Leslie Brisman, for example, maintains that George Darley, a canonically minor English Romantic poet, actually seeks poetic "smallness," but does so as if the very concept of producing minor literature were itself a Bloomian "revisionary ratio" which in the end resuscitates literary anxiety or uncovers "the frustration that must attend, or . . . motivate, the search for images of diminutiveness." Brisman asks the provocative question of whether writers can "wish to be small." He then proceeds to show how Darley realizes this wish through his different texts: how he "diminishes the power of the threatening precursor by re-presenting lost power as that of the plural 'tremendous dead'"; or how his "multiplying the weak [poets of the past] further protects as it diminishes the 'I' of the poet." That is, Darley "derives his originality from this posture of weakness" as he strives to empty his poems and tales "of even that minor anxiety, suspense," in this way revealing his "desire to rework richer, more traditional materials into a more benignant form."[26]

Yet these strategies to induce a sense of literary minority, an "exclusive authenticity of smallness," in order to escape "his distaste for the representation of anxiety," ultimately derive from Darley's wish to be great, his ambivalent "distaste for his own poetic smallness." Darley becomes for Brisman a metaphor for all poets who "desire . . . the power . . . to originate representative language," each of whom yet "senses his own voice to be weak, stuttering, or silent, and desires to be infused with a voice that will speak *through* him . . . to be original." Through his fiction, then, Darley inscribes his ambitious literary vision, or escapes "great" literary "precedents" by "retain[ing] his prime [literary] identity as derivative."[27]

Thus, in this Bloomian framework a writer's apparent desire for literary "smallness" must ironically fail; instead it signifies an overcompensation for the ineluctable desire to produce major literature. If Darley in one text "hoped to gain recognition not as a giant poet but as a small voice capable of stirring his readers into dramatic recognition of the 'pigmy nature' of all men," in this oedipalized, revisionary conception of canonicity he can be seen to work "some wondrous returns to the mysteriously self-transcending awareness of man's pigmy nature, and that awareness distinguishes poetry about weakness from weak poetry."[28] Darley here exhibits the revisionary ratio Bloom terms *kenosis* that he later associates with the trope of metonymy. By this ratio the writer is able to disguise the fact that he is repeating precursors: "The later poet, apparently emptying himself of his own . . . imaginative godhood, seems to humble himself as though he were ceasing to be a poet, but [does this] in relation to a precursor's poem-of-ebbing"; but in emptying the precursor text in this manner, he also makes his "later poem of deflation . . . not as absolute as it seems."[29] Shrinking every semiotic occasion that might signify what Brisman terms "anxiety about poetic stature"[30] constitutes a strategic rhetorical defense against producing major literature rather than an "absolute" sign of producing an anxiety-exempt minor literature.

This recanonified conception of minor literature, which also includes the premise that every literary work entails "a misinterpretation of what it might have been,"[31] clearly redounds to the "literary" credit of Bloomian criticism itself. Even *critical* writing quests for its own solipsistic space where it will have neutralized the priority or influence of another text on its own operations. The Bloomian critic no less than the writer he misreads writes "as though he were ceasing to be a poet," that is, as if he were writing in a diminished imaginative medium. Criticism, too, would seem to risk becoming an anxious avatar of minor literature. Yet Bloomian criticism, free from *kenosis,* admits rather than strives to evade the anxiety which subtends its praxis. In this way, it resembles more the kind of writing represented by Beelzebub, one that at least ambivalently supports the major precursor text's struggle for radical independence, than the kind the angel Abdiel represents in *Paradise Lost,* for example, which remains beholden to the "shared generosity" or "the decency of discourse," as Donoghue terms it, associated with the consensus-sanctified canonical tradition. Bloom thus explicitly names his critical enterprise a "severe poem."[32] He even suggests that the critic writes in a literarily more anxious context than poets: "Just as a poet must be found by the opening in a precursor poet, so must the critic. The difference is that a critic has more parents. His precursors are poets *and* critics" (my italics).[33] In his later work *Agon,* Bloom goes so far as to propose "that the idea of poetry is always more founded upon the idea of criticism than criticism is ever founded upon poetry."[34]

In short, Bloom makes explicit what Frye's systematic criticism leaves implicit. Moreover, criticism must "wrestle" not only with literature as a privileged vocational labor but also with rival critical concepts, in particular those of Frye and the New Criticism which at the time Bloom ventured his "anxiety" theory still exerted a pervasive influence within American academia.[35] By universalizing the competitive oedipal situation of all texts, Bloomian criticism seeks to withdraw itself from formalist criticism's lip-service acceptance of its fate as a minor literary genre. Even Eliot, the major modern poet of the American academy before Bloom supplanted him with Wallace Stevens, has a vested "literary" interest in writing his essays on canonically minor poets. His reintroduction of Donne and other metaphysical poets into "the direct current of English poetry" (at least, that is, "at their best") assumes that changes in taste as much as an unchanging or "objective" esthetic criterion account for canonical literary reputations.[36] This conception of canonicity effectively leaves literary accomplishment uncertain. Together with Eliot's defense of "minor poetry" as a benign foundation of, as well as continuing source of information about, our literary tradition, his notion of the uncertainty of canon formation, a notion that at one point even allows him to diminish the major status of Milton, establishes a bottom line beyond which serious literary efforts are bound not to fall. In other words, Eliot's critical disquisitions on minor poetry serve to ameliorate his anxiety over the canonical status of *his own* poetry.

The Bloomian perspective, then, would have us view criticism as well as "literary" writing as unconsciously motivated misreadings of prior major literary precedents. To Bloom, any reading constitutes "aggression", its supposed "innocence or primal virtue is a last social mystification."[37] Even his application of rhetorical revisionary ratios to literary works under the aegis of a necessarily misread oedipal thematic effectively raises his quasi-Freudian critical act over Frye's Jungian-oriented archetypal criticism — just as it also frees his act from the influence of orthodox and Lacanian Freudianisms. Likewise, his eclectic critical raids on tangential discursive disciplines, and especially his critical "plagiarisms" of Kabbalistic and Gnostic thought, transume, to use one of his ratios of misreading, Frye's critical "bricolage" of anthropological materials as well as his (and Eliot's) orthodox Judeo-Christian comprehension of Western literary texts within "the great code."[38] We could also argue that Bloom uses, even as he differentiates his "self"-grounded criticism from, deconstructive criticism's (un-)definition of the radically relativized "text" in order to dispel Eliot's notion of the individual "work of art" and Frye's notion of an organizable body of relatively stable (if variously interpretable) literary *works*. Bloom's critical position would overturn such idealistic, essentially nonhistorical or, as Geoffrey Hartman characterizes Frye's criticism, spatialized hypostases of literary works[39] by proposing a psychodynamic, radically temporal notion of intertextuality.

Yet if Bloomian criticism helps us highlight the anxiety of "becoming minor" that haunts the production of critical and poetic texts alike, such criticism also ironically justifies the conservative ideology of canonicity itself. Indeed, we could argue that Bloom's own anxious criticism is continually crossed by the imminent return of a repressed Frye-like criticism. In differentiating the character of his critical act from the "generosity" attending minor poetic works, Bloom verges on repeating Frye's self-interested consideration of minor literature as a mirror in which he can construe his own critical act as a more important "literary" event. As recent critics try to argue, Bloom's oedipalization of critical and poetic texts results merely in a defense of canonical distinctions or yet another version of the institutionalization of literary studies around a privileged body of major writers and texts.[40] Bloom's criticism also depends on the concept of a self-constitutive literary history as a "defense against chaos" or the sociocultural-historical context in which critical and poetic texts get produced.[41] Ideologically speaking, Bloom's criticism not only "represents an aspiration of power conceived as 'absolute freedom,'"[42] but, as Terry Eagleton argues, for example, makes Bloom liable to the charge that he himself is a critical "'latecomer' who has emptied out the revolutionary vision of his precursor [Walter Benjamin] and put the feeble *tessara* of literary history defensively in its place."[43]

From such perspectives, then, we can see the bourgeois or quasi-historical assumptions behind Bloom's oedipal literary-historical criticism. Bloom does not disguise his ideological conception of literary texts; for only in a bourgeois setting could it make sense to claim that poets and a critic like himself "sin against continuity, against the only authority that matters, property or the priority of having named something first. Poetry *is* property" (my italics).[44] What Bloom cannot condone about minor literature precisely concerns its failure to "sin against [literary] continuity," but perhaps more significant, its (to him) scandalous appearance as *public* property, the ideological connotation behind his aspersion of it as an act of "shared generosity." Even an apparently non-Bloomian critic like Denis Donoghue, who nevertheless adopts anxiety terminology when arguing that contemporary minor American poets have "turned back, in horror or in irony, from the occult demands usually and desperately glossed in terms of genius, mystery and madness," shows that critical conceptions of minor literature within a bourgeois setting tend to turn on its appearance as "a collective act rather than an individual assertion. Poems are written by individual poets, but . . . [minor poetry] is felt as issuing from a people. The constituents of experience are deemed to be . . . at best communal, even though they are privately enacted and suffered."[45]

Minor literature, or better, minor literary production, thus entails "a collective act" which has pejorative or at best neutral literary value for bourgeois criticism. Reflecting what Fredric Jameson would term an ideological narrative of "American myths of the self and of its identity crises and ultimate reintegration,"[46] Donoghue, not to mention Bloom, posits the freedom of minor literature to have become otherwise: "under different circumstances," his minor American poets "might make a leap toward greatness," but they "seem to have *decided* not to leap" (my italics).[47] But if it cannot imagine a nonpejorative or noncanonically pressured minor literature, such criticism can still lead us to the point where we could imagine such literature's desire to repress "the anxiety of influence" without itself registering anxiety. Bloom's theory inversely suggests that the production of minor literature is less a *texte accompli* than an *attempt* to surrender to the influence of its major precursors. At the same time, as a "collective act" within the context of canonical literary productions, it clearly stands as an exception to the rule of oedipalized literary praxis. From Bloom's ahistorical perspective, minor literature on the one hand exemplifies an *act* of writing which exists as a process of depersonalizing itself as the private "property" of its writer and/or as property appropriable by a Bloomian critic who wants to have "named something first." On the other hand, its "generosity," its apparent capitulation to conventions or established literary precedents, paradoxically argues for its "strong" ability to repress its competitive or bourgeois canonical setting.

Caught between a Bloomian and an ideological perspective, however, we may be forced to argue that in repressing this setting, minor literature appears more bourgeois than a bourgeois major literature. And how can criticism formulate the "shared generosity" of such literature except by itself accepting *its* minor or "collective" literary status or by depersonalizing its own activity? Indeed, Bloom's critics have tried to accept the "minor" value of their critical endeavors. Frank Lentricchia and Paul Bové, for example, seek to define their own criticism not as "severe" poetry but as social commodities in the cultural-historical "collective" marketplace. To Lentricchia minor literature serves as the precursor for major literature since the former provides the continuous literary-historical context "from which strong writers must wrest their identities at perilous points in their development."[48] But we can see how difficult it is for a would-be non-canonical or "minor" critic in the American academy to deny and not ironically corroborate the critical priority of Bloom in this very matter. Lentricchia can envisage minor literature only as an anxious or "perilous" possibility for a major writer to avoid. Contrary to his historicist or collectivist intentions, he effectively misreads Bloom's quasi-historical paradigm as one which he, Lentricchia, swerves from.

In a more self-conscious manner, Bové argues that the "critical act" should accept "the historical nature of hermeneutics and the comparative powerlessness of critical secondariness," even as he acknowledges Bloom as "perhaps the most brilliant critic the American academy has produced in this century."[49] But in Bové's effort to get beyond Bloomian criticism's "troping against time," he like Lentricchia ironically enacts Bloom's revisionary ratio, *kenosis*; both critics turn away from their already diminished narrative of his "brilliant" or ambitious "centripetal" critical acts to less personal and less ambitious "centrifugal" critical practices like historicism and hermeneutics. As I have suggested, by itself Bloom's quasi-systematic criticism inversely shows that one cannot guarantee a canonically transcendent, noncompetitive or anonymously "collective" praxis for producing minor literature *or* literary criticism.

It would appear, then, that a decisively nonbourgeois mode of criticism like Marxism, one fully aware of the ideological investment in canonical distinctions made by a bourgeois criticism like Bloom's, is better suited to discuss minor literature's "becoming minor." The very category of minor literature exemplifies bourgeois culture's refusal to consider artworks *as* "work," specifically, minor literature as *alienated* literary labor.[50] Yet as we have also seen, a minor literature produced in a bourgeois setting could easily exemplify a more reactionary mode of bourgeois literary production than so-called major literature. Given its "literary" investment in but also potential duplication of the devalued modus operandi of minor literature, a bourgeois mode of criticism could exploit Marxist notions of minor literature (an exploitation, of course, that Marxists would note as itself a reactionary appropriation) in order to repeat at the level of criticism the ways such literature affiliates itself with, and yet tries to become more minor in relation to, the labor criteria, i.e., the prevailing hierarchical literary canon, of its bourgeois scene of production.

3   In a different sense from that of Bloom's criticism, the Marxist perspective can also conceive of minor literature as a "becoming minor," this time in relation to the competitive canonical paradigms originating within bourgeois culture. The Marxist conception of "labor," the fact that all writing occurs within the "material" marketplace parameters of production and consumption, immediately serves to neutralize the competitive distinction between literary and critical modes of writing. For Marxist criticism, both activities—and I would here include Marxist-revised bourgeois criticisms—can be understood to perform similar counterbourgeois functions, albeit in nonhierarchically different discursive media.

Even in general, a socioeconomic framework can help us redefine the self-interested motives behind bourgeois criticism's conceptualization of minor literature and canonicity. In the modern literary-industrial complex where criticism has become an occupation more than a belletristic or honorific vocation, the topos "literature" is inevitably crossed with the critic's own demands for new materials with which to work and/or to exercise his role in discerning "quality" amidst textual quantity.[51] Charged with—and yet, as cultural custodian or theoretician of literature, desiring to deny—his function as consumer-consultant for students and institutional peers committed to a specialized kind of knowledge (an elitist division of labor), the modern academic critic in bourgeois culture tends to seek nonexhaustively critiqued literary works or perhaps new theoretical constructs which will justify further criticism on more recognized works.

In this bourgeois or late capitalist setting, minor more than major literature often provides material for additional critical labor and opportunities of professional recognition for the critic whose field lacks prestige in contemporary society at large. The minor literature perhaps most suitable to attract this kind of critical interest is that produced by the more canonical writer; the diaries of Virginia Woolf, for example, are preferable to Sarah Orne Jewett's canonically respected *The Country of the Pointed Firs*.[52] Under the guise of viewing this major writer's minor works the better to understand his or her major work, such criticism raises the value both of these minor works and of its own critical act within the academic community. A similar situation obtains in the case of a noncanonically respected minor literature. On the one hand, such literature affords the critic a less competitive because more untrammeled critical topic, one for which he can virtually dictate his own terms, as it were, of critical labor, and in this way assume privileged proprietary rights over his chosen text(s). Even Eliot reveals this socioeconomically motivated desire as critic-consumer when arguing that "some poets . . . are good investments for *some* people, though no prices are quoted for them on the market, and the stock may be unsaleable."[53] On the other hand, since the critic can deal with his minor literary materials only in the context of peer critical values, the prevailing major criteria of "criticism" as he understands them, he tends to inflate or "apologize" for the minor subject of his critical enterprise.

From a Marxist critical perspective, then, even this provisional socioeconomic depiction of bourgeois criticism's marketplace situation reveals how this criticism reproduces the alienated labor practices widely discernible in our workaday bourgeois society. In this setting, literary and critical activities both entail the production and consumption of signs, whose exchange value vis-à-vis other marketplace commodities is privileged over their use value as noncommodified products.[54] Only a radical transformation of bourgeois culture's "base" can restore these "superstructural" activities to their function as a communally self-referential labor quintessentially symbolizing man's humanization of nature. Short of this material transformation, bourgeois attempts to assert the use value of literature merely constitute one more disguise "for [that] ultimately scandalous fact of mindless alienated work and of the irremediable loss and waste of human energies [throughout history]."[55] Thus, bourgeois criticism deludes itself if it maintains that when a literary work, especially a modernist work, appears "to alter the structure of artistic discourse," such revi-

sion also suffices to alter those "realities to which [this discourse] corresponds" and according to which bourgeois criticism itself is little
more than a Veblenian commodity ripe for conspicuous consumption.[56] To maintain that a literary work's "change in style will help
us see the world in a new way and thus achieve a kind of cultural
or countercultural revolution of its own"[57] has the same reactionary
significance as a critical perspective which seeks to alter the ways we
apprehend so-called conventional literary works. For example, Bloom's
ratios of anxiety actually call for repressive sublimations of "mindless" social rather than psycholiterary realities. The pseudoalienated
posturing of these ratios represents a misreading of their own alienated social scene of production, a scene that Bloom's quasi-revisionary
criticism unwittingly serves.

The egalitarian strategies of bourgeois criticism to mitigate "the
scandalous fact" of alienated labor thus constitute what Jameson terms
an impotent "aestheticizing reaction against the sordid realities of a
business civilization."[58] Marxist analysis shows that they repress the
nonrepressible fact that all literature is "a commodity involved in a
system of exchange dominated by commodity-mediated relationships . . . [or] governed by the same laws that prevail in the economic
sphere."[59] Such strategies, in short, ideologically regard minor
literature as a debased literary commodity. At best, they can reinvigo-
rate its exchange value by assigning it, for example, with a moral-
existential charge as the early Sartre does when he argues that

> the engaged writer can be mediocre; he can even be conscious
> of being so; but as one can not write without the intention of
> succeeding perfectly, the modesty with which he envisages his
> work should not divert him from constructing it *as if* it were
> to have the greatest celebrity. He should . . . say to himself . . .
> "What would happen if everybody read what I wrote?"[60]

Sartre conceives of minor literature as a free or "conscious" act and
places it within a revised antibourgeois canon, one which views all
literature as willy-nilly "engaged" in the project of promoting the reader's freedom; it is in this sense that minor literature is charged with
"the intention of succeeding *perfectly*." Sartre's polemical stance
ironically represents a bourgeois antibourgeois revolutionary esthetic

in that it remains ideologically beholden to a conscious subject, one who can choose to write with "modesty," and of course in that it appeals to a nonsocioeconomic "freedom" defining literary perfection as well as the relation between even the minor literary text and its reader.[61] Moreover, since he here shifts from an ontological to an existential conception of minor literary praxis, from that writer who "can *be* mediocre" to one who can choose to be so, one could argue that Sartre assigns minor literature with a sociorevolutionary project in the face of its complacent or existentially debased *en soi* intention, i.e., its manifest but here concealed status as a commodity.

Viewing all literature *as* such a commodity, and recognizing even its own egalitarian relation to it as "labor" within a bourgeois context, the Marxist critical perspective seems best able to "deconstruct the received hierarchies of 'literature' and transvaluate received [critical] judgments and assumptions."[62] Its very methodology, the ways it recasts literary works according to their historical-ideological machinations, frees Marxist criticism from a canon-inducing focus on the esthetic value of literary works.[63] As Eagleton argues, Marxist scientific methodology not only manifests "an egalitarian unease about the 'elitism' of assigning certain works to second-class status," but also radically differentiates itself from bourgeois criticism's pseudoantielitist or "abstract egalitarianism" which always entails an "enshrinement of Literature itself as a reified value."[64] It would redefine the task of the critic as "not to range works upon an evaluative scale but to achieve scientific knowledge of the conditions of their historical possibility." This scientific labor theory of literary value recognizes its own historicity, hence unlike bourgeois criticism does not fetishize its theoretical formulations;[65] it focuses on the work's relations of production rather than its appearance as an abortive *or* successful self-producing, autonomous artifact.[66]

Of course, one could quickly object that such a shift in focus is also a shift from the bourgeois conceptualization of minor literature to an ideologically charged version of it. If bourgeois criticism places such literature in the context of the competitive marketplace, however honorifically understood, Marxist criticism would seem to subject it to the question of its relation to "the class struggle." It would enlist minor literature in its ongoing task to demystify "Literature

. . . as a reified value"— as somehow transcending historical-material practices as well as self-interested class motivations. Walter Benjamin, for example, can forestall his ideological demands on literature only when he methodologically seeks to regard it in nonesthetic, nonevaluative, and yet also nonvulgar Marxist terms:

> Instead of asking, "what is the attitude of a work to the relations of production of its time? Does it accept them, is it reactionary— or does it aim at overthrowing them, is it revolutionary?" . . . I should like to propose another. . . . "What is its *position* in them?" This question directly concerns the function the work has within the literary relations of production of its time.[67]

Benjamin's methodology here gives way to a Marxist socioeconomic imperative as he proceeds to interrogate the work's "position" in terms of how it manifests the writer's

> directing, instructing stance. . . . *An author who teaches writers nothing, teaches no one.* What matters . . . is the exemplary character of production, which is able . . . to induce other producers to produce, and . . . to put an improved apparatus at their disposal. And this apparatus is better the more consumers it is able to turn into producers— that is, readers . . . into collaborators. [his italics][68]

But to demand that a literary work become an "exemplary" model of collective labor relations is to reintroduce a criterion of literary evaluation, albeit an apparently noncanonical one. If all works appear theoretically revisable by Marxist criticism, the latter's scientific or objective perspective would still have to claim that certain works seem to struggle to repress (in a "reactionary" sense) their existence as commodities, and others seem to express (in a "revolutionary" sense) an "exemplary" transformation of their alienated "literary relations of production." Marxist critics thus tend to focus on the genres of drama or prose fiction rather than on poetry since the former foreground such "relations." Brecht's plays, for example, effectively teach spectators their productive relation to the dramatic performance, a relation suppressed by the passive consumerist-ideological expectancies of bourgeois drama. In this way, Brecht's plays heighten the spectator's sense of his complicity with and need to overturn bourgeois ideology as a whole. Similarly, certain novels lend themselves better than others to Marxist analysis inasmuch as they represent "kinds of social actions that reveal the contradictory conditions which result from efforts to live a whole life in the face of class divisions and conflict."[69] Even the so-called "great aesthetic productions of capitalism," as Jameson argues, "prove . . . to be the cries of pain of isolated individuals against the operation of transindividual laws, the invention of so many private languages and subcodes in the midst of reified speech, [and] the symptomatic expressions . . . of a damaged subject [in his] vain efforts to subvert an intolerable social order."[70]

Marxist criticism thus cannot help but privilege those "great" texts which emit Marxist-confirming bourgeois "cries of pain." Such criticism also tends to privilege "popular" bourgeois literature insofar as it manifests bourgeois ideology's "reified speech" habits, satisfies the sheer desire for consumption, that is, is produced exclusively for its exchange value in the marketplace. Yet what of a bourgeois literary work neither honorifically "great" nor "popular," one that, even to a favorably disposed bourgeois critic, fails to exhibit a "free" plurisignative or unconventional praxis, or, to a Marxist critic, hardly signifies the presence of "private languages" or otherwise exposes the "contradictory conditions" surrounding its production? Like a ventriloquist of its bourgeois setting, such minor literature seems to depend on what Jameson after Roland Barthes refers to as "the older narrative schemata, which are felt—rightly—to be indefensible conventional presuppositions about the nature of life and experience."[71]

Yet Marxist criticism can redeem this minor literature in at least two ways. Such criticism, after all, essays to "engage with the language and 'unconscious' of [all] literary texts, to reveal their role in the ideological construction of the subject; and mobilize such texts, if necessary by hermeneutic 'violence,' in a struggle to transform those subjects within a wider political context."[72] Even with a text that fails to manifest its "productive" seams, Marxist criticism can by "hermeneutic 'violence'" situate it against a bourgeois ideological background. For bourgeois ideology, it turns out, can produce only the *desire* for closure regarding the representation of the individual self or a "natural" a-historical order[73] which minor literature seems to endorse by its uncritical adoption of "conventional" narrative schemata. Despite this desire, such ideology functions as a kind of Lacanian Symbolic or endlessly deferring *langue* which precludes any literary text from becoming "identical with itself" or representing a closed, autonomous Imaginary world excused from the "contradictory conditions" endemic to its historical situation.[74] Following Pierre Macherey, Eagleton argues that every literary work before or during bourgeois societies "emerges into existence precisely by the repression of certain (ideological) determinants" that it then "begins to betray"; it ironically "throws ideology into disarray *by* fixing it" or by foregrounding its "limits and lacunae, that of which [the work] cannot speak," but which "necessarily evade (but also covertly *invade*) it."[75] In the same way, every literary work "within bourgeois ideology . . . plays its part in constituting the reader as [an] equivalently self-coherent 'subject,' centred on the privileged space of an entirely appropriable meaning,"[76] thus opening up even the minor literary work to an analysis of what we have seen Benjamin term "the literary relations of production of its time."

But more than revealing minor literature's unconscious reflection of "a network of signs inescapably caught up in specific social practices,"[77] Marxist criticism can insert such literature into its own dialectically valorized ideological project, and show how it actively if mutely resists its bourgeois ideological prison house at the level of its semiotic operations. Such criticism, for example, can emphasize the regionalist or feminist subcodes of Jewett's "A White Heron" to show how her narrative includes an authoritarian capitalist ideology, one that privileges an industrial and/or patriarchal class order, the better implicitly to undermine rather than comply with it. Or one can show how her tale strives to resist this ideology's Imaginary repression of its own Symbolic narrative conditions—how this ideology "incorporates within itself (not without ceaseless struggle) the codes and forms whereby subordinate classes 'practice' their relations to the social formation as a whole."[78] Thus, one could argue that the production of this oft-anthologized story as an indecisive popular *or* honorifically literary text reveals this "struggle" within Jewett's ideological situation and points to the work's sense of its own "subordinate" political class status.

Still, with Marxist criticism might not one also claim that Jewett's story "so fictionalizes the 'real' as to intend a set of effects conducive to certain practices that are deemed, in the light of a particular set of falsifiable hypotheses about the nature of society, to be desirable"?[79] Even here, however, Marxist criticism provides a way to spare such literature from "reactionary" ignominy. For example, it could also maintain that the story's "textual effect" depends on "an articulated set of social practices [of production and consumption]" as they were defined in a specific historical period.[80] Upon examining this historical context, we may discover that Jewett's story intended a different "set of effects" *not* "conducive" to the "practices" of bourgeois ideology, just as we may discover that works of literary "realism" within *their* historical setting would have had the effect of an antibourgeois heterogeneous and not a stable or "naturalized" signifier, the ideological semiotic distinction promoted by the early *Tel Quel* group.[81] Thus, Eagleton argues that "we should be wary of claiming to recognize the 'same' textual effect across two such historically divergent sets."[82]

Such potential redemptions of the merely apparently "bourgeois" or stable "narrative schemata" marking nineteenth-century American minor literature clearly establish the model for other kinds of ideological revisions. In the case of "A White Heron," we could adopt a feminist perspective and, aware of Jewett's minority situation in patriarchal American society, view what Tillie Olsen terms the "loss of quality, the minor work" that Jewett as a woman could *only* have produced in such a society as revisable in terms of the story's "hidden silences."[83] Or like Nina Baym we could expose patriarchal American criticism's canonical reduction of women's writing to "minor or trivial literature" simply because it "does not conform to the myth" of American male idealizations of a feminized and virgin nature.[84] Such examples of minor literature help identify and, through the work of the ideological critic, can retroactively weaken our attachment to the dominant and canon-minded ideology which this literature both inscribes and subtly resists. Indeed, for a Marxist critic, major literature can exemplify reactionary practices more than minor literature. If bourgeois major literature also struggles against its dominant ideology, it does so in a way that paradoxically strengthens the latter.

As Eagleton argues, major literary texts can "so . . . produce a constricted ideology as to 'renew' it or by virtue of its own 'second order' signifying labour . . . revivify the values and perceptions that ideology proffers."[85]

But clearly, these possible Marxist recuperations of bourgeois minor literature must still regard it as an "exemplary" pretext for the Marxist project to overcome its bourgeois ideological antagonist. At the very least, Marxism's canonical egalitarianism entails the internalization of a prima facie ideological struggle whose goal is to replace the dominant social "narrative" which defines the various labor relations of writing and reading in bourgeois society. Marxists can even conceive of a utopian mode of literary production that will supersede its bourgeois predecessors and reduce *both* their major and minor versions to the ideological equivalent of minor literature—to a past, if still "conceivable" and revisable, example of alienated literary labor.[86] A Marxist critical perspective does lead us to conceive of a minor literature in the process of eluding (but not revivifying) bourgeois modes of commodification, the fetishizing of works as autonomous, quasi-individualistic events or as evidence of some "ideal order" of texts. But in performing its canonical demystifications, Marxist criticism also addresses not the literature at hand so much as actual and possible bourgeois procedures of canonicity, bourgeois critical codes, so as radically to differentiate itself from the "false consciousness" underlying their assumptions.

Thus, if we were to substitute "bourgeois ideology" for "language" in the following observation, we might agree with the critical deconstructionist that the Marxist's "knowledge of . . . language's performative power is itself a [tropological] figure in its own right and, as such, [is] bound to repeat [its] disfigurations."[87] This problem with Marxist criticism—its teleological or dialectical identification with and supersession of bourgeois criticism, its ideologically sublated repetition of canonical thinking in spite of its rhetorical egalitarian premises—is for us secondary. What we must emphasize is its enlisting minor literature in a counterideological project that willy-nilly minimizes this literature's esthetic operations. Bypassing what to bourgeois criticism seems the esthetic conservatism of this literature, Marxist criticism still conceives the latter as possessing a kind of (ideological) "exchange value." In this way, it permits an unregenerate bourgeois criticism, one aware of the canonical revisions or anti-canonical stance Marxism can produce without, however, taking a leap of faith into the ideological self-certainty of this Marxist perspective. Such criticism is able to envisage a minor literature in the process of eluding both its commodity status in a vulgar bourgeois culture, and its alienated or revisionary "labor" status as an ideological pretext for the ongoing Marxist revolutionary project.

One can see intimations of this (to the Marxist) Imaginary, *residually* "esthetic" conception of minor literature even in the way Eliot seeks to depict minor poetry. Adopting a bourgeois brand of "use value," the possibility that some kinds of literature "may be unsaleable," Eliot argues that we read minor poetry just as we read "new poetry." We read it, that is, for "immediate pleasure," not caring that it "may not have that value for most people"; we absolve it from canonical or comparative competitive pressures since "there is nothing else to go by," our primary problem thus being "not . . . that of trying to like something you don't, but of leaving your sensibility free to react naturally. . . . For if I am alone, there is nobody to whom I am obliged to express an immediate opinion."[88] Eliot's conception, as we have seen, serves his own poetic interests, his anxiety over his own poetic station within the traditional literary canon. It also constitutes a reactionary strategy. Not only does it naively assume that one could become "free" and "react naturally" with minor poetry, it effectively postpones his awareness that other critic-consumers are reading the poetry which he wants to feel he "alone" reads, namely, as a fetishized private commodity.

Eliot's notion of minor literature as affording him "immediate pleasure" implies a suspension of the need to perform the (alienated) critical *work* coterminous with his ideological commitment to the ideal value of literary canonicity. As bourgeois recreation, minor literature is not subject to a labor theory of literary value—or to Marxism's counterideological project to dismantle bourgeois criticism. More than canonical major literature, minor literature, with its conservative esthetic operations as produced within bourgeois culture, phenomenologically resists honorifically literary, popular, populist, critical, and ideological "labor" alike.

In a Marxist critical theory no less than in formalist or psycholiterary theory, then, one could argue that minor literature, even the very *concept* of minor literature, appears in the process of becoming more minor than these perspectives rhetorically maintain. At some point, Marxist criticism would define minor literature as those works which "occlude and impoverish the elements of a positively enabling ideology [even certain aspects of bourgeois ideology] by [their] textual operations."[89] Moreover, minor literature's conservative "esthetic" abdication or disaffiliation from any critical codifications existing, like Marxism, in oppositional relation to another possible codification also seems to define it as an example of socioeconomically unearned "play," an idealized instance of nonalienated labor. But as Eagleton suggests, such literature precisely occludes and impoverishes this bourgeois idealization of art-as-play. In other words, because it fails to sustain the minimal Marxist demand for an at least provisional image of utopian modes of literary production, minor literature lacks the dialectical, "positively enabling" value of bourgeois esthetics when pitted against a specific historical relation to art as a (repressed) commodity.[90]

As it turns out, however, we have not exhausted the ways in which we can discuss a minor literature in the process of passively resisting systematic critical and ideological projects. If such literature balks at becoming understood in terms of the binary between ideological labor and sheer esthetic play, it calls for a critical perspective capable of entertaining the possible value of a mode of writing that seems narcissistic and quasi-collective. Such a criticism would have to regard minor literature as lying outside this binary Marxist/bourgeois opposition wherein, as Jean Baudrillard remarks, "play is always merely the esthetic sublimation of labor's constraints."[91]

4   Gilles Deleuze and Félix Guattari's *Kafka: Pour une littérature mineure* attempts to conceive of minor literature as an antiauthoritarian as well as anti-author-centered event. Such literature is politically and metaphorically a "third world" kind of writing which eludes the totalizing formulations of formalist, oedipal, and bourgeois or Marxist modes of organization. In its elusive relation to these modes and their critical representatives, this literature functionally

demystifies the way each one, to use Baudrillard's terms, "disinvests the body and social [including 'literary'] exchange of all ambivalent and symbolic qualities, reducing them to a rational, positive, unilateral investment."[92]

For Deleuze and Guattari, minor literature exemplifies the anarchistic noncategorizability of what they refer to in *Anti-Oedipus* as "desiring-machines," that is, the temporary loci of desire breaking into the flux or, as they term it, "the body without organs" whose desire "constantly couples continuous flows and partial objects that are by nature fragmentary and fragmented." Such "flows" preclude the humanistic view of fixed objects or subjects of desire; desiring-machines exist only in radical relation to other "partial objects, flows, and bodies." Themselves only junctures of identity, organization, or "territorialization," such *self*-demystified machines produce "intensities" at constantly vanishing sites which social systems (the "socius") no less constantly try to "codify . . . inscribe . . . record . . . see to it that no flow [of desire] exists that is not properly dammed up, channeled, regulated." To be sure, we can conceive of a socius like Marxism regulating desire in the name of freeing it from more reified modes of organization like those supporting bourgeois culture, and thus itself becoming a desiring-machine. But no socius is ever privileged. Insofar as Marxism ascetically denies or postpones the elicitation of desire by fetishizing the discourse of labor, it too becomes subject to "antioedipal" schizoanalysis. Putative revolutions against capitalist ideological systems sooner or later serve merely to "reterritorialize" the endless and variable "flows of desire," the appearing/disappearing loci of energy where "nothing . . . is representative" except nonrepresentational "bands of intensity" or "potentials." Thus, more than one socius or countersystem can liberate desiring-machines from the supporting discourses of capitalist cultures. For example, Freudian psychoanalysis initially uncovers the "autoproduction of the unconscious" before it becomes still one more official capitalist discourse which serves to incarcerate "the body without organs" in an energy-restrictive oedipalized "primal scene." For that matter, insofar as capitalist culture's systematic organization of "reality" includes an obsession with the surplus value of commodities, an obsession that results in self-evidently artificial modes of organization, it unwittingly leaves in its wake intimations of a *social* "body without organs . . . the ultimate residuum of a deterritorialized socius."[93]

More relevant to our present concerns, Deleuze and Guattari argue that certain artistic works operate in the manner of desiring-machines working to "short-circuit social production . . . by introducing an element of dysfunction."[94] Given its linguistic organizations of "reality," literature especially can generate questions about "how to produce, how to think about fragments whose sole relationship is sheer difference . . . without having recourse either to any sort of original totality."[95] The ideal "antioedipal" literary text turns out to be the "littérature mineure" of a writer like Kafka, specifically a literature that a "minority produces in a major [as opposed to a deracinated minor] language"; to Deleuze and Guattari the first characteristic of minor literature derives from its being written in a "language . . . affected by a strong coefficient of deterritorialization."[96] A Jew writing in Prague, Kafka writes in relation to a Czechoslovakian or "territorialized" language and culture; in relation to German or Prague's official language for commercial and other bureaucratic transactions that require written documents; and in relation to an already deterritorialized Yiddish language which he occasionally speaks in public, much to the annoyance of the Jewish bourgeoisie.[97]

Kafka thus exemplifies the "impossible" situation of the deterritorialized minority Jewish writer, a situation that equally obtains for black minority writers using the "major language" of whites in the United States. He clearly manifests his Jewish minority's need to produce literature insofar as any "national consciousness, uncertain or oppressed, necessarily passes through literature." But on the one hand, as a writer of his minority culture, he also needs to write in German, the "major language," otherwise this minority would experience "the sentiment of an irreducible distance from the primitive Czech territoriality"; on the other, he must resist writing in German since to do so would amount to the Jewish minority's impossible but here virtual identity with "the deterritorialization of the German population itself, the oppressive minority [in Prague] speaking a ['paper'] language separate from the [Czech] masses."[98]

A second characteristic of minor literature, then, involves its immediate "political" connotations *as an act of writing*. The "minor" writer's "deterritorialized" relation to the major language in which he writes inevitably diminishes his authority to represent situations which will have more or less the same esthetic or ideological effect for all readers beyond those of similar minority ilk. And here we could apply Deleuze and Guattari's understanding of Kafka's "political" scene of writing to Sarah Orne Jewett's minority situation; for example, the fact that as a nineteenth-century American, regionalist, and woman writer, she can write only in an *English* major language, a federalist American culture determined to "reterritorialize" signs of radical cultural difference, and a patriarchal social and literary milieu which diminishes her authority to represent anything more than what Deleuze and Guattari term "l'affaire individuelle." Thus, in Jewett's as well as Kafka's minority literature, "familial" and "conjugal" situations appear unnaturally large, as if seen through the distorted focus of a microscope ("grossie au microscope"), and with only an isolated or mere "local color" significance. Whereas in "great literature," say of her anglified yet also American and male contemporary, Henry James, such "individual affairs" take on a universal significance or organically "rejoin other affairs no less individual, the [assumed] social milieu serving as environment and background," in her minor literature they occur only in a radically circumscribed and particled space—"espace exigu."⁹⁹

The "great" writer can thus assume individual authority with his materials. Based on his immediate access to the major language, he can imagine a world with the valence of total representability, unlike the minor writer who cannot assume such an "énonciation individuée." Yet for this very reason, the minor writer can construct a fragmenting, idiosyncratic, imaginative world based on "l'énonciation collective." He or she can escape the "oedipean affairs" or topoi of the "great" writer and write as a "communal" or nonindividual figure which enables one to produce a literature "positively charged with the role and function of collective and even revolutionary utterance." Of course, the minor writer always reserves the option to "reterritorialize" his decentered relation to the so-called major language. He can assume authorial control over the text by writing in terms of a single narrator or even enrich this language by showing its "hidden" resonances, its not-yet-exhausted symbolic powers that "his very eccentric relation to the major language helps disclose." But instead of seeking to gain entrance into the individual or oedipean domain of "great" literature, Kafka renounces such options and chooses to accentuate his communal or minority bonds by writing more and more in a "deterritorialized" mode, that is, by fractionating the major language, making it "vibrate with intensity" as opposed to intensifying its symbolic possibilities. Like a child, he mimics this language or "actively neutralizes" its ordinary representational sense by means of certain de-representational inflections or accents. In short, Kafka produces stories by reducing them to elemental verbal elements, verbal desiring-machines which elicit a "sequence of intensive states" rather than representational scenes that devolve on individuals or oedipean affairs.[100]

For Deleuze and Guattari, then, minor literature is "schizo" literature in its subatomiclike antioedipal and self-deconstructing release of literary "intensities." We could say that it appears "at the very limit of the social codes" that govern the production of major literature, that is, literature "where a despotic Signifier destroys all the chains [of radically partial signifiers], linearizes . . . them," whereas minor literature "continually works them loose and carries them off in every direction in order to create a new polyvocity that is the code of desire."[101] Minor literature thus leads to a "third type of interruption"; it produces "the residual break" that "mobilizes Voluptas as residual energy" or a "something left over" in relation to the major language it dis-organizes.[102] Such literature subliminally attacks what it itself could have become, a representative, like major literature, of the major language and culture which serve as conduits for a desire-repressing political order. To this end, it enacts a passive-aggressive strategy that promotes parts over the whole and in this way exists in the process of becoming "the third linguistic world,"[103] a literature that de facto sabotages whatever social or systematic code happens to control the means of major literary production at the moment.

For example, Kafka resorts to the fissioning literary figure of "metamorphosis" as the modus operandi of his stories. Although (but even because) it seems synonymous with the more privileged figure of metaphor, i.e., with the desire for representability, metamorphosis in Kafka literally fails to make "proper [or] figurative sense," but rather reveals his desire "deliberately" to "kill all metaphor, all symbolism, all signification, no less than all [proper verbal functions of] naming"—in French, "designation." Human beings representationally transposed into subhuman species actually point to the radical transitional situation that defines Kafka's continually deterritorialized signifying practices, the way something is always and only in the process of becoming another ("devenue devenir"). Every representational situation transpires "in a conjunction of flux, in a continuum of reversible intensities" or "mutual becoming." Moreover, apart from Kafka's disintegrative use of this otherwise honorific trope, the most elementary linguistic procedures also define for Deleuze and Guattari his praxis as a minor writer: his "intensive or stretched" use of his major language's "linguistic elements"; his abuses and misuses or prepositions, pronouns, all-purpose words ("de verbes passe-partout"); his "distribution of consonants and vowels" as well as strings of adverbs that serve to produce an effective nonrepresentational "internal discord." In this context, these performative linguistic gestures induce both a "new sobriety" within the major language and the continuing deterritorialization of the latter for the purpose of eliciting a "new intensity."[104]

Unlike the formalist or Bloomian esthetic conceptions of minor literature, then, Deleuze and Guattari's includes an ideological element. And unlike the Marxist ideological conception of minor literature, theirs attempts to account for its particular esthetic operations. Yet no less than these other conceptions, Deleuze and Guattari's antioedipal or fissionary (but not "visionary") delineation of minor literature ends up inviting the return of a repressed desire for canonicity. Their brand of minor literature clearly becomes a privileged double of their antioedipal revolutionary desire to overthrow all versions of a here debased reactionary or reterritorializing major literature. Moreover, such deterritorialized literature requires the preexistence of a major literature or language it can deconstruct—or rather its criticism can deconstruct—so as to expose minor literature's heretofore underground political "intensity." Deleuze and Guattari thus privilege only a certain kind of minor literature, that which like Kafka's is in the process of interrogating the oedipean tropes of major literary praxis but which the major language or canonical critical codes can misrecognize as major according to their own standards. Is not Kafka (or Beckett, another writer they call minor) canonically honorific in modernist critical circles? Deleuze and Guattari's conception of minor literature, then, restrictively includes those "schizo" or marginal texts which they can wrest from the reterritorializing practices of established critical codes they associate with the major language and which they can redefine as examples of a politically subversive minority praxis.

But a minority major "minor literature" clearly leaves in its wake a "minor" minor literature. In the "intensive" critical force field of Deleuzian criteria, the works of Poe, for example, would qualify as "minor literature" more than those of a Sarah Orne Jewett. One could argue that her works manifest the desire to reterritorialize their incipient politically minor or "collective" minority context. To be sure, the Deleuzian critical perspective permits us to schizoanalyze the anorexic representations of a story like "A White Heron." We can regard them as "points of nonculture and underdevelopment, the zones of the linguistic third world" intent on sabotaging the major language of American patriarchal culture. But Poe's texts seem to perform such operations more incisively. So often dealing with the representational theme of doubles, his tales expect a double reading (e.g., the gradual and retroactive recognition that a narrator is insane) which throws into question the centrality of this representational theme, makes it seem possibly an effect rather than a cause of this semiotic repetition. And as with his later "reading" of "The Raven" in "The Philosophy of Composition," a text that expects such a second reading also expects its reduction to a mechanism, its becoming minor or unoriginal but in the context of a major Romantic language privileging Imagination *or* originality. Poe thus dehumanizes Imagination, exposes it as a desiring-*machine,* just as in Deleuzian fashion he represents a bird metamorphosing into a subhuman voice that mimics human speech ("Nevermore") and in this way demystifies the privileged notion of a unified, oedipean self which would distinguish itself from other creatures precisely by such linguistic ability. A marginal text with regard to its critical topic, Poe's "Philosophy of Composition" in effect converts "The Raven" into a marginal text and mimics the latter's intention to produce sheer "effects," i.e., Deleuzian "intensities."

Poe's deterritorialization of his major language undoubtedly occurs in other ways: decomposing his proper name through initials in the anagrammatic "ape" of "The Murders in the Rue Morgue"; or as in "Berenice," reducing representational identity to particle-ized teeth and, as regards the very name of the story, to what Deleuze and Guattari refer to as a *bodily* deterritorialization uncovered in the relations between mouth and eating, speaking and writing.[105] "Berenice," pronounced like "very spicey" according to Thomas Mabbott, besides punning on phrases like "barren ice" or "very icey," fissions into a "schizo" infantile or senile speaker without teeth saying "berry nicey."[106] Like Melville's Bartleby with his "I prefer not to" refrain, Poe's characters evince a design becoming a de-sign, a designification or disintegration of the major literary language. Words become *words* in his "minor and intensive usage" of this language; he uses, or more accurately abuses, this language, we could say, "to oppose its oppressed character to its oppressive character."[107]

These "minor" dialectical strategies also make clear the way a writer like Jewett becomes more minor from the Deleuzian perspective inasmuch as she uses, for example, dialect-ical linguistic elements merely to produce her regionalist or otherwise minority representations. Deleuze and Guattari specifically refer to the "rejuvenation of regionalism" as a "reterritorialization by dialect or argot," which often indicates "the most reactionary, the most oedipean" of humanistic tendencies. Such regionalist literature remains below even a reactionary major literature, not to mention that produced by a minority writer like Joyce who, by sheer verbal "exuberance and overdetermination," serves to regenerate and not revolt against his major (British) language. The Deleuzian privileging of a politicized, rhetorically inverted minor literature, a literature "neither great nor [systematically] revolutionary but minor," thus excludes a minor literature which does not show it can "hate all literature by masters." Without any question, Deleuze and Guattari's antioedipal schema would lead us to devalue further what we could term a bourgeois or oedipean brand of minor literature. At best such literature epitomizes one of those "styles, genres, literary movements, however small [or minor in the usual sense], that have only one dream: to fill a major function of language, to offer its services as the language of the state or official language."

Conversely, their antioedipal minor literature has universal or trans-
cultural significance insofar as "'minor' qualifies not only certain lit-
eratures, but the revolutionary conditions of all literature in relation
to literature called great (or established)." Better than the major literature on which it parasitically depends and a minor literature it
would consign to literary perdition, Deleuzian minor literature answers the question plaguing not only "immigrants" and "minorities"
but "all of us" and "minor literature" itself: "How does one become
the nomad and immigrant and gypsy of one's own language?"[108]

Despite Deleuze and Guattari's virtual canonization of an antioedipal minor literature, their position allows us to imagine a literature precisely in the process of *becoming* minor in relation to the
major possibilities proffered it by the language and codes subtending
its production. On the one hand, a Deleuzian critic could maintain
that even this example of minor literature manifests its "major" ambition, that is, its writer's interest in "the possibility of producing one's
own language," or his desire for his language "to be unique," to imagine "it is or has been a major language" as he writes. On the other,
given Deleuze and Guattari's view that the minor writer should not
"fill a major function of language" but "have the contrary dream: know
how to create a becoming-minor," we could argue that their implicit
devaluation of an oedipean minor literature ironically isolates *it* as
satisfying their requirements for a literature in the process of "becoming minor"—this time with regard to both a systematic *and* a Deleuzian
critical conception of it. If such literature seems to reproduce the
"official" major language in which it becomes inscribed, it does so,
as the preceding critical perspectives continually remind us, in attenu-
ated and thus in-significant ways. And aside from its possible production by a minority writer, such literature can emit signs of its merely
potential deterritorialized status through its repetition, its miming but
not Poe-esque mimicking, of conventional modes of expression, those
which major literature both establishes and violates, and which always already precede minor literature's every act of "becoming minor." Moreover, its self-effacing mode of representation must occur in
an unselfconscious manner or it could constitute either a "becoming-
major," that is, repeating major literature's reterritorializing ideological praxis, or a "becoming-minor" according to the aggressive anar-

chistic principle of canonicity that grounds Deleuze and Guattari's own deterritorializing critical activity.

Neither one nor the other; both one *and* the other. The charged perspective of Deleuzian criticism allows us to imagine a minor literature in the process of removing itself from all signs of binary canonical thinking, from all privileging of major literature or of antimajor literature. We can imagine a minor literature which exhibits a minor mode of reterritorialization and deterritorialization, a literature releasing the "intensities" of major literary conventions by attenuating them, and a literature unintentionally or passively disclosing the desiring machinations of language. Or we can imagine a minor literature grounding these "intensities," that is, not pressing but rather leaving these disclosures *in potentia*. Such a literature could be said to deterritorialize its major language up to a certain point, but then require a Deleuzian criticism to continue this process in its place. More, at this very point it seems to *reterritorialize* this language along with the major literary and critical codes the latter carries, the better to infect this would-be minor text "without organs." In resituating itself within the magnetic field of major literature, this bourgeois minor literature would also seem to preclude any de facto "major" revision along the lines of Deleuzian schizoanalysis.

In other words, we can imagine a minor literature that neither identifies its operations with whatever constitutes for it the productive operations of major literature, nor in critically revolutionary terms seeks to fracture the bureaucratic, formalist, psychohistorical, Marxist, and/or now the Deleuzian projections of minor literature. Such a literature, we could say, short-circuits even as it represents the possibility of a nonalienated, noncanonical "Voluptas" of literary production. This apparently chaste, retiring type of minor literature might well suggest to us a literary death wish were it not that this very conception coterminously constitutes a critical deathbed conversion of such literature to yet another possible avatar of canonicity, and again suggests criticism's own unwillingness to accept the possibility of a text's unregenerate desire for literary finitude.

5   These preceding conceptions of minor literature demonstrate, I think, the double motivation that haunts specific critical interpreta-

tions of it. The critical wish to regard minor literature from a non-canonical perspective collides with criticism's self-disguised or, in the case of Harold Bloom, openly professed "power" relation to such literature.[109] In this sense, a deconstructionist mode of criticism could at least provide us with a perspective from which to recognize the ways "canonicity" invades our acts of writing, reading, and interpreting minor literature. But this critical practice would ceaselessly have to deconstruct our canonical-ideological tendencies, for as Jacques Derrida argues in another context,

> To deconstruct the opposition . . . is to overturn the hierarchy at a given moment. To overlook this phase of overturning is to forget the conflictual and subordinating structure of opposition. Therefore one might proceed too quickly to a *neutralization* that *in practice* would leave the previous field untouched. [Derrida's italics][110]

Short of this ad infinitum critical (self-) deconstruction, canonical projections of minor literature intrude precisely at the moment when one has overturned another canonical projection.

In short, by definition and simply in its attempting to define minor literature as a datum of literary experience, criticism is condemned to interpret it in canonical terms. Poststructuralist critical practice, even as exemplified by the eclectically critical Roland Barthes, tends to bear out this problematic truism. We could argue, for example, that the kind of bourgeois minor literature we have been trying to isolate resembles Barthes's "text of pleasure." As such a text, minor literature can effectively suspend the act of critical evaluation: "If I [Barthes] agree to judge a text according to pleasure, I cannot go on to say: this one is good, that bad. No awards, no 'critique,' for this always implies a tactical aim, a social usage. . . . I cannot . . . imagine that the text is perfectible"[111] But as soon as one isolates this minor "text of pleasure," one produces a critical category which, because of its mercantilist setting, as Barthes notes in another work, frustrates our pleasure in *reading,* that is, our desire to apprehend it apart from the evaluative impulse. And this setting inevitably forces our critical narration to "construct, i.e., *complete,* a piece of merchandise," our potential rewriting of the minor text, so that both it and our critical narration become "banalized, made guilty by the work to which [they] must eventually contribute."[112]

In a more explicit manner, Barthes reintroduces the structure of canonical thinking into the semiotic virtuosity of *S/Z* where, through codifications we could just as easily apply to "A White Heron," he focuses his attention on a story by Balzac. By slicing Balzac's "Sarrasine" into semiotic pieces, Barthes effectively converts this "readable" story, a narrative whose mode of representation requires only conventional efforts to appropriate it, into a "writable" or discontinuous "text."[113] Barthes uses his five codes to detotalize "Sarrasine" and proceeds to write it himself as if for the first time; he rewrites it, that is, in relation to a superimposed field of expected linguistic, sexual, and economic binaries which endow the story with a multilayered but nevertheless stable appearance.[114] But more, in deconstructing this story Barthes also deconstructs his own imagined self-present or "realistic" reading of it and thus, as it were, effectively writes his reading, i.e., performs his *criticism,* as if for the first time. In this sense, Barthes's criticism reproduces a minor literary text by a major French writer in its own image and likeness and according to a conception of the modernist "text" as privileged over the classical "work." Despite its wish to deconstruct traditional canonical notions, then, Barthes's criticism both ends up corroborating Honoré de Balzac's honorific literary status in terms of his protomodernist capacities and, in its tautological tracing of this "text's" self-deconstructions, raises *itself* to the level of a literary "text."[115]

The pattern seems familiar but never more explicit. Beyond this example presented by Barthes, we can imagine a more explicit poststructuralist conception of minor literature, one that would endow it with the status of a Derridean "supplement," say, a contingent, inconspicuous event in literary history that eludes and in this way deconstructs the autonomous "presence" of a privileged major literature. Any literature capable of both supporting and desiring to remain apart from canonical apprehensions, any literature written for the sheer pleasure of writing or reading, would "disseminate" the criteria responsible for reducing itself to minor literary status. But in another sense, to regard minor literature in this way is to make it "work," i.e., to *de*-construct, make *in*-complete, logocentric ideological notions of canonicity. Moreover, as even Derrida himself appears to assume, certain texts like the ones privileged by Barthes can "disseminate" their canonical codifications "better than others."[116] If some texts virtually deconstruct themselves, if they depend on but also undercut their tropological illusions of self-presence, other texts, what we can term devalued brands of poststructuralist minor literature, remain vulnerable to acts of critical deconstruction alone.[117]

Clearly, then, what we need to imagine is a minor criticism of minor literature. Such a criticism would have to (self-)deconstruct its canonical tendencies in interpreting minor literary texts. No doubt this procedure would result in prolonged discussions reducible to what an epistemologically conservative notion of textuality would judge as egregious overreadings and as a criticism more literarily ambitious than the texts themselves. In inviting such judgments, however, this criticism would be in the process of adjusting its locus of production to that of the text it criticizes. One can imagine how the "major" critical setting surrounding a particular act of criticism, in whatever terms the critic identifies this setting, could duplicate the major literary setting of even a past canonically minor work. But from this common but also different locus of production, a minor criticism would still have to trace its own process of becoming minor in relation to an always already privileged, if indefinite, protean notion of major literature and/or criticism.

In short, a minor criticism of minor literature entails the critical intention to deny canonicity unselfconsciously. Any other mode of denying minor literature's status as a trope of canon formation institutes a counter- rather than noncanonical status for it, i.e., aborts the process by which we could consider it as existing in the process of becoming minor. Such criticism thus constitutes a virtually endless praxis as opposed to a theoretical propaedeutic. It requires continual lateral procrastinations, a critical-methodological catachresis that (self-) deconstructs revisions of canonicity by means of formalist self-demystifications (Frye), oedipal totalizations (Bloom), antioedipal detotalizations (Deleuze and Guattari), and ideological *Jetztzeiten* or the hypostases of literary texts within an "arrested moment of time forced to its revolutionary crisis."[118] And since the identification of minor literature effectively precedes the act of interpreting it, at the very least a minor criticism would have to try to ensure that the text it examines possesses the phenomenological consistency of seeming "minor" before and after this examination in order to diminish such criticism's inevitable revalorization or dramatization of its own and the text's *desiring* to become minor.

Yet even this constative articulation of a minor criticism obviously contradicts its performative intentions. Just as an imaginary minor criticism can state and only dream of taking back its thesis about a literary text's becoming minor, so any theoretical formulation of this criticism remains problematically motivated by the simultaneous desires to define and undefine this canonically anomalous topic. In the end, "minor literature," the conception of minor literary texts, comes down to a questioning of—as well as permanent question for—the act of criticism.

CHAPTER ONE   "A WHITE HERON"

AS A MAINE CURRENT

There shall . . . be a new friendship . . .
It shall circulate through the States, indifferent of places,
It shall twist and intertwist them through and through
    each other—Compact shall they be, showing new signs,
Affection shall solve every one of the problems of freedom,
Those who love each other shall be invincible,
They shall finally make America completely victorious. . . .
                                                    —Walt Whitman

I want to be lifted up
By some great white bird unknown to the police
And soar for a thousand miles and be carefully hidden
Modest and golden as one last corn grain. . . .
                                                    —James Wright

1   Any anthology of American literature will inform us that
Sarah Orne Jewett deserves honorable mention in American literary
history chiefly as a regionalist or "local color" writer of late-nineteenth-
century New England. Jewett herself "admitted a frank consciousness"
of this classification during her lifetime.[1] Her works turn almost exclusively on her actual experiences with people from small central
New England villages, and with the natural settings surrounding these

"country by-ways"—as she once entitled a collection of sketches and tales.[2] Like other local color writers, Jewett tries to portray the often idiosyncratic mannerisms, dialect, social customs, and homespun moral dramas of people like her own neighbors in South Berwick, Maine.

But such writing, notable for its unique and sometimes unconventional topical settings and characters, received its literary value more from sociological circumstances than from its claim to esthetic or thematic innovations within the American literary tradition. For one thing, it was produced in a radically changing post-Civil War United States which was committed to an urban and industrial, as well as centralized or federalist, mode of social organization. The source of regionalist topoi, namely the simply organized, communal, agrarian-like *Gemeinschaft* society was on the verge of becoming an already passé American myth in the face of the complex culture or *Gesellschaft* of postbellum American society. Unlike Dreiser's realistic *Sister Carrie*, for example, which begins with its heroine's leaving her regionalist culture, and coming to the city, that is, with the separation from the myth of America as an agrarian-centered society, Jewett's regionalist writing, as the ending of a tale like "A White Heron" suggests, seems to express a reactionary wish to deny the "revolutionary" implications of America's postbellum industrial capitalism. Indeed, the curiosity of the urban-oriented and genteel literary audiences about regional subcultures in the United States, the audiences of *Harper's* and the *Atlantic* magazines where Jewett published much of her work, already bespoke the reduction of such cultures to token or quaint pieces of Americana, or to the status of social impotence.

In other words, "regionalism" amounted to a kind of genteel evasion of the more complex if not sordid social realities of American society when Jewett was writing her sketches and stories. Such writing, we could claim, "knows its place," its setting and the secondary status of its merely transparent or esthetically uncomplicated transcription of it. For example, Jewett often noted that she wrote her stories according to a precept her father had given her when she first began to write: "Tell the things *just as they are.*"[3] For a regionalist writer to write "the things" she knew best was to court the literary limitations of her topos. American literary criticism makes us aware of this fact when it refers to such writing as produced mostly by "New England spinsters . . . driven to extremes of nostalgic fantasy" about "imaginary pasts."[4] In short, this "New England" brand of regionalist fiction and sketches constitutes a minor aberration or detour in mainstream American literary history.

Yet in the light of a more ideologically self-conscious critical position, one can ask whether Jewett's works simply accede to sociological explanations which reduce them to transitory literary as well as historical significance; or whether they resist such reductions to the point where this resistance comes to inform their use of narrative conventions, themes, and stylistic practices. At the very least, such resistance would suggest an attempt to lay the groundwork for a literature of enduring literary value. But one cannot begin to address this issue without first recognizing its place within the history of American literary criticism. As suggested, Jewett's works have remained subject to what semioticians term an "ideological bias" by which critical and popular readers alike tend to read and evaluate them. To question this "bias" and revise Jewett's works accordingly, we would have to employ a self-conscious ideology like Marxism or even American liberalism, either of which could help us "to read a given text in the light of 'aberrant codes'"—codes, that is, "different from the ones envisaged by the sender"—and thus "find out what in that text is ideologically presupposed, untold."[5] Thus, Jewett may have been aware of producing works earmarked for a regionalist coding, but this coding does not necessarily coincide with the "regionalism" that has become part of the teleologically comprehensive discourse of federalist or Union critical perspectives.

To be sure, during and since Jewett's time this federalist discourse has itself undergone transformations, variously privileging, say, Whitman's self-conscious democratic or "en masse" poetics, Howells's morally self-conscious American social realism, James's interrogation of the "American" character, and the "main currents" democratic and antigenteel liberalism of V. L. Parrington.[6] But however defined, these "main currents" discursive perspectives focus on the way texts concern themselves with the struggle to forge an American cultural union. They also ensure that we apprehend regionalist writing and subculture in terms of either their contribution to this struggle or their im-

practical "assertion of special fears and delusions, and of special privileges and immunities from the *main course* of our democratic, technological, acquisitive society" (my italics).[7] Not even the apologists
for Jewett's regionalist writing can quite resist this binary perspective. Richard Cary argues against the charge of Jewett's having written merely "idyllic" works by insisting on her capacity but also "maid-
enly decision" not to "stress . . . the dire experience" in these works.[8]
Cary here attempts to make Jewett compatible with the literary practitioners of realism which "main currents" critics have more often than
not associated with major American literature. In a similar manner,
other apologists tend to repeat the predilection of Union critics to
treat regionalist writing in terms of a totalizing ideological criterion,
even when this totality is understood as an ironic or unrealizable
American myth. Thus, Josephine Donovan argues for Jewett's successful "synthesis" of the rural/urban conflict in her novel *The Country of the Pointed Firs*.[9] Jay Martin attributes the success of this work
to its sustaining a narrative tension between nostalgia for a past America and the recognition of present American social realities.[10]

Such criticism, in other words, constitutes a political act. It represents the "political unconscious" of American criticism which tends
to project regionalism as an "ideologeme," to use Fredric Jameson's
term. In this context, regionalist writing becomes more than an iso-
latable school, a literary-historical or even social movement; it becomes part of a federalist ideological strategy serving to reinforce the
"belief system" of this "main currents" federalist position, a position
intent on repeating discursively its historical victory over and "class
fantasy" about geographical, ethnic, and racial subcultures or minorities that even today appear "in opposition" to it.[11] Simply said, "main
currents" critical assumptions about American social and literary
history presuppose a privileged teleological reading of American literary texts which strives to minimize the stubborn persistence of
"regionalist" attitudes in American life.

The question of whether Jewett's works accede to or resist sociological and therefore literary reduction thus appears alongside the
question of whether a federalist-oriented critical perspective isn't itself susceptible to reduction to a fantasy over what constitutes a major-
alias-mainstream American literature. What we could term the *Ge-*

sellschaft of a twentieth-century American criticism and literary history assumes it can define regionalist writing as a naively referential, genteel, or in other words, a self-evidently minor literature. The *Gemeinschaft* of Jewett's own regionalist writing, on the other hand, replaces "main currents" concerns with "Maine" currents or narratives concerning "country by-ways" or other local topoi; it refers to "things just as they are" in ways that possibly outflank, or at least differ from, those such criticism values. This very possibility could easily lift Jewett's works above an ideologically devalued concept of local color writing. The self-consciously regionalist tenor of her writings would here remain concealed or withheld from the federalist perspective that critical readers have adopted toward them and that has continually consigned her works to the de facto status of minor literature. It would be as if the secret defining the central action of "A White Heron" were also referrable to the story's own relation to its openly regionalist topos, ideology, and literary-historical value.

2   Perhaps the most explicit manifestation of the regionalist/ Union binary in Jewett's writings appears in her stories about people from cities or towns confronting people from small New England villages. Jewett herself would retrospectively claim that the impetus behind her earliest literary efforts had been to redress a regionalist grievance by extolling the universal or "grand" values of New England life to urbanites apt to dismiss them out of hand:

> When I was perhaps fifteen, the first city boarders began to make their appearance near Berwick, and the way they misconstrued the country people and made game of their peculiarities fired me with indignation. I determined to teach the world that country people were not the awkward, ignorant set those people seemed to think. I wanted the world to know their grand simple lives; and, so far as I had a mission, when I first began to write, I think that was it. [12]

One could easily argue that this grievance-spawned sense of literary vocation informs the thematic and referential concerns of both the sketches and stories she wrote during the 1880s when she herself experienced "the conflicting attractions of rural and urban life."[13] As late as 1892 she signals her greater attraction for the former when faced with the inevitable implications of the latter. In a letter to Annie Fields, one of her closest friends, whom she lived with in Boston during the winter months, Jewett expresses dismay over a "syndicate" that intends "to cut up and sell the river bank all in lots" in the Berwick area; if only someone she knew in town would buy it instead, that would "make such a difference to me. Sometimes I get such a hunted feeling like the last wild thing [] left in the fields."[14] A part-time inhabitant of South Berwick when she writes this letter, Jewett yet cannot tolerate the idea of her village's losing its rural ambience.

It seems clear that Jewett's consistent mode of resolving the rural/ urban conflict in her fiction was to privilege characters and themes as well as images synonymous with rural "primitivism" over those suggesting urban "sophistication."[15] Motivated by indignation, her desire to reclaim or at least preserve the values of her regionalist culture in the face of their devaluation and even abuse at the hands of an expansionist, capitalist American Union helps set the context by which we can read, for example, Sylvia's decisive silence in "A White Heron." The only question we might ask is whether this context exists as mere background to the story or as its primary ideological subtext. Since its heroine is but a little girl, does her decision amount to what Union critics like Berthoff refer to as a hysterical, unconscious, or simply sentimental assertion of regionalist values? Or can we claim that the story constitutes an ideological allegory wherein Sylvia's refusal to communicate the white heron's location to the hunter expresses a rejection of the postbellum federalist world, specifically its presumption that after having triumphed over one secessionist region, it can dispossess with impunity other regions of their right to exist according to their heterogeneous or particular subcultural values?

Jewett's "indignation" clearly seems to point to the latter reading of the story. Here, the little girl, the hunter, even the heron, represent less individual subjects than "actants" within an ideologically centered narrative which we could paraphrase as follows: her "regionalist" silence frustrates or sets limits upon his "federalist" relation to rural culture (the farmstead) and nature (the white heron); he egregiously presumes he can pursue the latter anywhere, buy it off for a small price (ten dollars), all for the sake of a self-evidently unnecessary project (to stuff and study the heron for his personal collection). In rejecting this federalist "great world" (p. xxii, above), albeit with "a sharp pang" (xxii), "A White Heron" does not so much aggressively assert as measuredly reclaim the values of regionalist mores and morals. Moreover, in making the heroine nine years old, it also suggests that this reclamation is permanently renewable—not, that is, fixated nostalgically upon an imaginary past way of life. Even the story's namesake *in* the story argues for this more activist regionalist interpretation. The hunter informs us that the white heron, a "rare bird" or species which is "never . . . found in this district at all" (xvii), has virtually adopted this region as its home; but the ideological subtext of the story informs us that the bird has migrated to this region not from a natural cause, not even because it has "been chased out of its own region by some bird of prey" (xviii), but rather as a result of an expanding and expansionist American society represented by the hunter himself. Indeed, we could argue that Sylvia's situation at the end of this story humanly repeats the heron's "dumb" situation before the story properly begins. Like the bird, she too *comes* to adopt this region as her home, the farmstead here standing as a metonym of regionalist culture, in preference to the "crowded manufacturing town" (xiv) as well as "the great world" of federalist culture which would destroy her regionalist innocence, regardless of this culture's rhetorically benign intentions.

We can corroborate this ideological rereading of the story by using Jay Martin's schematization of postbellum changes in American society, especially those pertaining to its explosive economic growth, the demographic shifts from country to city and East to West, and the increasing scientific as well as technological effects on human relationships and relations towards nature.[16] In her letters and sketches, Jewett frequently alludes to Berwick's past economic vitality centering on shipbuilding, the source of her own family inheritance, but now also indicative of Berwick's stagnant economy. Sylvia climbs a tree in "A White Heron" that appears to acknowledge this past *as* past, given its being "the last of its generation" (xix). On the other hand, in alluding to "the huge tree" as "asleep" (xx), the story suggests that this regionalist past remains alive, its spiritual vitality still accessible:

"It was like a great main-mast to the voyaging earth" (xx). More concretely, the economic state of Mrs. Tilley's farmstead alludes to New England's demographic plight after the Civil War. The fact that only two females are left to run this barely subsistent farm reflects New England's precipitous postbellum population loss, particularly of young males who migrated to other American regions, notably the West like Mrs. Tilley's son Dan, to seek their capitalist fortunes or simply escape the economic and climatological hardships of New England life.[17]

But "A White Heron" also depicts these women as exceptions, that is, as figures of a regionalist culture's continuing survival. Mrs. Tilley and Sylvia show how regionalist denizens can both endure *and* enjoy what to American urbanite readers might seem an economically and socially deprived if otherwise idyllic situation. Their modest way of life exists in contrast to that of the hunter who "would give ten dollars to anybody who could show [the white heron] to me," and who "desperately" intends "to spend my whole vacation hunting for it" (xviii). Uttered in a setting where the "so lightly spoken of" ten dollars seems like a lot of money (the little girl thinks it "can make them rich . . . and they are poor now" [xxii]), the word "spend" exposes his American capitalist background. To "spend" his "vacation" searching for the heron suggests his ideological propensity to view others, Mrs. Tilley, Sylvia and even himself, in terms of capitalistic or abstract labor relationships. Indeed, in contrast to both Sylvia and her grandmother, he is not referred to by name in the narrative; this reinforces his status as an anonymous "stranger" (as the narrative occasionally does refer to him) or a figure representing the anonymity produced by a growing industrial American society.

The story also promotes this binary regionalist/federalist reading through subtler maneuvers. We can easily apprehend the ideological significance of the distinction the narrative makes between Sylvia's former existence in the town, where the only sign of life seemed "a wretched dry geranium that belonged to a town neighbor," and her first feeling at the farm "as if she never had been alive at all before" (xiv). But the story also represents this distinction in imagistic terms. At its beginning, for example, we find a silent little girl walking a cow that wears "a loud bell" which "would not ring" (xiii). Here, si-

lence self-evidently signifies the peace or nonhectic pace of life associated with living in the country, especially when juxtaposed with
Sylvia's sudden recollection of the "noisy town" and "the great red-
faced boy who used to chase and frighten her" (xv). The hunter repeats this "noisy" and aggressive association when he makes Sylvia
suddenly "horror-stricken" at the sound of his "clear whistle" before
she even meets him (xv). This binary ideological trope becomes ironically repeated in the story's last paragraph when Sylvia herself associates "the sharp report" of this hunter's "gun" with "the piteous
sight of thrushes and sparrows dropping *silent* to the ground" (xxiii;
my italics). This contrast between a silence synonymous with the
innocence of Sylvia, nature, and regionalist culture itself, and the
deathly silence produced by his "noisy" gun, serves to represent the
hunter and his federalist culture in ominous, almost melodramati-
cally evil terms.

We can also construe the hunter's gun as another coded allusion
to Union or federalist ideology, this time as a metonym of its industrial technology. Josephine Donovan, for example, argues that his gun
symbolizes "the evils of the industrial city."[18] We could at least maintain that it alludes to the deleterious use of technology in postbellum
American society, for example, the way the telephone, for Jewett, de-
personalizes human communication.[19] But the trope that best projects the hunter as an "evil" ideological persona is his scientific or
naturalistic ambition—in the story, his ornithological ambition—to
know nature in an at best utilitarian, at worst Faustian, manner. Unlike the hunter cat, "fat with young robins" (xiv), or, for that matter,
Sylvia's uncle Dan who "was a great hand to go gunning" (xvi) whether
for food or recreation from the difficult tasks of farming, the hunter
has killed and taxonomically preserved "dozens and dozens" of birds,
making them into objects out of a gratuitously bourgeois motive (his
personal collection) and for the sake of an abstract scientific study.
Its villain an updated version of a Gothic scientist who comes to
"use" or murders to dissect nature, "A White Heron" here takes on
the trappings of an ideologically epistemological melodrama. Morally obtuse, the hunter would use Sylvia, the regionalist hospitality
of Mrs. Tilley, his own vacation, and of course the rare white heron
to realize his quest for knowledge. He takes pride in admitting he

collects birds not to "cage 'em up," as Mrs. Tilley first benignly assumes (caging them would imply at least keeping them alive), but to fix them as objects: "'. . . they're stuffed and preserved, dozens and dozens of them,' said the ornithologist, 'and I have shot or snared every one myself'" (xvii).

Thus, while the hunter superficially appears "kind" to Sylvia and even makes good rather than evil use of his knowledge when he teaches her, for example, "many things about the birds" (xviii), the narrative conveys to us the insensitive ideological position he stands for by having him refer to his own habitual ("dozens and dozens") denigration of nature. Never questioning whether it is moral to privilege knowledge above nature or to seek to (dis)possess the white heron for his mere "personal collection," he evokes the postbellum federalist hubris or presumption to know its subcultures and dispossess them of any separate identity. In the story, however, Sylvia symbolically thwarts this presumption and installs in its place an alternative spontaneous or even ecological vision of nature, and by extension, of regionalist subcultures. Where the hunter would preserve the heron by taxonomic death, Sylvia *does* preserve it by preferring a kind of Thoreauvian or antebellum mode of cognition. Like her own final silence which preserves *her* mystery in relation to the hunter's code of understanding, her knowledge of the heron's secret preserves *its* mystery; indeed, her knowledge of this secret almost literally signifies a transcendentalist vision, as when she recalls seeing the heron "*flying* through the golden air" and "how they watched the sea and the morning together" (xxii; my italics). This memory, cause of her final silence, clearly indicates a more immediate and total knowledge of nature than the ornithologist's.

Despite her preadolescent age, then, Sylvia appears within a "social" skein of signification which endows her with heroic if melodramatic stature. In exemplary fashion she represents the continual possibility of a "natural" as opposed to a "naturalist" or scientific relation to nature almost literally "in the face" of the latter's growing dominance. In other words, she refers us and especially contemporary readers to the Romantic or Victorian ideological code which both privileges childhood innocence over adult experience and identifies her as the metaphorical child within anyone. At the very least, her final silence represents the story's elevation of childhood imagination over scientific or utilitarian modes of knowing nature, here associated with adulthood and the "acquisitive" discursive habits of a progressivist republican culture.

Jewett herself seems to authorize this "regionalist" vision of resolution and independence, this reflective and not just reactionary triumph of nostalgia for a *Gemeinschaft* or Jeffersonian America. The narrative's authorial intrusions clarify the moral and cognitive perspective that we should adopt toward the ideologically coded melodrama of Sylvia's desire to please the hunter because her "woman's heart" is "vaguely thrilled by a dream of love" (xviii). Only seeming conventionally complacent, intrusions like the following perform a precise ideological function: "Alas, if the great wave of human interest which flooded for the first time this dull little life should sweep away the satisfactions of an existence heart to heart with nature and the dumb life of the forest!" (xx). Besides raising melodramatic alarm bells (will this little girl overcome the temptations of "the great world" represented by the stranger?), this intrusion dramatizes an intimate mode of cognition in relation to the protagonist. The ostensibly adult author here *shows* the adult reader how he or she can know Sylvia in the same way Sylvia comes to know the heron, i.e., as a living subject rather than an object at the mercy of a discursive viewpoint that would dismiss (as we have indeed seen Union critics dismiss) her believability as a heroine capable of making an exemplary moral choice. At the same time, the authorial persona also serves to acknowledge the fragility of "heart to heart" rural values as personified in this vulnerable little girl and dramatized through her coming to doubt her final decision (xxii–xxiii). Without such explicit authorial representation—without literary representation per se—the "dumb" truth of the "dull little" values differentiating regionalist culture from its republican surroundings might easily get swept away, become surrendered, ultimately forgotten.

Sylvia's choice thus takes place in a "social" binary field; her choice is for a poor but self-subsistent rural economy; for a preindustrial, pretechnological way of life; for "dull little" rural pleasures; for an imaginative and perhaps transcendentalist relation to nature, each as against that obtuse but also attractive power of Union or "great world" values. Still, one could also argue that this choice occurs in a "dumb," silent, and thus fragile representational manner for a less ideologically decisive or pro-regionalist reason. After all, the girl's final silence in the presence of the young hunter could signify a mere delay or postponement of the radical social threat posed by this harbinger of federalist culture. Yet here again an authorial intrusion helps us. Though her silence might signify not an active but a passive moral choice, namely that of a person who admits she "could have served and followed [the hunter] and loved him as a dog loves" (xxii), this apparent moral ambiguity serves as a foil again to emphasize both the active nature of this choice and the ideological "indignation" against minority sociocultural status that it polemically signifies. The story allows *us* if not the little girl to understand the decisive nature of her choice. It dramatizes this decisiveness by having Sylvia feel that the hunter "is so well worth making happy" (xxii) and informing us that she had intended to divulge the heron's secret up to the very moment when she "does not speak *after all*" (my italics). Such obstacles add definition as well as poignancy to Sylvia's decision, a definition the narrative reinforces when speaking for her: "No, she must keep silence!" (xxii). This exclamatory sentence indicates the moment not only when the heroine apparently decides to protect the heron's right to live, but when as narrator Jewett herself inscribes her regionalist-ideological resistance to the culture of the late-nineteenth-century American Union.

In short, the ideological coding which "A White Heron" explicitly invokes results in a story where Union values get rejected, albeit not without a "haunting" sense of loss such as Sylvia experiences when the hunter goes, for the sake of regionalist values which depend on truer if less sensational unions, i.e., with birds and other "secrets" of nature. Moreover, this rejection within the story could be said to duplicate the story's own rejection of the reader/critic who seeks to understand it as part of his or her critical or literary historical "collection." Either way, we can regard "A White Heron" as crossed with a nascent ideological ambition not only to express but to become itself a positive act of regionalist resistance—to veto a dominant American culture that would abuse and dispossess it of its independent regionalist vitality or belief in itself.

3   But if Jewett's writings seem to take sides in a specific sociohistorical as well as traditional opposition between rural and urban
cultures, one could argue that they do so with obvious equivocations.
In one sense, we could say that "A White Heron" resists the ideology
of Union cultural autonomy by displacing it with a reactionary illusion about *sub*-cultural autonomy. In another, more explicit sense,
the story seeks to redress a regionalist cultural grievance by means
of a nonaggressive, nonpolemical justification of the ways country
people are "misconstrued" by urban visitors. From these perspectives,
in other words, it seems clear that Jewett's writing propagandizes the
values of her regionalist culture in the very terms of a federalist value-
system or as if no serious ideological crisis existed. Intracultural divisions occur through ignorance rather than political contradictions.
In 1893, one year after she wrote to Annie Fields about her "hunted
feeling" concerning her village's losing its rural identity, Jewett informs
a would-be writer that her motto in writing had been "the great saying of Plato—that the best thing one could do for the people of a
State was to make them acquainted with each other."[20]

Jewett's here essentially *e pluribus unum* regionalist ideal—one
which has more universal application to the situation of later immigrants or all Americans who in a rapidly changing culture dwell nostalgically on a simpler American past way of life (a conventionally
"regionalist" motif)—suggests a zealous commitment rather than resistance or begrudging resignation to the realities of postbellum American society. Indeed, what American after the war could hope to deny
the supersession, by Union ideological values, of the defunct Jeffersonian vision of an agrarian-based American economic system and
a decentralized government?[21] Thoreau, for example, an antebellum
New England regionalist writer, could dream of ideological secession by Walden Pond. A human consciousness indulging in the possible dream of radical self-determination, he could assume *Walden*
was his own American experiment, a privately lived metaphor of an
ideal American life. By comparison, in "River Driftwood," an 1881
sketch, Jewett meditates on the possibility of "self-existing . . .
springs" of rivers, a thought that to her could lead to "confusion and
chaos" or "boundless speculation." She can contracept this subcoded
social as well as overt intellectual possibility of disorder or "natural"

secession only by accepting the truism of her river's, i.e., her regionalist culture's, leading "to the sea" or contributing—precisely in the displaced manner of this sketch—to the ideologically necessary order of a unified "State."

Jewett's writings simply avoid the occasions where they might be led to take a regionalist stance against the cultural realities threatening to absorb her tempting but dangerous vision of a "self-existing" regionalist way of life. One looks in vain in her writings for allusions to the mill town or industrial New England world, a conspicuous omission when one realizes that only a "mile away from Sarah's house the textile mills at Salmon Falls were employing larger and larger numbers, and rows of drab rickety houses were growing like mushrooms overnight," with the "village folk . . . slowly crowded out by Irish immigrants."[22] Occasionally we find an oblique but nonetheless evocative reference to "machinery" or, in "A White Heron," to a "crowded manufacturing town"; but this latter reference, like the hunter and his cultural perspective on the farmstead, ultimately remains marginal rather than exists in opposition to this story's rural resolution.[23]

Jewett's regionalist stance, in other words, seems typically "American." Her writings hardly reveal her as one of those hysterical New England spinsters, as Berthoff terms them, who were "driven to extremes of nostalgic fantasy" or fixated on "imaginary pasts with a violence matched only by their will to overlook the real one."[24] To be sure, she sometimes views the American past with a nostalgia that seems intent on privileging it: "People do not know what they lose when they make away with the reserve, the separateness, the sanctity of the front yard of their grandmothers. . . . [We] Americans had better build more fences than take any away from our lives."[25] Yet this sociological recommendation, a recommendation that will find its poetic fruition years later in Frost's "Mending Wall," seems to assume a nonironic federalist orientation ("we Americans"); its token project ("more fences") lacks the symbolic edge of its Frostian supersessor. It is possible to construe "We Americans had better build" as a subjunctive or optative rather than an imperative or even declarative utterance. Moreover, actually building more fences, regardless of their metaphorical applicability to "our [social or personal] lives," would amount to no more than a token gesture, or last stand, to minimize the effects of postbellum American society on regionalist culture. Intended to preserve a small space, the "sanctity" of front yards synonymous with such culture, these fences function as rhetorical de-fenses against, rather than resistances to, the realities of this late-nineteenth-century Union world.

This function also defines certain basic elements of "A White Heron." As a little girl, Sylvia hardly suffices as a credible vehicle for asserting a regionalist grievance; rather, according to the strictures of verisimilitude, both Jewett's heroine and the girl's final choice at most *suggest* such an assertion. As represented by the hunter, Union values, no doubt, would "make away with" the girl's as well as the heron's inalienable rights to a "separate" yet unobtrusive sanctuary. But the fact that "we Americans," the story's readers, can understand and sympathize with Sylvia's choice, can metaphorically adopt her perspective and, thanks to authorial orchestrations, appreciate the maturity involved in making it, shows how rural values can easily become part of—even as they would modestly reform—America's federal self-image as a humanitarian society. Both the fence in "From a Mournful Villager" and the little girl in "A White Heron" thus function as token figures suggesting the possibility of an American intra-cultural accommodation. They dramatize the authentic harmony, the *true* Union, to be gained when people from the dominant federalist culture become privy to the "grand simple lives" of people from America's minority rural cultures.

One could reinterpret the other "self-existing" assertions of regionalist culture in "A White Heron" in the same way. The tree, for example, allows Sylvia to see the ocean and "a vast and awesome world" for the first time, a socially coded allusion to how the Union would appear if seen from a regionalist perspective—as "awesome" rather than established. The farmstead, too, represents a beneficial rather than poverty-stricken way of life; even the hunter recognizes its Thoreauvian promise, how it represents "the best thrift of an old-fashioned farmstead" as opposed to the "dreary squalor" he initially expects to find (xvi). It also neutralizes any stereotypical prejudices he and other urbanites might have about the xenophobia of country people: "[Mrs. Tilley's] long slumbering hospitality seemed to be easily awakened" (xvi). And where the story represents Sylvia as being sorely tempted by the ten dollars the stranger offers, it also insinuates that hers is primarily a child's fantasy economics: "No amount of thought, that night, could decide how many wished-for treasures the ten dollars, so lightly spoken of, would buy" (xviii). Obviously meaning more to the little girl than the two adults, this ten dollars would hardly constitute a temptation or self-evidently signify "capitalism" even to the story's nineteenth-century reader. At best, this "amount" signifies the more frugal but not anticapitalist exchange-value system of regionalist culture—with access to "good milk and plenty of it"—that could provide a brake to the excesses of the federalist marketplace. But in either case, it does not signify the difference between being rich and poor as Sylvia imagines.

More important, the story portrays the hunter in other than pejoratively Faustian-epistemological terms. It variously refers to him as a friendly, communicative "*young* man" who teaches Sylvia "about the birds"; far from being unequivocally associated with the "noisy town," he appears as capable of silence as the girl when together they "traversed the solemn woodlands with soft-footed *silent* care" (xviii). It also represents him as not presuming or taking for granted the hospitality of the two women. One could say that from the very beginning he regards them with total respect: "He listened eagerly to the old woman's quaint talk, he watched Sylvia's pale face and shining gray eyes with ever growing enthusiasm, and insisted that this was the best supper he had eaten for a month" (xvi). And he appears sensitive, despite the fact that "Sylvia would have liked him vastly better without his gun" or "could not understand why he killed the very birds he seemed to like so much" (xviii). Although too old for this nine-year-old girl, the hunter still feels romantic affection for her, for if Sylvia "was vaguely thrilled by a dream of love," so too "some premonition of that great power stirred and swayed these young foresters" together (xviii). Nor does the story depict him as a representative of the self-certain, both progressive and aggressive aspects of scientific inquiry, an epistemological relation to nature in comparison with which Sylvia's regionalist "heart to heart" relation to it accrues heroic if fragile status. The story shows his relation to be no less vulnerable than hers. He himself admits he has "lost my way, and need[s] a friend very much" (xv). Moreover, we can see that his desire to capture or "objectify" the white heron depends on both the hospitality of his hostesses and particularly Sylvia's firsthand knowledge of its habitat.

Indeed, the ideological perspective of "A White Heron" seems to uphold a synthetic rather than antithetical mode of knowledge, that is, one which could accommodate both Sylvia's "dumb" or experiential relation to nature and the discursive enlightenment promised by the hunter's objective, scientific kind. Jewett had broached this perspective in "River Driftwood." There she asks for "the linguist who [could learn] the first word of an old crow's warning to his mate" (not unlike the white heron's warning "to his mate on the nest" [xxi]), or could "talk to the trees, and birds . . . in their own language"; then she wonders whether "science . . . will give us back the gift, or shall we owe it to the successors of those friendly old saints who talked with the birds and fishes? We could have schools for them, if we once could understand them, and could educate them into being more useful to us."[26] Similarly, one could argue that the hunter/ornithologist can teach Sylvia only "*about* the birds," and thus represents the beginning of a true knowledge of nature. But in the same way, in her capacity as saintlike child, who lives in what appears "like a *hermitage*" (xvi) and has squirrels and birds "come an' feed right out o' her hands" (xvii), Sylvia too remains a novitiate of nature, a figure who has yet to learn, not to mention learn how to communicate to others, the "gifts and graces" and "secrets" of nature that a "heart to heart" relation to it may *eventually* yield. In short, taken separately, both the hunter's and Sylvia's modes of knowing nature are inadequate; but together, they could indeed "educate [nature] into being more useful to us." If not grounded in a "heart to heart" or an intuitive knowledge, a purely discursive knowledge of nature will lead to its death. But as the story also suggests, the former without the latter results in a "dumb" if more preferable childlike state, a silence, that is, which cannot communicate its knowledge and thus becomes vulnerable — and makes nature vulnerable as well — to an only postponed and by itself limited scientific understanding.

One could even maintain that Jewett *privileges* a progressive mode of knowing nature that analogously signifies her support of federalist ideals: "The day will come for a more truly universal suffrage . . . when the meaning of every little thing is understood, and it is given the rights and accorded its true value."[27] From this perspective, we could claim that "A White Heron" privileges an egalitarian or democratic mode of knowledge that would reveal the "rights" of "*every* little thing." Here Sylvia rather than the hunter represents an authentic Union epistemological vision. She alone comes to see (and be seen by) the white heron; she alone becomes initiated into an ecological vision of nature in contrast to the hunter whose fixation on one aspect of it, the heron alone, prevents him from comprehending nature as a totality of parts. To his restricted perspective, nature indeed must be "secret" or as "elusive" as the heron. In contrast, Sylvia symbolizes the story's democratic epistemological perspective where the observer of nature can always become the observed as well, a position Jewett sometimes expresses in almost a Whitmanesque democratic manner: "The great gulls watch me float along the river curiously and sail in the air overhead. Who knows what they say of me when they talk together; and what are they thinking when they fly quickly out of sight?"[28]

But in the spirit of a revised Union rhetoric, we need not claim that Jewett's story privileges one above the other epistemological position. Instead, we could argue that at the end of the story, Sylvia *and* the hunter are at the beginning of knowledge not only because of their youth but because together they represent a synthesis of scientific and intuitive or "heart to heart" relations to nature. On the one hand, insofar as we think of ornithology as an avocation rather than a serious vocation, the story mitigates the hunter's potentially villainous ideological role. Like the little girl but in different terms, he too is an amateur of nature, someone who has collected birds "since I was a boy" (xvii). On the other, whatever else we wish to say about the hunter's quest to capture the white heron by means of his gun, this quest can result in sharable human knowledge about nature. The means, not the end, of ornithology will provoke our censure. Not killing birds for sheer egregious pleasure, then, the hunter quests for a certain kind of knowledge which dilutes the *radically* pejorative significance of such killing.

More important, perhaps, this quest provides the occasion for breaking down the potentially radical social barriers between federalist and regionalist ideologies in the American state. The quest unwittingly ("a surprise") leads him to "so clean and comfortable a little dwelling in the New England wilderness" (xvi) and, in the process, comes to demystify any ideologically hierarchical assumptions he may have had regarding country people. Obversely, this quest leads him to Sylvia, the narrative's regionalist persona who through this accidental meeting not only begins to know nature's "secrets" by the end of the story, but also comes to recognize the unnecessary opposition between her regionalist respect for nature and his federalist project which would destroy it. In other words, his federalist quest also serves to demystify any "self-existing" assumptions regionalist culture might have about itself. In both respects, then, Jewett's "A White Heron" could be said to turn this binary ideological opposition into one of mere intracultural, neutralized difference. If only ironically, the hunter's quest for the white heron initiates Sylvia into a new attentiveness toward nature. But her renewed regionalist vision also represents the "grand simple lives" of country people to the story's urbanite readers in the name of a more authentic understanding of an American democratic Union.

4   There remains yet another way we can interpret the story's ideologically coded revelations of the contradictions within as well as between a regionalist and federalist cultural vision of the American state. The accommodation as opposed to the "indignation" Jewett promotes in "A White Heron" could also be seen as a means to withdraw from the dramatic ideological implications of adopting a regionalist cultural perspective. Accommodation here becomes a rhetorical means to adopt this perspective without engaging in ideological conflict at all. In the coda of the story, for example, we read of Sylvia's sense of loss over the hunter and "the great world" he represents; but the narrative mitigates the "hauntedness" of her retrievals of the cow by suggesting that she will continue to discover other natural "secrets" which not only will minimize this loss but will justify her otherwise repetitive rural existence. By contrast, in "The Independent Thinker," a story published in the same year as "A White

Heron" by Mary Wilkins Freeman, another so-called New England local color writer alert to the contradictions within a "self-existing" regionalist culture, the conflict between an individual and her rural society becomes the story's *primary* focus.[29]

In short, the indeterminate pro-regionalist, pro-Union signs in Jewett's story could exist as part of a strategy to shun the very occasions of socially coded conflicts. This strategy, in other words, serves to neutralize the socioconflictual allusions that are called into play when one writes about regionalist "things just as they are." Indeed, this neutralization often occurs even within the syntagmatic process of writing on such topics. In a previously cited passage from "River Driftwood," for example, I suggested that given the fact of any text's allegorization of its "social" or ideological scene of writing (especially in the case of late-nineteenth-century American local color writing), Jewett's language about those "self-existing . . . springs" willy-nilly raises secessionist ideas that could result in "an awful confusion and chaos still," that is, a de facto Civil War "still" continuing within the superstructural activities of American society. And lest such ideas "[lead] one to think of the transmigration of souls and other puzzling subjects," i.e., the possibility of unsocializable elements within the body politic or the sense of cosmic order confirming a Unionist American ideology, Jewett quickly attempts to limit the analogical implications of her discourse: "My river, as I said at first, leads to the sea, and from any port one can push off toward another sea of boundless speculation."[30]

The virtual caesura here between "my river" and "any port" marks the difference between a personally specific, referential use of language and an analogical or universal usage inevitably underwritten by the passage's readers. Unlike the river in "my river," the port in "any port" becomes nonreferential, not an actual port on her river so much as a point of discursive-analogical departure for semantic destinations that include its own federalist ideological background. By admitting such analogical thinking into a passage that has just been on the verge of signifying secessionist ideas, Jewett's writing virtually surrenders to American Union demands that regionalist subcultures underwrite its *e pluribus unum* ethos, regardless that these demands will entail "boundless speculation," a radical dilution *or* transcendence of these cultures. But such "speculation" also functions as a distraction to the passage's probable Union readers. One cannot turn back to Jewett's personal reference to her avowed regionalist topos ("my river") except through the detour of the universalizing tendency of language which, of course, can *rhetorically* envision the possibility of radical contingency or particularity of place so that, for example, the general "my river" becomes the specifically referential "*my* river." Thus, the caesura between "my" and "any" in this passage could easily serve to conceal Jewett's attempt to retain *and regain* her reference to her region for herself alone, that is, *after* she acknowledges its necessary metaphorization and ideological reclamation by a federalist discursive praxis.

But if after reading this passage "my" becomes "any" to readers — and residually more "*my* river" or region to its writer than it was before being written — this reclamation does not necessarily suggest Jewett's reactionary repetition of a bourgeois or Union privatism, her desire, that is, to possess regionalist materials all for herself. For one thing, the act of writing makes this reclamation or "Region Regained" project by definition a transitory and at best subliminal possibility. For another, this rhetorical maneuver functions in Jewett's writing primarily to remove her regionalist topos from its conflicted social thematic, and thus from the very occasion for the expression of a minority indignation over, resignation to, or even positive acceptance of, the prevailing American state. Although it diminishes if not annihilates the social value of regional cultures in America, Jewett's historical situation partially (and here ironically) reproduces this function as well. From our late-twentieth-century perspective, the transition from a regionalist to federalist America has definitively occurred; from Jewett's, we could argue, this transition still was in process, thus affording her the occasional option to apprehend the changes it was producing as if they could paradoxically preserve the past through its arbitrary and postmetaphorical difference from the present.

We can see this strategy of reserving a regionalist past most explicitly in "From a Mournful Villager" where the very subject entails a wish for the "reserve" or "sanctity" of regionalist front yards. Jewett can refer to this past only from the standpoint of "we Americans" and through the token metonym of "more fences," a metonym that, because it must remain arbitrarily related to the "past" past which her act of writing invokes, leaves this past as if it were still to be signified. The effect of this stylistic reserve clause in Jewett's narrative is to make this already generically reserved sketch a reserved discourse on regionalist values, and to remove this discourse from its already indeterminate sociohistorical regionalist *or* federalist topos. But such stylistic maneuvers also attest to the fact that the ambiguous ideological positions of her writing are by themselves incapable of warding off the latent social conflicts her regionalist materials spontaneously invoke. These maneuvers, then, serve both to invite and to evade a subcodified "social" response which, since they foster the illusion of a determinate pro or contra federalist reading, in effect leaves unread a literally reserved and regionalist subtext—that is, a minor minority "regionalist" text whose virtual discursive silence a federalist majority culture, like the hunter faced with Sylvia's silent "secret," can never evaluate on its own ideological terms. In the same way, Jewett may seem elegiacally fixated on a New England regionalist past in "From a Mournful Villager"; but her persona remains not fully focused on this past (since she must advocate its token return), not fully committed to the present (since she desires to "fence" it away), and unconvinced as regards the American future ("we . . . had better . . .").

But nowhere in Jewett's works is this process of stylistic-ideological indeterminacy better exemplified than in "A White Heron." Its Union-accommodating not to mention antifederalist allusions work to induce its own misreading and in this way produce a regionalist text that, like the white heron itself, ultimately eludes the "social" grid of both perspectives. In this sense, the ten dollars the hunter offers Sylvia for information about the heron only apparently signifies the real *or* imaginary, the pejoratively *or* neutrally regarded, exchange-value system of postbellum American capitalism. We can now see how the narrative quickly translates this monetary amount into an indefinite "amount of *thought*" focused on the girl's "wished-for treasures." A rather blatant "social" seme becomes displaced here from its material significance for both a child and an adult, to "thought" and the vague, immaterial musings relevant to a child alone who "had all the time [i.e., leisure] there was, and very little use to make of it" (xiii). Indeed, as the story progresses, the money's melodramatic value, its constituting an obstacle to Sylvia's final choice, dissipates before her no less "vaguely" defined romantic interest in the hunter who "is so well worth making happy" (xxii).

The same holds true for the story's setting and for its provocative allusion to industrial technology through the hunter's gun. The regional setting of "A White Heron" seems conspicuously unspecified, as if it were merely a provisional place-referent in the process of becoming more indefinite. The story "locates" the farm by a mode of dis-location; it exists somewhere between total "wilderness" and a "town" (itself a modified or displaced allusion to a city). The narrative also describes the farm as a "clean and comfortable . . . little dwelling," distinguishing it from a possible exemplification of "primitive housekeeping"; but even as it represents "the best thrift of an old-fashioned farmstead," an allusion which excuses it from its social significance in postbellum New England, it appears "on such a small scale that it seemed like a hermitage" (xvi). These reductive or asocial determinations of the farm also apply to the hunter's gun. A gun hardly constitutes a synecdoche of the new industrial technology of postbellum America; the hunter, after all, uses it in a countryside setting, a "New England wilderness," where, as Mrs. Tilley suggests when she remarks how "Dan, my boy, was a great hand to go gunning" (xvi), both it and the activity of hunting must seem as natural as farming. The story also places the gun on a spectrum of possible minitechnological relations to nature. It has Sylvia accept the hunter's "jack-knife, which she thought as great a treasure as if she were a desert-islander" (xviii). For the hunter, the jackknife and gun represent practical implements for dealing respectively with inanimate and animate nature; for Sylvia, they appear as part of her fantasy world, one a romantic "treasure" supporting this world, the other a "sharp" reminder of a reality that threatens it.

Thus, while sympathizing with Sylvia's attitude toward the hunter's gun, the adult readers of the story cannot help but perceive blurred distinctions where she perceives vivid ones. Indeed, the reader has to ask how else the hunter could capture the heron—a project Sylvia accepts as worthwhile throughout most of the story—*except* by means of this practical gun. More important, the story further displaces the "social" significance of the gun by unconsciously crossing it with its unavoidable sexual connotations. Sylvia, we could say, accepts the phallic jackknife, i.e., a sexual knowledge whose harmlessness and indefiniteness the story conveys through indefinite phraseology like "*some* premonition of *that great power*" or "*vaguely* thrilled by *a dream* of love" (xviii). But of course she rejects the more imminent phallic sexuality connoted by the hunter's gun. Its effect on birds is made analogous to a female virgin's sexual anxiety: Sylvia feels sorrow at "the sharp report of *his* gun and . . . pretty feathers *stained and wet with blood*" (xxiii). In this context, the hunter represents not so much a Union presumption to know and (ab)use its subcultures as a male quest-hero who, as Annis Pratt argues, tends to know and (ab)use the woman — much in the way we can claim male critics do with Jewett's story — as an object of his patriarchal quest.[31]

But even if it leads the story into other areas of ideological conflict, such code switching serves to divert attention from the more explicitly social conflict posed by Jewett's regionalist topos. Moreover, the switch from explicitly social semes to the more implicitly social allusions to epistemological conflict further dissipates the story's already displaced expressions of ideological conflict. In one sense, by representing two modes of knowing nature, the story calls up the contemporary Huxley-Arnold debate between science and religion, Jewett's allusion to "old saints" in "River Driftwood," for example.[32] But this intellectual or more generalized epistemological conflict gets resolved, as we noted, by a "synthetic" synthesis in Jewett's writing that leaves "every little thing" *not yet* "understood," and which thus represents the hunter as a pre-mature scientist and Sylvia a premature transcendentalist visionary.

"A White Heron" also withdraws the socioepistemological allusion endemic to its regionalist topos in more specific fashion. Mrs. Tilley has lost "four children, so that Sylvia's mother, and a son (who might be dead) in California were all the children she had left" (xvi). But "this hint of family sorrows" conspicuously omits reference to the fact that at least one if not all of the lost children must have lived through or even died in the Civil War, i.e., precisely the locus of conflict pertaining to the American Union. The story does more than pass over this war generation (for whom guns indeed might have signified death); the three generations and the potentially conflictual generation gap the story does represent clearly exemplify a kind of democratic ignorance that again suspends the question of an existing, privileged mode of knowledge. Monetary circumstances as opposed to regionalist-ideological values have prevented Mrs. Tilley from migrating west with her son Dan: "I'd ha' seen the world myself if it had been so I could" (xvi). And like Sylvia and the hunter, Mrs. Tilley also exemplifies a limited epistemological perspective. Her age alone, if not her sorrows as a mother, argues for her having gained knowledge from experience. Yet she fails to understand her granddaughter, whom she needs for "assistance" to run the farm, when she "rebukes" her for not telling the heron's secret to the hunter, even though she understands Sylvia's special affinity for birds: "Last winter she got the jay-birds to bangeing here, and I believe she'd 'a scanted herself of her own meals to have plenty to throw out amongst 'em, if I had n't kep' watch" (xvii). Experienced or innocent, male or female, child, young adult, or elder, the nonwar generational representatives in "A White Heron" cannot claim special access to wisdom or knowledge about life, hence cannot represent any privileged ideological perspective.[33]

In short, Jewett's story withdraws not only from the social ramifications of the topoi associated with regionalist writing, but also from the region of "regionalist" writing itself and/or its possible ideological perspectives. Even the narration, for example, after adopting a conventional, selectively omniscient but also empathetic stance toward its protagonist—"Now look down again, Sylvia . . . there where you saw the white heron once you will see him again" (xxi)—seems to retreat from a determinate or knowledgeable representation of the girl's plight. On the one hand, Sylvia remains silent because she knows the hunter will kill the heron; she comes to realize "she cannot . . . give its life away" (xxii). On the other, this otherwise definitive moral choice, made in the face of the hunter's "kind appealing eyes . . . looking straight in her own" (xxii), is mitigated by earlier narrative information. From the very beginning, silence is Sylvia's primary characteristic. Mrs. Tilley suggests she had chosen Sylvia from her daughter's "houseful of children" to live on the farm precisely because of the girl's reticence before people: "'Afraid of folks,' old Mrs. Tilley said to herself . . . after she had made the unlikely choice of Sylvia" (xiv). To live in the country, we recall, requires a preference for its peaceful silence over the town's "noisy" society.

But Sylvia's silence represents an extreme behavioral trait as much as a temperamental compatibility with rural modes of life. Even Mrs. Tilley, who represents country life and regionalist mores in the story if anyone does, seems easily hospitable and talkative to the stranger: ". . . the hostess gossiped frankly . . ." (xvi). In contrast, "Sylvia kept an awed silence" in presenting the hunter to her grandmother (xv). She literally fails to utter a word in the story except to speak "almost inaudibly" (xv), to give her name "'Sylvy,' with much effort" in her first meeting with the hunter (xv), and to call "Co'! Co'!" to the cow which, like herself later before the hunter, does not respond to impatient human requests (xiii). The narrative propagates the illusion that Sylvia converses with others. But the illusion is broken when the narrator must speak in the place of Sylvia's speech and thoughts. Like Mrs. Tilley who informs the hunter that her granddaughter knows the woods so well that "the wild creatur's counts her as one o' themselves" (xvii), the narrator in her self-restricting omniscience—her limited epistemological position—mediates, makes indeterminate, her protagonist's thinking. When the question is asked, "Were the birds better friends than their hunter might have been,—who can tell?" (xxiii), we cannot determine whether it belongs to the narrator's overvoice or Sylvia's own thinking. Believable or not, Sylvia's final silence is conspicuously ambiguous because the narrative keeps this silence silent; the girl's decision is indecisive even to herself.

In short, the latent xenophobia and virtual aphasia of this girl and perhaps the narrative itself attenuate not only the nature of this apparent choice but also the story's politically unconscious allegiance either to regionalist or federalist ideology. The narrative informs us that she speaks to the hunter, for example; but it also sets up a contrast between his voluntary *act* of teaching her "many things about the birds" and her passive or *re*-active behavior: "She did not dare to look boldly at the tall young man" (xv). Where he initiates conversations, she only responds to his words: "There was no such thing as speaking first. The sound of her own unquestioned voice would have terrified her" (xix). This characterization clearly suggests that, riddled with ambiguity ("who can tell?") and reluctance ("now, when the great world for the first time puts out a hand to her, must she thrust it aside for a bird's sake?" [xxii]), Sylvia's decision is less a choice of life over death, nature over society, let alone regionalist over federalist *or* authentic federalist over debased regionalist and federalist values, than a resolve to accept the necessity of making a decision. This decision, in other words, occurs outside herself; at best it connotes a passive moral choice, one that both she and the narrative (she "*must* keep silence" [xxii], and she "*cannot* speak" and *cannot* tell" [xxii]) inertly, rather than through some sudden enlightenment, weigh on the side of the heron. For this reason, Sylvia's putative moral act quickly becomes estranged from its result. Soon after the stranger leaves "disappointed," she "forgot even her sorrow at the sharp report of his gun" (xxiii).

Yet from our present perspective, this attenuation of Sylvia's credibility or believability as a moral heroine should be regarded as but another strategy for the story itself to withdraw from the ideological dialectics of its topos. Indeed, the convention of verisimilitude serves to absolve Sylvia from representing the Romantic metaphor of the child recalling adult readers to their own possibly innocent relation to nature or to the enduring value of regionalist ways of life. As a child, the protagonist is actually spared making "adult" choices which in the end both we and the narrative seem inclined to make for her. Insofar as we become privy to her otherwise unspoken romantic attraction to and desire to please the hunter, we readers no less than the adult authorial narrator will likely interpret Sylvia's passive silence as a positive moral and "social" sign. But even this romantic framework that could make Sylvia's decision appear decisive for more than a child loses its validity in the face of her preadolescent, preerotic age. Whatever it means to the hunter, "that great power" which stirs Sylvia remains mere "premonition," only an indefinite or "vaguely" experienced feeling that, were it more definitive, would justify our attributing serious moral and perhaps ideological significance to her final refusal to tell the heron's secret.

"A White Heron" further emphasizes the preerotic status of the girl when it reduces her feelings for the hunter literally to childish infatuation or mere puppy love: "[She] could have served and followed him and loved him as a dog loves!" This allusion not only neutralizes the latent sexual significance of Sylvia's anxiety over the hunter's gun, the sexual conflict we suggested previously, but also shows how the story deploys her status as a nine-year-old child to retract her metaphorical function as a pivotal ideological actant or semiotic pretext for the story's protest against or confirmation of Union and/or regionalist cultural values. Or put another way, Sylvia's identity as a minor constitutes a reserve clause in the contract that requires her to signify a regionalist vision, a reserve clause that ultimately seeks to elude this binary cultural topos. Because she is yet to come of age or be recognized as an adult, she can represent a consciousness that, as it were, *comes before* any awareness of the ideological conflict of the kind subtending local color stories and sketches.

Jewett's "minor" ideological symbols, then, whether a little girl or a New England fence, become more minor when we apprehend them against the mixed social as well as literary codes her writing calls into play. Her works ironically *work* to defer their serious if latent "social" meanings, that is, their identity or locus within specific postbellum American "harvests of change" that willy-nilly infiltrate the style and topoi of local color writing. Fence, little girl, or white heron, Jewett's subjects appear within the nexus of an unavoidable "social" discourse which requests determinate readings in the way one symptomatically tends to say "The" when citing "A White Heron." [34] But occurring, so to speak, after requesting a relatively self-evident "regionalist" response, the continuous *process* of indeterminacy that Jewett's texts practice has the effect of suspending such responses. In other words, it is as if her narratives were in the process of expecting but then withdrawing from their inescapable "social" registers of significance. We think we know the "social" significance of Sylvia's final decision; but then it dissipates via the reserve clause of verisimilitude or becomes no less an "accident" than her first encounter with the hunter (xv). If in spite of this intentional/unintentional self-indeterminacy, the story, like Sylvia's final decision, accrues such significance, then in turn it too becomes indecisive, provisional, or irresolute: "Were the birds better friends than their hunter might have been,—who can tell?"

Of course, to avoid the definitive social ramifications of Jewett's regionalist topos, or to represent "things just as they are" in her Maine countryside from the point of view of a child's preconflictual social awareness, is not actually to escape, except by rhetorical repression, the dialectical comprehensiveness of the ideological context in which this story necessarily becomes inscribed. But with its irresolute "silent" and "secret" resistance to or confirmation of the country's founding federal Constitution, "A White Heron" seeks to elude this context, especially as pertains to its socioliterary reception. That is, like the heron in the story, "A White Heron," whether from some migratory or mutational accident that dilutes its sense of ideological pressure, attempts to separate itself from its "local color" context of reception. In commenting on this story, Jewett herself would acknowledge its anomalous literary identity:

> Mr. Howells thinks that this age frowns upon the romantic, that it is no use to write romance any more; but dear me, how much of it there is left in every-day life after all. It must be the fault of the writers that such writing is dull, but what shall I do with my "White Heron" now she is written? She isn't a very good magazine story, but I love her.[35]

Howells could support local color writing insofar as it conformed to his notion of a federalist or "main currents" social realism. The fact that Jewett regards "A White Heron" as "romance" or not "a very good magazine story" thus doubly situates it as — at its "social" best — the story of a minor's minor righting of a major American cultural conflict, expressed within a minor literary genre. But "romance" is even further removed from social realism than is the contemporary mode of local color writing for which she herself was accorded a measure of recognition. And so one could read her comment as a virtual confession of her desire to have written "A White Heron" completely outside the socioliterary setting of her times, namely as a text that would possess minor value whether to a regionalist or a federalist mode of reception.

Folktales, we know from structuralist critics, operate according to binary oppositions in various codified guises. If not a folktale per se, "A White Heron" at least calls our attention to a certain "social" opposition which until recently has constituted the story's most typical codified response. But examining this response has led us to appreciate the way "A White Heron," in what seems a continuous process of self-indeterminacy, referential *and* figurative, phenomenologically withdraws from its otherwise aggrieved, subversive, or moderate position within Jewett's inevitably conflicted "American" discourse. Still, the story's virtual self-subtraction of one "social" seme, suggesting its desire to determine itself as of minor thematic importance, makes way for another which could be using the former as a minor pretext to express an even more major minority grievance.

CHAPTER TWO "A WHITE HERON"

AS A NUN-SUCH

They shut me up in Prose—
As when a little Girl
They put me in the Closet
Because they liked me "still"—

Still! Could themself have peeped—
And seen my Brain—go round—
They might as wise have lodged a Bird
For Treason—in the Pound—

Himself has but to will
And easy as a Star
Abolish his Captivity—
And laugh—No more have I—

—Emily Dickinson

This is my birthday and I am always nine years old.
—Sarah Orne Jewett (circa 1897)

A child draws the outline of a body
She draws what she can, but it is white all through,
she cannot fill in what she knows is there.
—Louise Glück

1   The ideological climate established by recent feminist critical theories regarding the "revision" of women's fiction, its writers
as well as characters, encourages and even requires us to read "A White
Heron" as a latent feminist document. To be sure, the story itself does
not seem to request this kind of reading. From its publication in 1886
to the present, most critics have codified it in terms of the "local color"
binary which we have discussed in the preceding chapter. But this codification too, called for by the story's topos, theme, and the literary-
historical setting in which it appears, can be apperceived as a screen
partially concealing a nineteenth-century woman writer's protest
against a patriarchal American society which controlled her means
of literary production as well as her legal social status. Such a society
undoubtedly would have made Jewett feel little older than her story's
nine-year-old "minor" protagonist.[1]

To support this feminist rereading of Jewett's story, we can first
point to her undoubtable awareness of the nineteenth-century woman's movement. John Neal, a fellow Maine writer who died in 1876,
was one of this movements' most outspoken and prolific proponents.[2]
Jewett herself was more than likely aware of Stanton's 1848 declaration at the Seneca Falls Convention; she was certainly aware of Mary
Wollstonecraft's *Rights of Woman* and Margaret Fuller's *Woman in
the Nineteenth Century,* both of which were reviewed in 1855 by
George Eliot, an author whose "major" works she owned in her library.[3] Indeed, when she first began to write, Jewett had used the
pseudonym "Alice Eliot," a name Cary thinks derives from the pseudonym of Mary Ann Evans.[4] Do we glimpse even here Jewett's early
wish to reclaim feminine literary authority for her writing? "Alice
Eliot" could easily constitute a refeminization of "George Eliot," itself representing the nineteenth-century woman writer's strategic use
of a male signature to receive a fair reading of her works in a patriarchal society where women were precluded from being taken as "serious" writers.[5] In any case, we also find Jewett making a coded
feminist allusion to the ideal of "universal suffrage" in a previously
cited passage from "River Driftwood"; or in the 1881 "From a Mournful Villager," arguing that "the sanctity of the front yard of . . . grandmothers" once connoted woman's secondary status, her "restricted
and narrowly limited life," but now the "disappearance of many of

the village front yards may come to be typical of the altered position of woman, and mark a stronghold on her way from the *much talked-of* slavery and subjection to a coveted equality."[6]

But the most telling sign of Jewett's ongoing concern with the nineteenth-century woman's grievance against, and attempt to rectify her position in, patriarchal society occurs in her 1884 work *A Country Doctor,* a novel which she later said she liked the "best" of all her "books."[7] As many critics have noted, in depicting the relationship between Nan Prince, the protagonist of this novel, and Dr. Leslie, the country doctor who becomes her mentor, Jewett here indirectly represents her own relationship with *her* country doctor father.[8] It is significant, then, that the story focuses on Nan's struggle to declare her female vocational independence, that is, to become a doctor in a male-dominated profession. As a child whose mother and grandmother have died, Nan becomes a member of Dr. Leslie's household. She eventually follows this childless widower on his rounds, just as Jewett did with her father, and gets smitten with the idea of becoming a doctor, an idea Dr. Leslie supports but, recognizing the difficulty she will encounter in trying to enter a male-dominated profession, encourages only cautiously. Nan ultimately realizes her desire, though not before she is made to doubt her vocational choice through the resistance of patriarchal males and females who think "a woman's proper place" is marriage. A woman, in fact, presents Nan with the greatest obstacle to realizing her vocational ambition. Nan's relatively wealthy paternal aunt Nancy, who lives in a city and whom Nan discovers after she has become an adult, not only tries to woo her away from the rural culture represented by Dr. Leslie, but staunchly maintains that Nan should get married.

The nineteenth-century feminist elements of *A Country Doctor* thus seem rather clear. On the one hand, we have a female protagonist who expresses her rights to enter a privileged profession from which women are systematically excluded and for which men are prepared from birth. Or as Nan herself remarks, given the same childhood backgrounds, still

"everything helps a young man to follow his bent; he has an honored place in society, and just because he is a student of one of the learned professions, he ranks above the men who follow other pursuits. I don't see why it should be a shame and dishonor to a girl who is trying to do the same thing and to be of equal use in the world. God would not give us the same talents if what were right for men were wrong for women."[9]

On the other hand, Nan's reliance on a benign father figure (or on "God") to help her realize her social equality with men, however much it may have indicated one of "the larger effects of socialization, which . . . may govern the limits of expression or even of perception and experience itself" for women in other periods,[10] in this case reads like a gloss on Margaret Fuller. Unlike Nan's male suitor, for example, Dr. Leslie does not treat Nan as what Fuller termed an "article of property" or "an adopted child," i.e., in the way nineteenth-century men treated women.[11] Instead of treating the very young Nan with the deferential affection of a parent, "[he] did not like children *because* they were children" and thus comes to view her in the same light as one of his own "grown friends" (my italics).[12] In Dr. Leslie, Nan finds that "good father's early trust" that gives one of Fuller's enlightened woman friends "the first bias" for her "self-dependence, which was honored [in her by her father]," though "deprecated as a fault in most women" by other men.[13]

One could argue, then, that in fact and fiction Jewett perceived the woman's struggle for "self-dependence" along the same lines as her New England feminist precursor. Fuller had noted how feminine autonomy found its "preliminary [in] the increase of the class contemptuously designated as 'old maids.'"[14] Unmarried herself, her closest friends women, most especially Annie Fields, Jewett represents Nan's desire to become a doctor as requiring the rejection of marriage, an institution that Fuller and other nineteenth-century feminists deemed a patriarchal means for keeping women from realizing their own "spiritual" potential.[15] This desire is clearly that of a conscious feminist, although presented as that of a "New England nun." Nan thus does not make her vocational choice before entertaining serious doubts and being attracted to the possibility of marriage.[16] Moreover, in the sociohistorical context in which it appears, Nan's desire to become a physician also inescapably signifies a desire for

a distinctively feminine as opposed to a general, i.e., less sexually conflictual, "self"-independence. Nan Prince's professional ambition
clearly exists in precise opposition to established patriarchal norms
of social behavior, an instance of which occurs when George Gerry,
a prospective suitor, becomes threatened by her "unnatural" self-
reliance: "It is in human nature to respect power; but all his manli-
ness was at stake, and his natural rights would be degraded and lost,
if he could not show his power to be greater than her own."[17]

But although Nan represents the ideal of female autonomy in *A
Country Doctor,* the "virgin" who, in Fuller's words, would escape
"the very fault of marriage . . . [namely] that the woman *does* belong to the man," her claim to social equality or the right to enter
a male-dominated profession effectively buttresses rather than challenges the "power" of this patriarchically valued profession itself. Fuller
had argued that the truly autonomous woman would remain radically "unrelated" to the established cultural roles valued by males. To
become a doctor, after all, would hardly dispose of the elitist hierarchical comparisons Nan associates with patriarchal institutions:
"Just because [one male] is a student of one of the learned profes
sions, he ranks above the men who follow other pursuits." Nan's wish
to become a *country* doctor like Dr. Leslie mitigates her complicity
with such institutional elitism but remains no less related to the latter. Even the confrontational aspects of Nan's feminist ambition, and
therefore of Jewett's novel, could frustrate the realization of a nonheterosexual or "virgin" female autonomy. Such confrontation would
amount to engaging or even wanting to accept patriarchal values — a
more moderate feminist idea which Fuller opposed but which also
has radical feminist ramifications, as we shall see — and thus would
retard women's attempts to develop a totally "unrelated" feminine
culture or value system.[18]

What better way, then, to promulgate transcendentalist feminist
values to other women than in an innocuous story with a nonadult
and therefore nonfeminist "virgin" heroine whose silent refusal to be
conscripted by a patriarchal ethos is bound to go unnoticed by male
readers as a radical feminist declaration of independence? Precisely
because it "isn't a very good magazine story" to Jewett, "A White
Heron," like the white heron in the story, eludes the determinate de-

mands of the patriarchal "great world." In this sense, Jewett's story at once corroborates and exploits the fact that within a patriarchal society, women lead secret lives; that they have become used to concealing and suppressing their ideas; that instead of eliminating they should cultivate this secret apartness, that is, work to "leave off asking [men] and being influenced by them" and rather "retire within themselves" as women in "virgin loneliness."[19] Surely it is this "virgin loneliness," apt to be misread as a sentimental, even narcissistic denouement, that Sylvia represents with authorial encouragement at the story's end: "Bring your gifts and graces and tell your secrets to this lonely country child!" (xxiii).

At first, to be sure, the story does not seem to reverberate with coded feminist "secrets" so much as with modest feminist allusions. The exception to this surface modesty may occur in the "canine servitude" that we have seen Annis Pratt argue Sylvia escapes, servitude to a hunter who here represents a rapacious patriarchal world that would make women as well as nature into objects of sexual and intellectual pleasure (see p. xxvii above). But with this possible exception, we do not need to rely heavily on feminist literary-critical tenets, such as Elaine Showalter's idea that women's fiction is a "double-voiced discourse, containing a 'dominant' and a 'muted' story" (the latter normally comprising the work's subcoded feminist connotations), to unearth the tale's images of female independence.[20] The cultural world Sylvia inhabits is a de facto matriarchy. Her father is dead or has left her mother; Mrs. Tilley's husband is dead, her son Dan gone off to seek his fortune in the West. Conversely, not only are the two adult women spared direct relations with patriarchal families—and relations to aggressive males within these families as exemplified by Dan and his father who "did n't hitch" (xvii)—they actively head these households as if men were unnecessary. Mrs. Tilley runs the farm at what appears to be a subsistent if not profit-making level: a "clean and comfortable" place suggesting "the best thrift of an old-fashioned farmstead, though on . . . a small scale" (xvi). Sylvia's mother supports a "houseful of children" back in that "crowded manufacturing town" (xiv), presumably by working in a factory. If only in a working-class way, both women demonstrate they can perform the economic functions traditionally assigned to *both* sexes.[21]

But the clearest indication of a feminist thematic in "A White Heron" lies in the little girl's encounter with the hunter. However benign he seems, in teaching Sylvia "about the birds," he also unconsciously comes to teach her "about the bees"—about a sublimated, aggressive male sexuality symbolized by his very project as well as the use of his gun. Where for the male critic, Sylvia's choice most often manifests her Thel-like turning away from the harsh realities of (a patriarchal American) society and/or sexuality, for the feminist critic this choice likely signifies a special brand of "heroinism."[22] By the end of the story, Sylvia, at the price of loneliness, has learned to recognize and avoid the ideologically coded willingness of even a "kind appealing" young male to violate a symbolically feminine and virginal nature for the sake of controlling "her," i.e., making her part of his "collection." As suggested by the etymology of her name (woods or forest) and her activities at the farm ("the wild creatur's counts her one o' themselves" [xvii]), this "nature" includes Sylvia herself.[23] Thus, both heron and heroine exist as mere objects within the hunter's field of perception; in terms of Fuller's definition of the woman's situation in patriarchal marriage, each is an interchangeable "article of property," items to be bought for ten dollars or seduced by the vague promise of romance. What Sylvia learns is that the hunter's quest for the heron "means murder" for herself as well as the bird; in turn, her identification with the heron comes to symbolize the desire of "the imprisoned girl-child to become a free adult."[24]

Ultimately, Jewett's narrative isolates Sylvia as the sole signifier of feminist ideology. Her mother and Mrs. Tilley, who will "rebuke" the girl for not telling the heron's secret to the hunter, show how women can duplicate male social roles but not act radically independent of American patriarchal values. Both women are not "free" but clearly if involuntarily remain inscribed within a patriarchal situation that thwarts their desires. Mrs. Tilley, for example, would "ha' seen the world . . . if it had been so I could" (xvi). It is against this stratum of feminine options as much as against the hunter's project that Sylvia appears as a "minor" because disguised symbol of radical feminist ideals. Precisely because she appears as no more than a child, she serves as a metaphorical "free *adult*" woman in whom female readers can see their only marginal relation to patriarchal determinations of their secondary social place. Thus, the "muted" story within Jewett's "A White Heron" concerns a white or pure feminine heroine who at the narrative's "dominant" level is described as "paler than ever," and thus subtly associated with the story's white heron. Or said another way, the little girl not only constitutes the story's secret and feminist anagrammatic title (white heron / white heroine), but also conveys its secret ideological life for those female readers who can revise what happens to her at the story's "dominant" or self-censored level. Like Annis Pratt, for example, such readers will immediately apprehend that Sylvia's feeling disappointment at not being able to "have served and . . . loved [the hunter] as a dog loves" (xxii–xxiii) signifies a deferred enslavement to a pejoratively construed patriarchal "great world."

More important, a strategic "mimetism," to use Mary Jacobus's term, pervades Jewett's representation of her feminist heroine's actions in the story. Mimetism entails the woman writer's "reproduction" of a "deliberately assumed" discursive practice pre-occupied by patriarchal values and myths about women; because she is unable to write "outside" a male literary tradition, there is no "alternative practice available to the woman writer apart from the process of undoing itself," even with regard to representing female heroines.[25] In this sense, we could argue that Jewett represents Sylvia with certain male-defined qualities in order to subtract them from or even reverse their assumed significance within the patriarchal ideological tradition which governs nineteenth-century literary representations. For example, by associating Sylvia with nature and especially the white heron, Jewett puts her in the role of the hunted object and thus seems to accede to the myth of the male as the active hunter, the traditional literary trope of males as the pursuers of women as well as natural creatures. Yet from the very beginning of the story, Jewett depicts *Sylvia* as a kind of hunter who becomes more successful in this activity than the hunter himself. She "had to hunt for" the cow, a *female* cow whose "pranks" she in turn assigns with "intelligent" or *active* meaning. Moreover, she knows the rural area around the farmstead as well as her uncle Dan whom Mrs. Tilley notes "she takes after": "There ain't a foot o' ground she don't know her way over" (xvii). And in attributing to her an ability to find the white heron, an ability that makes the hunter all but dependent on *her* prowess as a hunter, the story subliminally defines Sylvia as an incomparable huntress and woodland explorer. In short, coupled with her "virgin" identity, these depictions allusively associate her with Artemis—a figure of radical feminine independence in the classical patriarchal tradition.[26]

This "muted" metamorphosis of a minor into a major female heroine, a metamorphosis that suggests both the ongoing feminist goal to live "outside" stereotypical patriarchal definitions of a woman's "proper place" and the story's own "secret" literary ambition, repeats itself in relation to two other patriarchal myths. One could argue that the hunter and Sylvia, for example, reenact the story of Apollo and Daphne from Ovid's *Metamorphoses*. In mythological tradition, Apollo is the archer, the overseer of birds (notably of the *white* swan), the inspirer of divine knowledge, and in Ovid's story, the love-obsessed god who pursues Daphne, a wood nymph, until she escapes from him by becoming a tree, thanks to the power of her river god father.[27] The mysterious "handsome stranger" of "A White Heron" is an expert marksman with his gun, as "when he brought down some unsuspecting singing creature from its bough" (xviii); an "ornithologist"; someone who knows all "about the birds and what they knew and where they lived and what they did with themselves" (xviii); and a godlike figure to Sylvia who, even though he inexplicably "killed the very birds he seemed to like so much" (and so holds the power of life and death in his hands), looks up to him "with loving admiration" (xviii) and treats him with awestruck deference, "the young man going first and Sylvia following, fascinated . . . her gray eyes dark with excitement" (xix). Most especially, of course, the hunter is obsessed with capturing the white heron which, as we have seen in this feminist reading of the story, becomes all but synonymous with the "white heroine."

But this last "muted" metamorphosis should alert us to how "A White Heron" itself becomes a marginal feminist version of a myth that effectively reduces the woman to a fixed or knowable natural object. The story quite clearly assigns Sylvia with Daphne-like attributes. Her name, her climbing the "great pine-tree," her final (treelike) silent stance before the hunter, even the "woodlands" the narrative suggests she will indefinitely inhabit as the story ends, all allude to this girl's virtual transformation into a tree. Yet Sylvia's transformation results from but is not the result of the Apollonian hunter's quest;

it originates not out of anxiety, the sense of patriarchal pursuit, but out of her desire to "see all the world" from the tree, a desire, then, which like her name precedes and eventually supersedes the hunter's invasion of the farmstead. Thus, like the tree itself, the tree she regards "wistfully" not as a vehicle of escape but as a positive adventure, "the last of its generation," unaccountably left standing in the woods by (one assumes) past male settlers or shipbuilders, Sylvia remains beyond—or in Fuller's terms, "unrelated" to—the hunter's patriarchal code of understanding. But here she also replicates the status of the white heron that remains secret and literally beyond the hunter's vision. Sylvia *alone* climbs the tree, spots the heron and its secret nest, and ultimately refuses to divulge this experience to the hunter, i.e., to the patriarchal world both he and Sylvia's grandmother (as if she were a distraction from the confrontational sexual thematic of the story with its Apollo/Daphne allusion) represent.

In short, Sylvia's metamorphosis is variable, "free," elusive to any "proper" code of understanding. Indeed, the trope of "metamorphosis" may be considered a means for women writers to undo more traditional tropes like metaphor or simile which, for example, would make us perceive Sylvia *as* a displaced Daphne-like figure with a relatively stable significance.[28] No less than the story which allusively traces Ovid's, Sylvia becomes a site of purely possible signification, an interpretable "shy little" figure whose feminist significance remains secret but does not run away from male and female patriarchal readers.

But this "deliberately assumed" or traced revision of a classical patriarchal myth itself metamorphoses into a more major feminist revision of a less forgettable patriarchal myth. The tree that Sylvia climbs and which serves as the pivotal vehicle of her decision to save the heron obviously evokes comparison with the biblical Tree of Knowledge. In believing that "whoever climbed to the top of [the tree] could see the ocean . . . all the world" (xix), she assumes the trappings of an American Eve whose experience overturns the expectancies of the Puritan Judeo-Christian tradition that indicts the woman as the cause of Man's Fall, that is, because of her fatal curiosity about the Tree of Knowledge or Death.[29] The knowledge that the little girl gains from the tree results in life rather than death, in moral integrity rather than duplicity. Indeed, the heron Sylvia saves bears comparison with the peaceful "bird of paradise" found in many matriarchal creation myths. In this sense her action, far from being a sentimental Christian, i.e., patriarchal, homily on the value of life in general, symbolizes the return of a repressed feminine intentionality of nature.[30] Thus, both the story and Jewett's very writing of it could primarily concern this imaginary return to radical feminine origins or to a feminist perspective from which the "great pine-tree," say, symbolizes a gynocentric Tree of Knowledge precisely in opposition to its phallocentric usurpation and distortion in Western biblical tradition. Or just as the girl alone climbs the tree and sees the heron, so Jewett's "shy little" story entails a "secret" rhetorical transumption by which women can reclaim a gender-exclusive relation to the origins of life or the Edenic Garden in the face of patriarchal propaganda which would reduce such "knowledge" to a Fallen or ontological fetishism of nature — or to mere ontological naiveté.[31]

Of course, the relatively quiescent surface of "A White Heron" emits only faint signals of this sexual-biblical war; yet they appear in ways which bear the most extreme feminist interpretation. In Sylvia's tree-climbing episode, we hear echoes of Milton's rendition of Eve's experience in Book V of *Paradise Lost* where, thanks to the intervention of Satan disguised as a handsome "Guide" or "one of those from Heav'n," she dreams of being transported to the top of the forbidden Tree of Knowledge:

> Forthwith up to the clouds
> With him I flew, and underneath behold
> The earth outstretched immense, a prospect wide
> And various: wond'ring at my flight and change
> To this high exaltation. . . . (*Paradise Lost*, V, 86–90)

> . . . when the last thorny bough was past . . . [Sylvia] stood trembling and tired but wholly triumphant, high in the tree-top. Yes, there was the sea with the dawning sun . . . and toward that glorious east flew two hawks. . . . [They] seemed only a little way from the tree, and Sylvia felt as if she too could go flying away among the clouds. Westward, the woodlands and farms reached miles and miles into the distance . . . truly it was a vast and awesome world. (xxi)

The passage from Jewett's story glosses the Miltonic passage with strategic, ideologically motivated differences. Where Milton's Eve tells Adam of her dream (as she will later tell him of her disobedient deed), Sylvia will not tell the Adamic hunter what "knowledge" she has gained from this "flying away" experience despite her initial intention to do so. In fact, Jewett's "Eve" climbs the tree voluntarily and literally awake ("She forgot to think of sleep" [xix]), whereas it is "Adam" who has rehearsed within a dream the temptation of a sinful if pleasurable "knowledge": "The guest waked from a dream, and remembering his day's pleasure [i.e., to capture the heron] hurried to dress" (xxii). Jewett's Adam here represents the curiosity and desire for a kind of knowledge — of the heron he intends to kill and place in his ornithological collection — which almost, but not quite, seduces her feminist Eve into a Fall from her innocent relation to nature, and results in the latter's Fall as well, the reification of nature implicit in his stuffing birds. More, with his money and knowledge "about the birds" which, like Eve's knowledge after she eats the forbidden fruit, temporarily promotes an illusory or "vaguely thrilled" (xviii) intimacy with a sexual partner, *he* tempts the *woman* in this revised version of the biblical primal scene. Even Milton's masculine Satan, who produces Eve's dream by first disguising himself as a "Toad" (*Paradise Lost,* IV, 800), becomes neutralized and distanced as a tempter by the story's reduction of him to a mere "hop-toad in the narrow footpath" (xvii).

"A White Heron," then, (re)tells the story of how an exceptional woman — exceptional since even Mrs. Tilley accedes to the hunter's intention to "cage up" nature — resists such temptation and becomes representative of the woman radically "unrelated" to patriarchal stories of her inferior station in the order of creation. The male story of *Paradise Lost* here becomes a pretext for the female story of *Paradise Regained.* From the vantage of a subtly allusive Tree of Knowledge which the girl climbs by her "free will" or by her own "great design [which] kept her . . . awake and watching" (xix) — not, then, as in the Miltonic Eve's patriarchally produced dream — Jewett's Eve literally sees the "sea" for the first time; she sees "the *dawning* sun . . . and toward *that glorious east* . . . two hawks," images, like the child herself, resonating with prelapsarian echoes. In climbing this "great" tree, Sylvia encounters and triumphs over its phallic power and resistance to becoming occupied by a girl, "her thin little fingers clumsy and stiff as she" goes "round and round the tree's great stem, higher and higher upward" (xx). We could argue that the woman here symbolically overcomes the patriarchal tradition's phallocentrically privileged claim on all modes of knowledge and comes to know "a vast and awesome world" outside this tradition. And so, aside from the story's substituting a feminist heroic Eve for a dominant, privileged Adam, we find it also substituting the exclusive value of a feminine regenerative relation to a traditionally feminine nature for a woman-provoked Fallen relation to a traditionally patriarchal God. We could also argue that it performs these substitutions through the effective agency of a female authorial persona who appeals to this nature to assuage the necessary loneliness incurred by the vision of radical feminine independence, a vision that continually requires nature to "tell your secrets to this lonely country child!" (xxiii). Such an agency itself exists as a revision of Milton's surrogate male agency in *Paradise Lost*, the Raphaelite messenger of the Judeo-Christian patriarchal God who can promise Adam and Eve only a deferred surcease from their present spiritual loneliness, their alienation from a prelapsarian awareness of nature which in Jewett's story pertains *only* to the "disappointed" hunter.

As I have suggested, recent feminist critical theories not only license but request that we ascribe such unlikely, ideologically motivated revisions to texts written by women writers. These ascriptions pertain especially to fiction by and for women of the nineteenth century whose "feminism" would not likely lead them to be fully aware of the extent to which they indeed were revising patriarchal ideological norms of their social identity both within and outside their fiction. In this context, the implausibility of such revisions must itself be regarded as evidence for the "degraded" position of women in Western patriarchal society, a position Fuller registers when she paraphrases Plato's view "that Man, if he misuse the privileges of one life, shall be degraded into the form of Woman; and then, if he do not redeem himself, into that of a bird."[32] Through Sylvia's figurative and anagrammatic association with the white heron, Jewett clearly "mimics" this descent — but in order to create a space for the woman to declare her radical sociosexual independence. And further, she could be said to reinforce this strategic mimetism through her "elusive" (xix) representation of both heron and heroine. As we have seen, Sylvia becomes allusively associated with major feminine figures borrowed and revised from patriarchal tradition: Artemis, Daphne, and Eve. And were we to emphasize how Sylvia alone seeks and finds this white heron, she also would become a kind of Virgin Mary who here generates her own immaculate conception, namely through the agency of a Holy Ghost-like bird which both inspires her with a self-dependent vision of nature precluding intercourse with the values of "the great world," and itself eludes the discursive designs of patriarchal understanding as symbolized in "muted" fashion by the hunter's ornithological intentions.[33]

At the very least, as the tree-climbing episode almost literally proves, Sylvia as feminist heroine does not exhibit any fear of flying, that is, of determining her relation to life in terms which transcend her attraction to patriarchal terms, the "fancied triumph and delight and glory for the later morning when she could make known the secret!" (xix). Quite clearly a "child . . . brought up amid the teachings of the woods and fields, kept fancy-free by useful employment and a free flight into the heaven of thought,"[34] she exemplifies the ideal feminist "maiden" which Fuller had compared to a bird not unlike the "rare bird" that Sylvia becomes associated with in "A White Heron." Mothers, Fuller had gone on to say, should never "clip the wings of any bird that . . . finds in itself the strength of pinion for migratory flight unusual to its kind."[35] As mother to her story which she also refers to as a "her" (see p. 71 above), Jewett seems to have written a tale whose thematic referent interchangeably metamorphoses into a "heron," a "heroine," and a "her." Could there be a better way to demonstrate the "migratory flight" of a feminist literary text?

2   But at least three problems arise with this radical feminist revision of "A White Heron." The first has to do with the way even a feminist criticism can just as easily interpret the "secret," nonconfrontational feminist propaedeutic and the story's allusive feminist revisions in terms of it as signs of an impotent capitulation to, co-

option by, or perhaps de facto complicity with a patriarchal ethos. The second concerns the desire of such criticism to posit the feminist allegorical subtext of Jewett's production of her story as the "secret" site of its true textuality; this displacement occurs not only in defiance of the story's reduced and revised representational signs suggesting its own allusive feminist subtext, but also in spite or in the face of this criticism's awareness of the difference between the "muted" and "dominant" elements of the text in question. The third problem relates to a contemporary critical aporia, namely the necessity of any critical theory to reproduce the text it criticizes in its own blind and insightful terms. Thus, one can question the radical or, in Adrienne Rich's terms, "lesbian" feminist critic's tendency to replace patriarchal standards of major literature, standards which have been invoked to reduce the value of women's writing, by gender-exclusive feminist standards which willy-nilly place a greater value on the act of feminist critical revision than on the literary text thus being used as a pretext for this critical narrative. In what if any sense could we maintain that "A White Heron" "deconstructs" its radical feminist meta-narrative—*after*, that is, one acknowledges its "deconstruction" of patriarchal appropriations?

As regards the first problem, radical feminist criticism should be only momentarily thwarted by a reactionary feminist interpretation of "A White Heron." Such an interpretation could doubtless stress the implausibility or even egregious misreading which our exposition of the story's feminist revisions clearly entails when compared with its spare narrative surface; could perhaps cite the story's own implausible elements such as the child heroine's temptation by a mere ten dollars, or the unrealistic possibility of romance with an older, at least adolescent, "young *man*"; finally could point to the genteel literary context in which Jewett wrote her stories, one of whose ideologemes was a sentimentalized notion of childhood innocence.[36] Thus, the girl's silent decision, a represented silence that the narrative doubles by its own hesitant ("who can tell?") paratactic silence regarding this decision, could be understood as a regressive *retreat* from any putative revisionary feminist thematic. Instead of indicating "redemptive possibilities" or proffering an alternative feminine social model to a profit-oriented patriarchal American society through, say, an ideologically charged domestic topos, a viewpoint Nina Baym adopts when reading American women novelists before 1868, the "muted" ideological silences of this 1886 story concerning a farm run by an elderly woman may exemplify what Baym terms the "decline of women's fiction into girl's fiction."[37] Or these silences may serve to corroborate Ann Douglas's thesis about the "feminization" of American patriarchal culture. Jewett's heroine, who effectively chooses to remain in her "hermitage" at the end of the story, and even Jewett herself who relies on Margaret Fuller's *Woman in the Nineteenth Century,* a text virtually disregarded by late-nineteenth-century feminists concerned with more practical political matters, here seem to deserve the pejorative rubric of "New England nun" insofar as they privilege a sentimentalized, idealistic moral code and remain silent about the "real" social issues facing contemporary adult women.[38]

Yet with Nancy Miller, we could regard the story's silences as signs of its antipatriarchal inscriptions. We could "italicize" both them and the story's *apparently* "unmotivated and unconvincing" depiction of Sylvia and the hunter's romantic relationship and claim they are only "inaudible to the dominant [i.e., patriarchal] mode of reception."[39] The little girl's silence throughout the story and especially when she refuses to tell the heron's secret would then touch on what Gilbert and Gubar identify as the "aphasia and amnesia . . . which symbolically represent (*and parody*) the sort of intellectual incapacity patriarchal culture has traditionally required of women."[40] Similarly, even Sylvia's "vaguely" drawn erotic feelings toward the hunter, feelings that generate the dilemma which frames the girl's decision as decisive, also lead us to a feminist register of meaning. Such erotic themes in women's fiction, according to Nancy Miller, actually conceal and serve to repress the woman writer's own "impulse to power . . . that would revise the social grammar in which women are never defined as subjects."[41] Moreover, far from constituting a descent "into girl's fiction" or representing Jewett's genteel acceptance of her proper, which is to say minor, literary place, both the story's child heroine and its diminutive genre invite us to revise them along the lines of Adrienne Rich's interpretation of Emily Dickinson's abbreviated poems. Such poems constitute *acts* of "self-diminutivization, almost to offset and deny—or even disguise—[Dickinson's] actual dimensions as she must have experienced them," that is, "under pressure of concealment" from a patriarchal world.[42]

Feminist literary criticism, then, compels us to regard "A White Heron" as a "muted" feminist story within an already "muted" feminist story. The heroine's dilemma concerns Jewett's own need to construct, in Myra Jehlen's terms, "an enabling relationship with a language that of itself would deny [the woman writer] the ability to use it creatively."[43] We saw evidence of this need in Jewett's *A Country Doctor* where Nan Prince's obstacle-ridden attempt to become a physician — a vocation, like writing, which was restrictively available to women in the nineteenth century — more than likely reflects the obstacles Jewett encountered in choosing writing as a serious vocation.[44] Even the way Dr. Leslie encourages Nan to become a doctor resembles the way Jewett's father encouraged her to read books and especially "tell the things just as they are" when writing them. Significantly for our present discussion, the novel ends at the point where Nan has not yet begun a practice of her own — as if, that is, the choice of vocation and not the vocational practice itself were its primary topic.

We could argue that "A White Heron" internalizes this prevocational topic even more. In this context, Sylvia's refusal to tell the heron's secret locale to the hunter represents Jewett's own refusal to write a story she identifies as feminine ("she isn't a very good magazine story, but I love her") in terms of the prevailing esthetic mandates of the patriarchal "great world" as represented by W. D. Howells and others. Howells's preference for social realism, for example, presupposes access to major social issues from which, as Virginia Woolf would later note, nineteenth-century women were barred.[45] Jewett's story, then, here becomes definable as an inverted feminist work which allegorizes its very mode of production. Her remarks in the letter cited in the previous chapter (p. 71) suggest that as a "romance" that deals with "every-day life after all," "she" gets written precisely *not* to become "a very good magazine story," i.e., for the marketplace pre-occupied by male editors, but rather to secure a "room of her own" for "her" author. Moreover, even with regard to "her" diminutive literary genre, "she" reproduces or secretly parodies a mode of fiction ironically intended to guarantee "her" minor literary fate before Jewett's canonically minded patriarchal literary contemporaries and twentieth-century supersessors.[46] For the very reason that "A White Heron" could so easily be reduced in terms of patriarchal literary standards, its secret feminist allegorization of its production suggests that Jewett herself partakes of the girl's "spirit of adventure [and] wild ambition" (xix). In other words, inscribed within the story is Jewett's wish to produce major literature.[47]

In the end, however, such speculation about the story's doubly subsumed feminist identity and its status as an allegorical prolegomenon to Sarah Orne Jewett's own "major" literary ambition belongs more to radical feminist criticism's discursive wish to transform "A White Heron" into an ironic minor literary text than to the "muted" sexual signals traced in the tale itself. A lesbian-feminist criticism like that espoused by Adrienne Rich must perform a supererogatory critical act that, even as it resituates Jewett's text within a recoverable "lesbian continuum," contradicts that same secret (and not merely "muted") feminist thematic which justifies the consideration of this text as a text of "major" feminist importance. Rich's perspective suggests that Jewett could not have written her stories except by converting the everyday moral and local color topics, topics with which she was most familiar as a restricted nineteenth-century woman, into the topic of the ways "women have always resisted male tyranny," or the "compulsory" (for the woman writer) patriarchal topic of heterosexual romance.[48] This perspective allows feminist critics alone to "ask how [a past woman writer] came to be for-herself and how she identified with and was able to use women's culture, a women's tradition"; and it allows women critics to "identify images, codes, metaphors, strategies, points of stress, unrevealed by conventional criticism which works from a male mainstream perspective."[49] Surely Sylvia's silent sacrifice of heterosexual romance with the hunter, not to mention her anxious memory of a "great red-faced boy who used to chase and frighten her," reveals such a point of stress, and thus justifies a radical feminist revision of Jewett's story.

But as Annette Kolodny argues, even a would-be revisionary feminist critic "must . . . be wary of reading literature as though it were a polemic and hence treating it as [she] would a manifesto or political tract."[50] To claim that Sylvia's silence has immanent gender-significant meaning in and through the narrative is not the same as claiming it has imminent referential meaning for women alone given their common experience of an underground secret life in patriarchal society. More important, to claim that this silence is gender determined as opposed to simply gender inflected within "a male mainstream perspective" is to violate its secret semiotic confrontation with male culture and/or its "lesbian" declaration of independence from this culture. The self-conscious metaphoricity that this self-conscious feminist critique would attribute to Sylvia's silence denies the very condition in terms of which it only *may* be appealing to a radical feminist mode of reception. For only if this secret *is* radical could it appear "unrelated" to any "male mainstream perspective." Or what amounts to the same thing, only if it can be read as if it were immediately accessible to such a perspective—after all, even patriarchal readers can apprehend the *relative* feminist significance of Sylvia's secret—can the story paradoxically signify its *doubly* secret or *radically* feminist scene of writing to women readers intent on constructing "her" coherent feminist subtext.

The danger for such criticism, then, lies in the way its self-conscious methodology risks opening up an irreconcilable breach between its own reflective act and the putative "lesbian" reading of the story which conditions this act on pain of its reduction to mere speculation. Such criticism must maintain the radical value of the story's esthetic surface, no matter how self-coherent and persuasive its ideological revision may seem to a feminist critical audience, lest it become exposed *to itself* as a *de facto* "polemic," a polemic that by definition would be no better than the variable critical avatars of "a male mainstream perspective." Can feminist criticism, for example, avoid transferring the meaning of Sylvia's silence from a patriarchal mode of reception to a feminist counterpatriarchal mode of reception whose "secret" significance ultimately depends on its contingent, literally and self-consciously maintained sexual inaccessibility to the male critic or reader?

Some recent feminist critics assert the impossibility of such a task. "In claiming value for the devalued term of an opposition," according to Elizabeth Berg, "one still allows the opposition to remain in place and to perpetuate the same order of relations."[51] In its "French" form, a feminist literary criticism would bracket women's writing as determined by literal gender differences, whether of authorship or characterizations. "Writing" alone expresses these differences, hence remains inaccessible both to traditional patriarchal modes of understanding and to their counterpatriarchal feminist revisions insofar as they polarize women's "essential" sexual identity. But even this notion of "writing," which views woman as a trope or a "reading effect . . . never stable, without identity," is comprehensible, as Alice Jardine argues, only to "the woman (feminist) reader."[52] Thus, although a feminist critic can recognize that her criticism "remains imbricated within the forms of [patriarchal] intelligibility . . . against which it pushes," she still insists on interpreting "a text that seems to do her arguing . . . for her," a text which—as Luce Irigaray claims, for example—"can only signify an excess or a deranging power" vis-à-vis patriarchal modes of writing.[53] It is the woman author's, critic's, and/or story's relation to what seems an always already prior patriarchal network of writing that prompts, and defines as such, the woman's perpetual deconstruction of such writing. In ideological terms, women's "writing" transumes rather than is consumed by naturalized images of women and women's writing purveyed by a repeated patriarchal discursive practice. Indeed, since the woman suppressed in society through patriarchal discourse constitutes a secret to herself as well as others, she has the unique if ironic ability to experience a dialectically privileged priority in relation to this discourse that would fix her identity to herself and other women.

"Mimetism," then, can apply to radical feminist critical practice as much as to the text it purports to explicate in feminist terms. And what looks like the conspicuous antithetical relation between a self-conscious feminist methodology and the "reading experience" of "A White Heron" here becomes feminist criticism's mimicking, at the level of critical discourse, of the story's esthetic expression of a secret feminism. The radical feminist codification of Jewett's story in terms of a counterpatriarchal critical discourse signifies less a self-conscious disagreement with what a patriarchal criticism would say or misrecognize about this story than a dialectically regained distance in "excess" of such criticism. In this sense, Jewett's heroine serves as an emblem for feminist criticism itself. On the one hand, she "*only followed* [the hunter], and there was no such thing as speaking first" (xix).

On the other, she climbs the tree in secret and establishes a secret relation to the white heron. In the same way, the postgendered feminist critic mimics the teleological direction of patriarchal critical discourse to the extent of sometimes seeming complicit with it; but given her inconspicuous, relatively secret — even childlike — status within such discursive practice, she can climb above its openly propagated intentionalities of literary texts, intentionalities which minimize the value of literary texts written by and about women. More, she can establish a secret relation to "A White Heron" itself that remains beyond the epistemological ken of patriarchal understanding and critical discourse. Both feminist critic and woman writer thus concern themselves with uncovering discursive rooms of their own, secret spaces in excess of whatever critical paradigms exist at some given moment in literary as well as social patriarchal history. If only from this perspective, it becomes possible for the woman's literary text to communicate "without identity" to "the woman (feminist) reader" alone.[54]

But this postgendered feminist criticism must still signify to itself its act of tracing male-associated critical practices. To its women readers, it must emphasize its own unconventional citations of what Rich regards as already unconventional codes, metaphors, and strategies that permeate all women's literature. Otherwise, it would once more engage in the equivalent of a heterosexual romance with patriarchal criticism, albeit an unwitting, unwilling, if also subtly reactionary one. As it becomes more and more potentially misreadable by its own women readers, such criticism must acknowledge its "secret" relation to male-identifiable modes of criticism, that is, in ways that not only suggest its transcendence of them but also ensure that patriarchal criticisms can *never* know male *or* female literary texts as women readers and critics have ironically learned to do from their "compulsory" or coerced familiarity with masculine epistemologies. Thus, even a postgendered feminist criticism comes to depend on the gender-inflected signatures of its practitioners or tends to thematize its deconstructions of patriarchal projections of literary texts in gender-specific terms. And if only for the sake of economy, it concentrates its attention on women's literature traditionally overlooked in patriarchal canonical histories, a literature it would inversely elevate to "major" literary status according to standards immediately accessible to and apprehensible by women alone. Such self-identifying marks of an otherwise "without identity" or postgendered feminist criticism suggest that even the practice of mimetism, or, as Mary Jacobus recommends, ceaseless deconstruction, assumes a relatively secured or centered self-image of "woman" to perform such operations and to realize the sophisticated desideratum of a radically secret or "lesbian" relation to a story, say, like Jewett's "A White Heron."

But perhaps such deconstruction could also lead to the extinction of the "woman," person or trope, as a pretext for subtly reprivileging or fetishizing the hierarchical binary of major and minor literature. After all, such a resurgent binary not only would bar male critics from custody rights over Jewett's story, but would ironically place these critics virtually in the same "minor" discursive position as feminist criticism would argue defines Jewett's in producing this story. In that case, who indeed could claim ideological custody of "her"? The question comes down to whether writers or critics, male or female, can ever arrive at a sex-less and not merely nonsexist relation to a literary text and the issue of literary canonicity it seems perpetually to broach.

3   We could take the "muted" feminist elements of Jewett's story as one among other signs of its phenomenological retreat from radical feminist as well as patriarchal appropriations. A novitiate in her rural "hermitage," the little girl comes to exemplify the values of "virtuous womanhood," the reformist self-image of so-called nineteenth-century protestant nuns setting out to "tame" the perceived antisocial proclivities of males who would undermine the moral fabric of the family and, by extension, society at large.[55] These values, especially respect for the other, whether human or natural, are shown to endure in the face of male-caused crises, for example the conflict between Dan and his father; Dan's abandonment of the farm due to his wanderlust or fortune hunting; and the Civil War which perhaps accounts for the absence, i.e., death, of Sylvia's father, and her mother's need to support her family alone. Yet as seems quite obvious, Sylvia's choice has only a tangential sociological applicability to the situation of magazine readers in the city for whom male promiscuity and/or the disintegration of family values were more explicit concerns.

In affirming Sylvia's life in the country ("Bring your gifts . . ."), the story's unidentified narrator also seems to affirm Jewett's stated preference for "persons [who] could make themselves quiet and solitary nests"—not unlike the white heron's "hidden nest"—"and never wish to go out into the busy world again."[56]

Jewett's writing thus seems to retreat from even the modest feminist elements suggested by her story. And this retreat becomes more noticeable in her representations of suggested adult heterosexual relationships. Writing to Willa Cather, she would later argue that the woman writer was unable to write from the first-person position of a "man's character," for to do so "must always, I believe, be something of a masquerade."[57] But this admission about her nonheterosexual imagination does not account for the way her third-person narrative representations of heterosexual relationships tend to be not only deeroticized but blurred by certain verbal maneuvers which further mitigate the "otherness" of characters to each other and to the reader. George Gerry, the prospective suitor of Nan Prince in *A Country Doctor,* has a name as "two-dimensional" as Richard Cary argues Jewett's characterization of him is.[58] In *A Marsh Island,* a novel published one year before "A White Heron," Jewett has two male characters— Dick Dale, a city-bred would-be artist, and Dan, a country boy—vie for the affections of Doris Owen, the daughter of a farmer who functions as a benign patriarchal figure for all three characters. Doris eventually chooses to marry Dan, but not before Dale's relationship to her is characterized as one of "brotherly" affection and her relationship to Dan Lester is based on his familiarity with the Owens' culture and family, particularly his having been the last person to see "his playmate," Doris's *brother,* "fall" during a Civil War battle.[59] Even these alliterative names, Doris, Dan, Dick Dale, George Gerry, strike one as unimaginative, blurring their gender distinctions or else underwriting their unimagined otherness as characters—as if they were children within the protective confines of a family rather than independent adults.

This process of regression to a childlike mode of representation, or said another way, this tendency of Jewett's writing to drift away from even the "virtuous" or modest feminist thematic, or the conventional heterosexual one, that *A Country Doctor* and *A Marsh Island* respectively invoke in the most explicit terms indicates Jewett's wish to produce a radical minor literature. Such literature *becomes* minor by the way she imagines its production, for example in the way she traces and tries to mitigate the feminist resonances of her representations. One way to write as if she were a child or literally a minor writer, that is, an ungendered persona whose imaginations are fictively in the process of avoiding impressment by adult sexual codes, is to reproduce a predominant child/parent relation either within her texts or in the very mode of her producing them. The expressions of this relation remain, of course, only latently autobiographical. Thus, the apparent irony of the feminist reference to the little girl's feeling in "A White Heron" that she could "have served and followed [the hunter] and loved him as a dog loves" becomes neutralized for Jewett, if not for the feminist critic, when apprehended first against the fictional precedent of the male Dan Lester's having "followed [Doris] about like a dog,"[60] and second against the precedent of her own childhood experience with her beloved father as he visited his patients: "I used to follow him about silently, like an undemanding dog."[61]

In her fiction written roughly around the time of "A White Heron," this relation becomes thematically expressed in the way that Israel Owen, for example, the patriarch who defines the values in terms of which the other characters in *A Marsh Island* are judged, justifies his daughter's erratic behavior toward Dan by what could be apprehended as a stereotypical view of women: "Women's a kind of game: you've got to hunt 'em their own track, an' when you've caught 'em they've got to be tamed some."[62] Embedded in this stereotype of the male as hunter and the woman as huntable object lies the father's defending his daughter as an unconventional character—a subject who can only be "tamed *some*" and for whom marriage, an option that she must concern herself with, "goes sort of against [her] natur'."[63] To Dr. Leslie in *A Country Doctor*, Nan Prince also exhibits "untamed wildnesses" as she is growing up.[64] As Nan's de facto father, he too appreciates his de facto daughter's difference from the other "village children," regardless of their gender; he thus tells Mrs. Graham, his longtime confidante in Oldfields who will later serve as Nan's reading companion, that given Nan's native "self-dependence and unnatural self-reliance," it "is a mistake for such a woman to marry. Nan's feeling toward her boy playmates is exactly the same as toward the girls she knows."[65] In both cases, then, though to different degrees, Jewett represents fathers whose "untamed" daughters they exempt from patriarchal institutions or conventions which these fathers thus only *appear* to represent by virtue of their social and/or sexual identities. And in the case of Dr. Leslie, as we have already seen, this exemption leads to the daughter's entering an elite profession by the end of the novel, but a profession which has not yet removed her from the "old fields" of his "country doctor" world.

Nan's daughterly relation to Dr. Leslie and his mode of professional practice quite obviously reflects Jewett's relation to her father and his homespun poetic advice to her to "tell the things just as they are," that is, in terms of her regionalist experiences or her familiarity as a woman with "every-day" topics. But *A Country Doctor* suggests that this relation itself can become the primary focus of Jewett's writing. In "A White Heron," for example, Jewett-as-narrator, just like Dr. Leslie with Nan, allows Sylvia time to absorb the "gifts and graces" and "secrets" of nature by herself or before she will have to enter "the great world" of heterosexually defined relationships prefigured by her experience with the hunter. In this sense, the narrational modus operandi of the story thus internalizes the father/daughter relation.

But even supposing that a child/parent relation not only effectively displaces adult heterosexual and antiheterosexual representational occasions in Jewett's writing, but also generates the conditions which facilitate a phenomenological scene of "minor" writing at a step removed from being understood as a scene of minor or major feminist *righting*, why would a woman writer adopt a paternal as opposed to maternal authorial relation to a little girl character? Certainly Jewett's avowed "love" for her story—for "her"—suggests such a maternal relation.[66] Biographically speaking, though Jewett seldom refers to her in letters, her relation to her mother, an intelligent woman who encouraged her children to read,[67] hardly seems to have been troubled. And yet in the two novels and story under consideration, mothers and mother figures play secondary roles, and even appear as obstacles to their daughter's or daughter figure's "untamed wildnesses." The materialistically motivated Mrs. Owen, with her "undercurrent of dislike," encourages a match between Doris and the wealthy Dale, then accepts Dan as a mate for Doris when she learns he has inherited property.[68] Aunt Nancy, as I have suggested, functions as *A Country Doctor*'s melodramatic antagonist in attempting to make Nan abandon her vocational ambition for marriage. Mrs. Graham, who Cary thinks functions as Nan's mother and was in fact modeled after Jewett's mother,[69] exercises only an indirect influence on Nan and serves as a foil to Dr. Leslie who has a more central fatherly relation to her, as when she predicts the girl "will be a most lovely, daughterly, friendly girl, who will keep you from being lonely as you grow older."[70] And of course the otherwise benign Mrs. Tilley, the mother-substitute grandmother in "A White Heron" who in feminist terms could help the daughter gain her independence from her actual mother without devaluing the latter, "rebukes" Sylvia for her silence or failure to speak the language of "the great world."[71] Indeed, in this story and *A Country Doctor,* the mother per se literally vanishes from the text. Sylvia has left her mother and siblings to live with a grandmother from whom the girl becomes figuratively separate. Nan's mother dies in the first pages of the novel, her maternal grandmother a few pages later. Thus are emphasized Sylvia's exclusive relation to the narrator, and the widowed and childless Dr. Leslie's exclusive fatherly relation to Nan.

Doubtless we could account for Jewett's aversion in these works to representing the mother/daughter relation in neo-Freudian as well as ideological feminist terms. In a patriarchal society such as Jewett's, the father and not the mother holds privileged ("phallic") access to its forms. The girl thus wishes to identify with her father rather than with the socially castrated mother whom she can "resent" and come to "turn away from . . . altogether."[72] Or in more strict psychoanalytic terms, at the oedipal stage, a stage which establishes the paradigm that will govern her future adult relationships with men and women, the girl but not the boy "can transfer her sexual attentions from her mother to her father [and] can want first his phallus, and then by . . . analogy, his baby"[73] — or in the displaced sexual medium of a female literary artist, "his" text. But such a situation need mandate not so much the girl's resentment as her ambivalence toward the mother since, as Nancy Chodorow has argued, the daughter can more easily identify with her mother than the son with his father; only the

son, that is, must give up or postpone the narcissistic project of wanting the mother.[74] In the normal course of ego development the girl
must liberate herself from her infantile or egoless relation to the preoedipal mother so that at the oedipal stage she can desire the father's
phallus, the symbol of power (rather than object of envy) which allows
this liberation to occur.[75] The girl here splits her "internal image [of
the preoedipal mother] into good and bad aspects" and goes on to
free herself or gain self-identity from this "overwhelming" mother by
"project[ing] all the good-object qualities . . . onto her father as an
external object and onto her relationship to him."[76] But again, this
transference of "libidinal" attachment from preoedipal mother to oedipal father does not require the devaluation of the female child's sense
of her feminine identity; on the contrary, her love for her father literally depends on her prior relation to the mother, so that this love does
not take place "at the expense of, or [as] a substitute for, her attachment to her mother."[77]

As her other works — especially *The Country of the Pointed Firs* —
and her benign relation to her mother show in fact, so these explanations show in theory that the mother/daughter relation exists as a
viable option for Jewett to have adopted in reproducing a "minor"
relation to writing. If she privileges the father/daughter relation in
these three works, it probably concerns more her wish to postpone
her identification with adult or postoedipal mother figures than some
outright aversion to such figures. For an adult woman, of course, such
postponement would entail a fantasized regression, a replay of the
little girl's energic transfer of love onto the father and also a return
to a time when she could still postpone her "real" conscription into
an adult womanhood which, as her women friends and close relationship to her two sisters show, she otherwise accepts and even embraces.[78] In imaginative terms, mother figures like Mrs. Owen, Mrs.
Graham, Aunt Nancy, Sylvia's mother and grandmother signify the
inevitability of the daughter's fate to become an adult woman. This
fate, no doubt, seems all the more onerous because of its patriarchal
restrictions and/or the possibility of the girl's becoming a mother herself with its attendant losses, as suggested by Mrs. Tilley's "family
sorrows" and Sylvia's mother's economic plight in supporting her family by herself.[79] Conversely, a father figure like Dr. Leslie, though iden-

tifiable with this same fate, signifies a threshold situation for the daughter, that is, only the *possibility* of entering a world of adult heterosexual relationships. Indeed, Dr. Leslie's "country" practice entails a choice not to enter this world, for he rejects the advice of his medical colleagues to realize his scientific abilities in the city.[80]

Thus, we can argue that both Nan's prevocational status at the end of *A Country Doctor* and Sylvia's choice effectively to remain a preadolescent in "A White Heron" reflect their exclusive relations to "fathers"—the narrator in the case of this story. Such relations serve as screen images, in psychoanalytic terms, of these daughter figures's respective desires to return to and remain within that transitional psychosexual space between preoedipal and oedipal self-identity. Jewett's fictional fathers allow Nan, Sylvia, and to a lesser extent Doris (Mr. Owen accepts the possibility of her relationship to the cosmopolitan Dale even as she comes to choose the world of her father's Marsh Island through the brotherlike Dan) to glimpse and even choose "the great world" of adult heterosexual relationships, but in the end also to retain their preadult "untamed wildnesses" or identities.

Yet for Jewett, clearly, the presence of a father figure in either a representational *or* a concealed narrational sense must strike an incestuous semiotic note as well as connote, if only unconsciously, literal sex differentiations to an adult woman writer who so exclusively privileges the father/daughter relation. One could argue that the incest taboo functionally precludes, for example, her production of a text as "his" substitute "baby," in Mitchell's words. But at the same time, such oedipal repression of a fantasized, fictionally mediated project of regression still leads the daughter to seek male substitutes, especially the adult "man . . . to give her [her father's] baby."[81] That this project appears *as* a project is clear from the way Jewett not only represents her heroines's choices of an exclusive father/daughter relationship over other adult hetero- and nonheterosexual options, but stresses these choices by banishing literal fathers just as much as mothers, without, nevertheless, erasing the crucial function of the father figure. In order *not* to write a "baby" text, in other words to distance her own awareness of the exclusive father/daughter relation, she tries to make it a substitutive or only allusively inscribed relation, in this way pushing its immediate connotations of adult sexual differentiation out of representational sight.

Thus, like her mother, Nan's actual father is dead but substitutively present through her patronymic name, Prince. This patronymic further reminds us that her daughterly relation to Dr. Leslie is nonbiological, nonmandatory, hence a "distant" relation, also emphasized by the fact that he neither tries to adopt her legally nor assumes the conventional role of the authoritative patriarchal father in bringing her up. Moreover, Nan in effect rejects her patrimony by refusing to live permanently with her *paternal* Aunt Nancy, and in this way becomes distanced even further from her already dead father. A similar distancing relation obtains in "A White Heron" where a surnameless Sylvia, whose father may be dead but is in any case absent from the narrative, lives with her *maternal* grandmother, i.e., without a grandfather and apart from a mother whose husband the narrative would have had to account for as it does for Mrs. Tilley's husband. Even in *A Marsh Island* where a father plays a dominant role, we could argue that Doris's attraction to Dick Dale and Dan, both of whose fathers are dead, concerns, as we have seen, a "brotherly" duo that reminds us how in this patriarchal world the father/daughter relation has less value than what would have been a more primary father/son relation.

Still, as Mr. Owen and Dr. Leslie show, even the distanced substitute father figure can turn into a signifier of the daughter's inevitable transformation into an adult woman in fact (marriage) or in effect (vocation). Simply for a prose writer to "name the behavior of an individual," according to Sartre, involves "naming it to all others" who, at least in the case with Jewett's two novels, are synonymous with an adult understanding of these works.[82] Such naming, the sheer fact of representing father figures, inevitably must affect her very imagination of these works' putatively regressive projects. In an autobiographical sense, this "adult" recovery of the father as a median figure who helps introduce the daughter to nonpejorative heterosexual "behavior" but mitigates the necessity of her conforming to it equally applies to Jewett's representation of her substitute daughters. For example, on one level the already distanced daughter Nan's distanced relation to her patrimony works to repress — but in order, here, to *express* — the absent presence of a pure or preadult father/daughter relation. But on another level, Dr. Leslie's support of her vocational desire — albeit a desire that must lead to a self-reliant kind of heterosexual adulthood—and her rejection of her patrimony would each risk reminding Jewett of her own situation as a writer, namely of *her* country doctor father's support of her vocation, and of the patrimony which, from the beginning of her career, allowed her to regard writing as "not a bread and butter affair with me."[83]

If the literal-minded "substitute" strategies of the two pre–"A White Heron" novels conspire to make fragile Jewett's desire to produce literature as a "minor" as opposed to an adult woman writer, that is, through a mantra-like projection of the father/daughter relation, such does not appear to be the case with "A White Heron" itself. Here, we have argued, a purely narrational or *anonymous* father/daughter relation helps constitute the story's "minor" mode of production. Or here Jewett relies on writing per se, writing in the (Lacanian) "name of the father" or of the linguistically dispersing Symbolic, to misrecognize the adult associations tied to any explicit representation of the father/daughter relation; to shred potential Imaginary identifications with maternal *or* paternal figures; in short, to elude "the biologistic reduction of the Law of the Dead Father to the rule of the actual, living male" or what amounts to the occasion of adult gender differentiations, even of a feminist or counterpatriarchal cast.[84] The Lacanian notion of "writing" can help us see how the story disperses rather than substitutes an explicit paternal position, if only to include this (non)position in a repressed or unconscious manner.

Doubtless we can attempt to rewrite "A White Heron" in terms of such "wild" psychoanalytic behavior. But if writing, in the words of Geoffrey Hartman, attenuates all "fixative spectral event[s]," and instead induces the writer to accept "the (absent) father . . . basically . . . the mediacy of words [and] a genuine recognition of difference," we will need to question even our identification of Jewett's anonymous, only surmisably paternal narrator as the fixed locus from which she inscribes a dyadic father/daughter relation in this story.[85] Writing endlessly refracts rather than compulsively repeats Imaginary projects like Jewett's; at the very least, writing in the name of the father should avert any unconscious desire to fetishize this "(absent)" paternal muse. In writing, then, Jewett cannot produce a guaranteed, unmitigated "minor" literature. Since writing precludes "some unique reduction to . . . one fixative spectral event,"[86] she cannot use it to reestablish even a discursively defined daughterly relation toward a metafatherly narrator who—just like the elliptically androgynous neo-Freudian father who represents, even as he displaces, the preoedipal mother for the little girl,—would regressively postpone her identity as a gender-differentiated, adult woman writer.

If Jewett cannot "write" from any secured position of the absent father, in this way becoming interchangeably "his" daughterly amanuensis, neither can she even indirectly represent this static but reversible dyadic relation through a writing-induced identification with Sylvia alone. This identification becomes apparent through her substitute narrator's "pathetic" interjections throughout the story (e.g., "look, look! . . . wait! wait! . . . little girl" [xxi]; through her avowed "love" for "her," the heroine-identified story itself; and through Jewett's middle-aged birthday confession of feeling "always nine years old," the age of Sylvia. Indeed, this identification verges on explicit self-reference, hence subject to Jewett's *adult* understanding and the demise of her "minor" project, that is, to write as if she *were* a minor shielded from adulthood by the protective father. Her own father died in 1878, a father whose poetic advice ("tell the things") we find her reiterating throughout her life—a father thus quite literally associated with her writing per se. If we date her own life from the date of her father's absence or death, she would have been virtually the same age as Sylvia when writing "A White Heron" in 1886.

In short, we could maintain that just as Sylvia can "look upon the cow's pranks as an intelligent attempt to play hide and seek" (xiii), so does Jewett need to deploy "writing" in relation to her feminized text. "Writing" serves to repress by dispersing and defetishizing the recognizable verbal sites of the father/daughter relation which would otherwise regenerate an apperceivable specular project, a compulsive narcissistic quest that in effect would promise to repeat her ensuing oedipalized growth into a sex-differentiated adult woman. Thus, the writing of "A White Heron" at best can realize her project to produce a "minor" literature only subliminally, whether because of the sexual-ideological allusions and possible readings of her text, or because of her own psychic temptations to specularize the dyad that would veto this "adult" semiosis.

In a sense, the precedent for examining "A White Heron" in such terms is afforded by *A Country Doctor*. There Jewett retreats from her father/daughter substitutions by "writing" and not only by mere representational distancing. There she inscribes her "minor" project by virtually tearing up her proper name, a "specular name" whose "repetition . . . gives rise to texts that seem to be anagrammatic or to conceal an unknown-unknowable key, a 'pure' signifier."[87] Nan Prince's very name suggests the father/daughter relation. "Prince" signifies both a patriarchal surname and superior masculine status in relation to other males, precisely the formulation used by Nan to defend the woman's right to enter a male-dominated profession (pp. 75–76 above). The feminine name "Nan" constitutes a diminutive form of "Nancy," the adult name by which the narrative refers to the already distanced mother figure, Aunt Nancy. "Nan Prince" thus virtually signifies daughter and father.

We could also maintain that since "Sarah" means "princess," Nan's last name reflects Jewett's unconscious paternalization of *her* first name, a paternalization rather than heterosexual masculinization since "*Prince*" points to a daughter's barely disguised sense of the father's privileged, capitalized—but not King-like—identity in relation to other adult males who are effectively excluded from this relation. Thus, "Nan Prince" figuratively tears up its already submerged "specular" allusion to a father/daughter relation and instead inscribes Jewett's own "unknown-unknowable" self-reference to a more intimate, more linguistically concealed father/daughter relation. Indeed, Jewett's actual but unused first name was Theodora, the feminization of her father's name Theodore. Quite literally, then, she would always be writing her name in the name of her absent father; or what here comes down to the same thing, she would always be reinvoking a relation whose unconscious "repetition" in a fictional character like Nan Prince remains as concealed from her as from friends and readers bound to identify her in terms of her sex-differentiating first name, the feminine "Sarah," and the patronymic "Jewett." Jewett's very signature thus helps her reproduce a childlike authorial anonymity, an absent father/daughter relation, which, far from indicating a "muted" feminist grievance, here momentarily eludes would-be feminist and patriarchal ideological conscriptions alike.

4   Turning the dead father into the Dead Father, Jewett unconsciously deconstructs her story's potentially adult, which is to say potentially "major," sexual-ideological signs precisely in the act of writing "her." But Jewett's text must also deconstruct this deconstructive
project lest *it* confess the adult perspective from which she desires to
produce a pure minor literature. Otherwise, "A White Heron" would
again become subject to the adult or major hierarchical codes of ideological significance that always have engendered this desire, codes
which the story already seeks to displace by the more neutralized and
neuterized binary thematic of a child's versus an adult's (Mrs. Tilley's
as well as the hunter's) relation to nature. To be sure, "A White Heron,"
as we have seen, invites the imposition of such adult codes. But it
does so in a way that throws the burden on the reader, as if leaving
the writer a space, albeit only momentarily since even this space can
be ideologically reappropriated--for example, by feminist narratives
of the woman writer's situation--in which she alone can sense the
in-significance of her representations.

   Thus, Jewett's text relies on a series of word-scattering tropes inviting, according to the conventions of her time, closures both simple and sophisticated. On one level, for example, Sylvia's decision
not to tell either the hunter or Mrs. Tilley the heron's habitat strikes
us as an adult decision in a possibly antipatriarchal as well as probably moral sense. Yet both the narrator's rhetorical question ("who
can tell?") concerning the value of this decision and the girl's silence
which "represents" it suggest its provisional status for the story's
anonymously removed writer. More crucial is the narrative ellipsis
between the time Sylvia climbs down from the tree intending to tell
the stranger the heron's secret—she thinks about "what he would think
when she told him" (xxii)—and the dramatic last scene where "she
cannot tell the heron's secret and give its life away" (xxii). Again, the
reader can attribute her change of mind to morality, sentiment, and/or
American transcendentalism, in short the conventional ideological
respect for nature indigenous to the historical and geographical situation of the story. But considering Jewett's avowed awareness of the
conventions of "realism" surrounding this story's resistant "romance"
identity, this ellipsis, marked as such by the text's spacing, signifies
a narrative silence which not only duplicates Sylvia's in the next scene,

but equally points to a withheld space in which the decision occurs not to represent her decision-making process, i.e., to let the reader do the decision making instead of the writer. Moreover, in the next scene the reader becomes further distracted from the elliptical or absent locus of "real" decision making when the narrative displaces Sylvia's decision by implying that it took place before her initial silence as she faces both her "fretfully" rebuking grandmother and "the young man's kind appealing eyes" (xxii). Only after this first silence, the putative result of her (unrepresented) thoughts when returning to the farm, does Sylvia remember "how the white heron came flying through the golden air" or the narrative suggest why she "cannot . . . give its life away" (xxii).

Such motivated rhetorical spacing occurs especially in relation to Jewett's inscription of the father/daughter relation. We could argue that Jewett first identifies and disidentifies with Sylvia by means of her name. The surnameless "Sylvia" stands as a torn up homonymic of "Sarah"—"S____a(h)"—a phonetic surrogate which the narrative deemphasizes by having Sylvia, no less than the two adults, refer to herself as "Sylvy." Such unnaming or even nonnaming reinvokes even as it invokes the father-as-author/daughter-as-character relation. It allows Jewett to unimagine herself *en passant* in the place of Sylvia, just as "writing" allows her to unimagine a paternalistic relation to the girl when as narrator she effectively adopts the position of Sylvia whom she helps discover the heron ("Now look down again, Sylvia . . . there where you saw the white heron once you will see him again" [xxi]) and both underwrites and identifies the moment the little girl makes her (contextually indeterminate) decision: "No, she must keep silence!" (xxii). Able to serve as a conduit through which the reader has the illusion of an unmediated apprehension of Sylvia in such scenes, Jewett's "pathetic" narrator also literally displaces the reader's proximity to the girl's thoughts or actions. This rhetorical stratagem interposes a space, a space occupied by a narrator bound to be overlooked as such and so still a space to the writer, that protects both the girl and the writer's relation to her from being regarded in adult, i.e., in explicit child/parent, terms, Moreover, in the scene where Sylvia climbs the tree, the narrative deploys an elusive spatiolinguistic imagery which refracts further the implicit child/parent relation be-

tween Sylvia and the narrator. Here the narrator adopts a childlike
position and places Sylvia in the parental position by describing the
girl at the top of the tree as if perceiving her "from the ground" (xxi).

Incipient metaphors and metamorphoses reducible to metonymies
that displace the former's only possible and in any case prerepresen-
tational objectifications of the father/daughter relation, such define
the tropological strategies of "A White Heron," its flight from adult
determinations becoming as "elusive" as the bird it represents.[88] The
story assiduously multiplies the various metaphorical adumbrations
of this relation beyond the narrator's relation to Sylvia. For example,
we have already seen how the narrative rhetorically tends to identify
the "pale" heroine with the heron. Her birdlike associations are made
explicit: when she climbs the tree, "her bare feet and fingers . . .
pinched and held like bird's claws to the monstrous ladder reaching
up" (xx). Atop the tree, "the solitary *gray*-eyed child" with a "brave,
beating heart" like a bird's sees hawks with "*gray* feathers" and feels
"as if she too could go flying away among the clouds" (xxi). But the
possible metaphorical identification between Sylvia and the heron occurs most clearly when both of them perch on similar trees: "[the
heron] comes close at last, and goes by the landmark pine with steady
sweep of wing and outstretched slender neck and crested head. And
wait! wait! . . . for the heron has perched on a pine bough not far
beyond yours" (xxi).

This juxtaposition, this literal metonymy verging on metaphor
or metamorphosis of Sylvia and the heron, could easily resolve itself
into a metaphor of the father/daughter relation. Sylvia's "longed-for
white heron" that here flies "beyond" her is not only male but assumes a royal or "crested" appearance to the girl and the narrator.
He adumbrates a kind of princelike father figure previously discussed,
in this story a figure to whom the daughter will—on the basis of a
privileged, literally exclusive and privately witnessed relation to him—
express more "loyalty" than to the adult hunter, the would-be heterosexual substitute of the father. At the same time, however, the vulnerability of the heron to the hunter, his obvious but also unconscious
dependence on her for protection from adult designs and sheer survival, puts him in a childlike relation to her. Moreover, just as the
reader begins to focus on this "close" spatiosymbolic identification

of the heron and heroine in this scene, one also encounters the fact that he "goes by" and perches on another tree. In short, their potentially metaphorical relation literally *becomes* metonymical or contiguous. Even *this* relation gets displaced onto another when the heron "cries back to his mate on the nest" (xxi), a displacement which further subsumes yet one more possible father/daughter relation. After all, Sylvia must first "look down" to see "the white heron's nest in the sea of green branches" (xxi). Atop contiguous trees, then, both Sylvia and the male heron, like parents, are in the process of looking down to this necessarily smaller-appearing—and so childlike—"mate." Another white heron whose sex we can infer as female and whose nest will lead the reader quickly to suppose she is a mother or mother-to-be (since no young are mentioned), she nevertheless remains representationally sexless, thus a possible if improbable (hence "secret") adumbration of a daughter figure.

Jewett's story also traces this configuration with its other protagonistic "character," the "great pine-tree." As we have seen, Sylvia's name etymologically associates her with this tree; but more important, no less than the "longed-for white heron" the tree appears as an object of desire for her, especially at the moment she begins to climb it:

> She had always believed that whoever climbed to the top of it could see the ocean; and the little girl had often laid her hand on the great rough trunk and looked up wistfully at those dark boughs that the wind always stirred, no matter how hot and still the air might be below. Now she thought of the tree with a new excitement, for why, if one climbed it at break of day, could not one see all the world, and easily discover whence the white heron flew, and mark the place . . . ? (xix)

As I argued earlier, just as this tree becomes the means by which she sees the white heron, so in thematic terms does her implacable, tree-like silence become the means by which the reader apprehends the value of "A White Heron" itself.

But it is the narrative's deployment of the trope prosopopoeia, here, which "marks the place" or traces the Imaginary locus of "A White Heron." The male-personified tree resembles the trees Jewett in her earlier sketches often regards in parent/child and particularly fatherly terms: poplar trees that look like "a little procession of a father and mother and . . . children out for an afternoon walk";[89] a tree that, although apparently "stunted and dwarfed" when young, comes to "grow tall and strong, and in [its] wealth of usefulness [has become] like some of the world's great men who rose from poverty to kingliness. . . . The great tree is a protection to a thousand lesser interests."[90] In fact this "great tree" could easily be "an ancient pitch pine," the kind which Jewett likes "better than any trees in the world."[91] Clearly, the "stately head" of the "great" masculinized pitch pine in "A White Heron" that "towered above" all other trees in his vicinity (xix) could similarly connote attributes of fatherly "kingliness." Metaphorically speaking, like a father who "must have loved his *new dependent*," the "*old* pine" (xxi) also protects the little girl from "lesser interests" by exclusively taking her above the "hot and still" world synonymous with both the hunter's and Mrs. Tilley's human society.

But whether pertaining to the heron or the tree, this rhetorical figure of prosopopoeia humanizes and virtually makes present its non-human referent even as it invokes an "imaginary or absent person . . . represented as speaking or acting."[92] If it here invokes the absent father in relation to a little "solitary" daughterlike girl, Jewett's narrative also absents an already absent father by assigning the "*old* pine" with *grand*-fatherly connotations. Moreover, the narrative (dis)places this (absent) fatherly tree in relation to "the white oak tree that grew alongside" it (xx), in other words, in the same manner as the heron with his mate. Again the spatial arrangement of the two trees metonymically situates Sylvia and the paternal object above a smaller and non-sex-denominated object. The unpersonified oak tree's nestlike features (a bird nests there and Sylvia herself "was almost lost among the dark branches and the green leaves" [xx]), along with its much lesser physical size, also could suggest a maternal figuration. Indeed, we could maintain that in climbing this tree to get to the pine tree, Sylvia in effect outlines the daughter's process of eclipsing the mother (the mother whose presence in family romance interferes with the girl's exclusive claims on the father) here represented by the oak tree, one of whose "upper branches chafed against the pine trunk" (xx). Yet the tropological scattering of this relational situation also allows us to surmise that this genderless "*white* oak" represents an elusive signifier of the daughter, like Sylvia and like the white heron's mate in relation to their *en passant* (merely possible) father-personified signifiers.

In both cases, Sylvia as transcending the mother or as retracing her own daughterhood, the narrative focus here remains on the daughter's experience of the transition from a mother to father nature, an experience that will become doubled in her sighting of the white heron. This transition, this interchangeable occupation of the roles of father to daughter or daughter to father in the crucial scenes of the story and which we could thus cite as "her" displaced Imaginary scene of writing, ritualistically repeats an absent primal transfer of the daughter's affection from preoedipal mother to oedipal father. This transfer is fraught with the possibility that the tropologically subsumed father might disappear altogether, that is, might cancel the project before it has even begun to realize the daughter's regression to a presexual self-identity: "There, when [Sylvia] made the dangerous pass from one tree to the other, the great enterprise would really begin" (xx). Akin to a regression from a more immediate symbol of regression, the absent-fatherly pine tree itself constitutes only a transition to the absent-fatherly white heron whom Sylvia at this point in the story cannot be certain she will see.

In the second place, the very tropes which elicit this regression to a preadult-alias-preadolescent moment of self-identity could defeat this project by also serving as memos of co-possible configurations of adult sexuality. Who can miss not merely the general significance but the phenomenologically evocative details of Sylvia's climbing the phallic tree? She begins "with tingling, eager blood coursing the channels of her whole frame"; once begun, "the pitch made her thin little fingers clumsy and stiff as she went round and round the tree's great stem" until the "tree seemed to lengthen itself out as she went up" (xx). And once up the tree, quite clearly, she experiences a kind of climax, first with the two hawks, when she feels "as if she too could go flying away among the clouds," and then with the equally phallic white heron at the moment when to Sylvia he "grows larger, and rises, and comes close at last . . . with steady sweep of wing and outstretched slender neck and crested head." Such libidinal investments of the two central fatherly tropes of Jewett's story could be regarded as paradoxically lessening its psychosexual associations. For example, they also serve to displace the little girl's "vaguely thrilled" sexual relation to the adult hunter whose gun poses an explicit phallic threat to her and explicit sexual issue to "her," the narrative itself. Whereas the hunter's "determined, and somewhat aggressive" whistle (xv) and "the sharp report of his gun" overtly threaten Sylvia even by their very sounds, the tree's "sharp dry twigs" that "scratched her like angry talons" (xx) and the heron's sudden resurrection from the "dark hemlocks" (xxi) lead her to experience a sex-muted exclusive relation to nature in the guise of a radically sublimated absent father who, in the merely speculative terms of the narrative, "*must* have loved his new dependent."

Representationally, her closest physical contact with a phallus-associated figure occurs with the tree, that is, an inanimate object *least* associated with adult human sexuality. Similarly, as we have seen, the narrative displaces the phallic heron's epiphanic appearance before Sylvia by calling attention to his relation to his mate, his "cries" of love for another, an exclusive relation which, insofar as it also signifies a possible sexual relation, gets dispersed when "the solemn heron goes away" because "of shouting cat-birds" (xxi). More important, Sylvia's climactic apprehension of the heron's resurrected appearance occurs through metonymized or peripheral representations rather than as a focused metaphorical epiphany: "a white *spot* of him *like a single floating feather* comes up from the dead hemlock and grows larger" (xxi). Both Sylvia and the narrator do not properly focus on him until his sexual motion, as it were, has become quieted into the visually neutralized image of him "perched on a pine bough not far beyond." Indeed, the force of this scene as a climactic scene for the little girl's sublimated sexual desire, an unconscious desire to lose her virginity and thus enter the world of adolescence, has all along been deprivileged by prior narrative information that she "had once stolen softly near where [the heron] stood in some bright green swamp grass" (xvii) and that "where you saw the white heron once you will see him *again*" (xxi).

In short, the narrative's sex-lessening tropological movements, not to mention the girl herself, identify "her" as a "harmless housebreaker" (xx) into the sexual thematic associated with producing adult literature, a thematic the story simultaneously traces and withdraws from.

No doubt we could add "emphasis," in Nancy Miller's words, to this withdrawal, just as we could revise Sylvia's climactic experience with the heron according to the aforementioned radical feminist positions. We could even displace it by an archetypal interpretation of this experience. Thus, Sylvia's climbing the "great main-mast to the voyaging earth" (xx), itself an archetypal figuration of primal intercourse between the sky and earth, leads to her divine, Leda-like rape by a swanlike heron from which she gains a transcendental or sacred vision of nature that she is incapable of communicating (hence, her silence) to the profane ears of the hunter and Mrs. Tilley.[93] But such an interpretation already constitutes a sublimation of the more phenomenologically contingent sexual connotations of the passage. And insofar as the story withdraws from this sexual thematic by reiterative tropological options, its absenting projections of the absent-father/absent-daughter relation, whether in terms of the trans-parental narrator, personified tree, or white heron, outline the narrative's project to tell its story from the Imaginary perspective of a time before such feminist and/or archetypal codifications would become necessary.

In this sense, the "lonely country girl" at the end of the story stands as the story's own desire for preoedipal or sex-less self-identity. If the girl's climbing the fatherly tree connotes anything, it is the "tingling, eager blood coursing the channels of" the *narrative's* "whole frame." In the same way, Sylvia's private climactic experience with the fatherly white heron allegorizes the narrative's own autoerotic impulses, its exclusion from this representational scene not only of the hunter and Mrs. Tilley but also of the reader who putatively witnesses it with the narrator. As we have argued, the narrator's "look, look!" preempts the reader's position, his or her direct apprehension of the girl's here climactic moment. The narrator effectively keeps this scene private in the process of writing it. And insofar as the narrative attempts to situate itself in a time before sexual time began, this narrational masturbatory activity can also deny the supersession of masturbation within a woman's psychosexual history, its reduction to secondary status in adult women subliminally cognizant of its regressive, i.e., not vaginal, significance.[94] Indeed, this narrational figuration of a private masturbatory act "in the name of the father" can be considered yet another strategy for returning to the locus of the preoedipal daughter's effort "to differentiate her body from her mother's and to establish herself as an active, autonomous source of satisfaction."⁹⁵

We can argue, then, that in "A White Heron" Jewett inscribes her wish to realize a sex-less site of literary production by substituting her heroine's experience with the heron, whom she chooses over the adult male hunter and Mrs. Tilley, and by means of tropes that objectify the father/daughter relation in veritably unconscious ways. But this objectification remains participial rather than "fixative." If Sylvia's tree climbing surrealistically outlines climbing the father from a child daughter's point of view, it also outlines a would-be daughterly writer's writing in terms of the metonymical proximity of an absent paternal figure "who" will allow her to grow up — just as Sylvia literally grows up when climbing the tree — in a way that quells any adult definitions of sexual self-identity. As long as she writes in terms of this adult-excluding dyad, Jewett can play at writing, can write as if she were indeed a "minor" writer in the same way that Sylvia plays with the cow as "amusement with a good deal of zest." She can even inscribe her name through the story's three protagonistic images: S-y-l-v-i-a as S-a-r-a-h; *heron* as anagram of *Orne;* the tree as a veritable *family* tree, a "great main-mast" metonym of the "Jewett" patrimony as first established by early patriarchal shipbuilders.⁹⁶ Significantly, this patrimony gives Jewett financial independence — a room of her own, as it were — to write without working and more important without getting married or entering "the great world" of heterosexuality and/or its feminist discontents.

On the one hand, the absent father allows such unconscious anagrammatic inscriptions to take place — here the scattered inscription of her name that signifies Jewett's desire to identify herself as a "minor" writer of this story once and for all. But on the other hand, as we have seen, this absent father requires constant invocation of his minimum still small voice, resurrected through submerged metonymies and prosopopoeias as well as narrational silences, lest "he" disappear and thus frustrate this project by leaving it open to adult sexual determinations — including Jewett's own — and leaving it also minus the (only past) father/daughter intentionality which once defined the production of "A White Heron." In short, here the issue of adult sexuality becomes coterminous with the issue of the story's possible textuality before others, a quite literal textuality that supersedes her "writing" and will lead Jewett defensively to remark, "But I love her," after she has written the story. As an allegory of its own production, "A White Heron" ultimately encounters the materiality of discourse interfering with its thus only contingent allegorization. Jewett's identification with Sylvia, for example, would reflect her desire to gain a "secret" relation to her story in the same way that the girl herself witnesses, but for some indefinite reason cannot tell, the white heron's secret: "What is it that suddenly forbids her and makes her dumb?" (xxii). Like Sylvia, Jewett cannot give away the secret father/daughter relation of the story without at the same time giving "*its* life away"; she cannot express without destroying her private relation to a paternal muse that "came flying through the golden air and how they watched the sea and the morning together" as she writes, that is, her unconscious memory of the pristine moment or "morning" of the girl's transition from preoedipal to oedipal daughter. The story, in fact, "forbids" these allegorical doublings. Jewett's identification with Sylvia remains possible, contingent, *en passant;* for otherwise it would betray the serious or explicit rather than secret "minor" intentionality of a story that in effect was being written *by* a minor, and not merely in the sense of one who, as a woman in patriarchal society, has a minority social self-identity.

In the same way, the relation between "writing" and its residual representational correlatives remains asymmetrically allegorical, allegorical in the sense of a discourse subsuming but not negating another discursive possibility. It is this possibility that makes Jewett's sex-lessening tropological maneuvers in "A White Heron" inadequate as ways to produce a totally pure minor literature. While it helps to neutralize all the imminent adult-alias-sexual ideological conscriptions of her text, writing in the name of the absent father in this particular intentional context cannot fully account for "her" coterminous exposure to other kinds of adult appropriations, especially those pertaining to the story's appearance as a literary text. Here the sheer exteriority of the *written* text makes it subject to such appropriations. And in turn, they make the "secret" intentionality of "her" production—an intentionality which constitutes this story's very "life," and which allows Jewett to "love her"—a continuing project that Jewett will have to reproduce in terms of these deferred possible readings.

In the end, to transpose the absent-father/absent-daughter relation to these other unaccounted-for discursive possibilities may lead us to regard Jewett as a kind of nun after all. "A White Heron" absolves her from identification as a genteel, reformist, or an ideologically protesting "New England nun." Instead it identifies her as a woman writer who would suspend the discourses of the great and busy world by constructing a verbal "hermitage" or scripting a private prayer. Or more precisely, "she," the story itself, would suspend discourses of any kind that strive to enlist "her" in a "great enterprise" greater than Jewett desires to propose here. Like the "shouting cat-birds" that chase away the white heron, these discourses would vex her project to produce a pure minor literature "in the name of the father."

CHAPTER THREE   "A WHITE HERON"

AS A RARE BIRD OF PASTORAL

The back of the picture, the unheard melodies, the dull
and the stale . . . are all of infinite value.—R. H. Blyth

May you stay forever young.—Bob Dylan

I   It seems apparent that in "A White Heron" Jewett primarily
relies on the tradition of pastoral literature, a preestablished discursive space which effectively neutralizes ahead of time the more referentially explicit ideological issues the story coterminously broaches.
This textual strategy would at once postpone the story's imminent
adult appropriations and propagate the illusion of producing literature in a "minor" mode, that is, outside the context of a comparatively determined minor literature. It would allow Jewett to prerepress
the historical temporality connected to the local color and/or feminist topoi consequent to the story's representations; it would allow
her to prerepress the phenomenological temporality that surrounds
her act of writing this story within the horizon of its becoming a public text—a text always about to become rife with adult significance.
And so not just Sylvia but the story and its imagined production end
as well as begin with the promise of remaining in endless "woodlands and summer-time" (xxiii), a pastoral veto of any kind of future
which, different from the imagined deictic presence of the story's
linguistic events, would require them to grow up or "mean" in adult

terms. In this sense, the narrator at the end of the story appeals to a timeless nature, a nature underwritten by the literary pastoral tradition, to continue to grant the heroine childhood experiences like her experience with the white heron: "Bring your gifts and graces and tell your secrets to this lonely country child!" As metaphorical emblem of the story's own literary identity, Sylvia, already a "sylvan" allusion to the pastoral tradition, quite literally becomes a perpetually silent girl child, a Keatsian "still unravished bride of quietness" which the narrative both preserves and doubles.

But as Keats's Grecian Urn poem shows, the pastoral tradition in Western literature by no means endorses a simple realizable state of timelessness or timeless present. For one thing, literary pastorals depend on privileged binary oppositions—Nature/civilization, Child/adult, Timelessness/mutability, Innocence/experience—which mitigate this state's representability and, because language itself occurs in time, always cross pastoral projects with elegiac intimations. At best, such pastorals try to represent, in Leo Marx's words, an ideal "middle landscape," a fictional space "located in a middle ground somewhere 'between,' yet in transcendent relation to, the opposing forces of civilization and nature."[1] This middle landscape defines both the literal setting of "A White Heron," the farmstead which seems "so clean and comfortable a little dwelling in this New England wilderness" (xvi), and Sylvia's ambivalent position between the civilized hunter and purely natural white heron. In choosing the heron's life over "loyalty" to the hunter, the girl effectively reaffirms as well as earns this "middle" pastoral ideal; her pastoral innocence becomes even more meaningful when she doubts whether "the birds [were] better friends than their hunter might have been" (xxiii). Moreover, the narrator's immediately ensuing "who can tell?" and the fact that Sylvia does not even know she *has* resisted a pejoratively defined temptation from "the great world" (and so stands as a doubly innocent figure of the pastoral ideal) further consolidate the "middle" locus of the story's pastoral identity. Thus, despite its apparent total faith in a nature that will perpetually endow its heroine with "gifts and graces" or with the capacity to remain forever young, "A White Heron" duplicates the way pastoral works "call into question, or bring irony to bear against the illusion of peace and harmony in a green pasture."[2]

In more specific generic terms, Jewett's story affiliates itself with an American literary pastoral tradition which subjects the European mode to the "real" historical and ideological circumstances of nineteenth-century American pastoral idealism. The story clearly delineates the "unprecedented" American situation where the "machine" entered the "garden" and a collision occurred, producing the need for a revised pastoral thematic, between the ideal of timelessness on the one hand, and on the other the suddenly intruding fact of time, the "sense of history as an unpredictable, irreversible sequence of unique events."[3] To Sylvia, used to loitering like the cow "occasionally on her own account" (xiv), it seems as if the hunter whom she meets by "accident" is suddenly intruding on her gardenlike existence with his machinelike gun. He also seems to us to become synonymous with the girl's sense of the anxious pace of life in the town—where a boy "used to chase and frighten her [and] made her *hurry*" (xv)—in his somewhat obsessional quest for a heron that itself has already "been chased out of its own region" (xviii). By keeping the secret of the heron's timeless habitat "where the green marsh is set among the shining birches and dark hemlocks" (xxi), Sylvia chooses the garden or "green pasture" over the implications of the hunter's but also American society's machines. In short, the story addresses the ideological split between nineteenth-century America's idealized notion of itself as "the virgin land," to use Henry Nash Smith's famous terms, and its contrary commitment to social progress, which is the more probable reason for the heron's dislocation.[4] In the context of this specific ideological conundrum, Sylvia's preservation of the heron's secret reflects not a purely "imaginative" or European pastoral idealism so much as historically grounded option associated with Jewett's "regionalist" situation. That is, Jewett can imagine the girl's choice as a viable possibility since her writing involves actual or "native materials."[5] She can refer to an actual place and a specific nineteenth-century American cultural situation which let her recuperate the fading reality of the "American frontier," the frontier more often associated with "the West as primitive agricultural region,"[6] but here appearing in the guise of a synecdochical, as yet unsettled pastoral "New England wilderness."[7] Sylvia's choice, then, stands for a renewed and still youthful pastoral vision of what thus becomes a veritable *American* "middle landscape."

Indeed, the keynoting scene of "A White Heron" suggests just how "American" this story proposes to be: Sylvia and the cow "were going away from the western light, and striking deep into the dark woods, but their feet were familiar with the path, and it was no matter whether their eyes could see it or not" (xiii). In metapastoral terms, both girl and cow signify pastoral images per se; their familiarity "with the path" signifies the narrative's own reliance on a familiar topos—regionalist as well as pastoral—in order to leave behind the imminent death of pastoral imagination itself ("the western light"). Only apparently a self-image of a New England culture's retreat from the direction of mainstream American culture, this eastering movement suggests the heroic attempt to renew ("striking deep into . . . dark woods") the American pastoral ideal of "the virgin land" by relating it to a biblically eastern Eden. Jewett's story thus begins by suggesting it intends to reverse the westward symbolic-ideological direction of European and American sociohistorical expansionism, but on a more metapastoral level, also the "westering" movement of British and European poetic ideology.[8] In contrast to such expansionism, this story constitutes a strategic regression to "a simple society of the middle landscape";[9] and in contrast to traditional pastoral writing, it constitutes the continuing "American" revision of Old World literary forms as well as ideals. In this context, Sylvia's tree-climbing episode alludes to and revises the Miltonic narrative's Tree of Knowledge less in feminist than in American pastoral terms. She here reclaims a tree symbolic of the American pastoral vision itself, the American possibility, grounded in the "unprecedented" American situation, of regarding nature as if for the first time.

"A White Heron," then, doubly displaces traditional pastoral literature's governing myth as Northrop Frye defines it, the full "paradisal garden" and "the body of the Virgin as *hortus conclusus*."[10] In its topos of a heron's "green" world and woods "full of little birds and beasts" in which a (literally) virgin girl feels "as if she were a part of the gray shadows and the moving leaves" (xv) and to which she maintains privileged access, Jewett's story seeks not only to make literarily credible a specific American historical context but also to accommodate it to the myth of pastoral literature. This American ideological context effectively converts the girl's virgin status, her borderline preadolescent identity, into an interchangeable signifier of "frontier" epistemology. Through her as well as *with* her, we encounter the American garden as if seen for the first time: "that *strange* white bird," his habitat "an open place where the sunshine always seemed *strangely* yellow and hot" (xviii). Sylvia's choice, in fact, reconfirms her virginal perceptions of a reanimated frontier nature: the dumb but as if "intelligent" cow; "the sea which Sylvia wondered and dreamed about," having previously heard "its great voice" (xviii); the "boundary" tree which has lost the practical significance ("for what reason, no one could say") it once had for the now-dead "woodchoppers" of civilization, and which comes to love its *"new* dependent." An empty, hence figuratively virginal, signifier to the two adults in the story, Sylvia's silence here suggests she cannot communicate the *first-time* aspect of her vision of the heron "flying through the golden air." By epistemological definition, the adults who cannot view nature as if for the first time as does this child, herself a borderline or "middle" figure between nature and civilization, are excluded from the American pastoral vision of "the virgin land" *as* virgin land.[11]

Indeed, located "away over at the other side of the woods" (xvii), the white heron's "green" place becomes a more privileged figure of the American frontier than both the traditional pastoral image of the farmstead's "middle landscape" and traditional American pastoral settings such as Irving's Sleepy Hollow. From the start of her career, Jewett clearly shows the affiliation of her works with this American tradition. The very title of her first collection of stories, *Deephaven* (1877), alludes to this mythical "sleepy hollow," a place set apart from the civilized or nonagrarian society of a changing America. A self-evident fantasy setting, Irving's topos frees him as an American pastoral writer from the pressure of serious as opposed to pastoral modes of literary production. Likewise, Jewett's "deep haven" projects a place outside the traumas of social-historical changes, changes that Irving detraumatizes by having his Rip Van Winkle sleep for twenty years and wake up to resume his pastoral style of life in a post-Revolutionary America. Even the indefinite asocial place "at the other end of the woods" in "A White Heron" could easily signify the story's supererogatory movement toward a deeper American pastoral identity (yet another significance of "deep into the dark woods") than Sleepy Hollow or Deephaven already indicates. As fictional settings or literary topoi, these recessive places allow their writers to represent pastoral heroes like Rip Van Winkle, Brom Bones, and Sylvia as, in Annette Kolodny's words, perpetual "psychological adolescent[s]."[12]

Moreover, one could also argue that her otherwise pejorative ideological situation as an American woman writer ironically grants Jewett a privileged access to pastoral modes of writing whether of the Old World or American tradition. According to Margaret Fuller writing about this situation some forty years earlier, "no traditions chain [American women], and few conventionalities. . . . There is no reason why they should not discover that the secrets of nature are open, the revelations of the spirit waiting."[13] A preadolescent virgin, Sylvia in "A White Heron" marks the American woman writer's ideologically virginal ability—re-marked by the narrational apostrophe to nature to "tell [this girl] your secrets"—to write exclusively in terms of such "secrets of nature."

In the second place, as a figure of the virgin woman writer and "virgin land" as well, Sylvia and through her Jewett herself could be said to double as the traditional objects of American patriarchal literature. The texts of early American explorers, settlers, and writers like Irving and Cooper show a psychosexual ambivalence in their representation of a feminized nature as bountiful mother on the one hand, and on the other hand as an unviolated virgin which they guiltily exploit. A central dilemma for these male pastoral writers concerns their wish both to express "filial homage" toward nature and not to exhibit "erotic desire" for her at the same time, a desire that would negate such homage. But where Jewett's male American precursors fail to effect what Kolodny terms a "pastoral compromise" with regard to their ambivalent relation to American nature, virtually confessing this failure in their texts, we can argue that Jewett succeeds precisely because of her ideological interchangeability with this nature.[14] As a writer whose gender congruence with both her heroine and the personified feminine topos of previous American patriarchal pastoral narratives allows her to imagine "the virgin land" without psychosexual ambivalence, Jewett can declare her literary-pastoral priority and effect "the pastoral compromise," as it were, for the first time. And so she projects a heroine who indeed pays "filial homage" to nature, whether in the guise of feminine cows or oak trees or masculine trees and herons; and who in being a preadolescent girl averts the semiotic locus of an "erotic" relation to these parentalized tropes of American nature. In this sense or for this "pastoral" reason, Sylvia is spared being identified as a Crèvecoeur-like American farmer who unavoidably exploits American nature—like Mrs. Tilley who uses husks and goose-feathers to construct beds, or the Bumppo-like hunter in the story who doubles as an allusion to the American pastoral tradition itself and in the end violates the pastoral American nature he otherwise "seemed to like so much" (xviii).

In producing a pastoral text as if for the first time, away over at the other side of traditional American pastoral woods, Jewett herself becomes "this lonely country child" (xxiii). She can write pastoral pastorally; she can bask as if forever in the "minor" pleasure afforded by a pastoral thematic which accounts for and preempts this story's adult ideological reverberations. Writing in relation to a male, American pastoral tradition that seeks to ground such pastoral pleasures in the actual world and not merely in imagination, she can apparently produce a pastoral text which avoids this tradition's inability to avoid invoking adult binary issues, such as an awareness of time and the inevitable discontinuity with nature versus a sense of child-like timelessness—a perpetual "summer-time" vacation—and a believable because gender-congruent relation to American nature. In this sense too, "A White Heron" can avoid the binary intentionality of minor literature, that is, avoid being subject to adult social, historical, literary categorizations of human experience.

2   But this strategy to protect "A White Heron" from any serious adult ideological appropriations and to consolidate its unique literary-pastoral self-identity, because it is grounded in a literary-historical transumption of the Old World and American pastoral tradition, of course forces Jewett's textual production to participate in the unconsciously charged field of literary history. In short, it reintroduces the here-intrinsic problematic binary field of a major-versus-minor literature.

In the same way, Jewett's would-be "feminism" is no escape from this psychodynamic literary-historical problem where even pastoral significations themselves are haunted by time or with becoming past in relation to previous modes of signifying timeless states. For it is not only her "feminine" ideological perspective that differentiates her project from past masculine American failures, but also her position in literary history, which precludes her from writing like Irving, for example, for whom a nonpastoral "reality" was still an unresolved, i.e., a "frontier," issue. Irving could write pastoral tales without the anxiety that either a self-evident, totally contradictory American reality principle, or native literary precedents, would impinge on his transumptions of Old World literary-pastoral materials such as the German folktales that comprise the literary origins of "Rip Van Winkle" and "The Legend of Sleepy Hollow."

It is from this perspective that we can regard the "frontier" images of "A White Heron," its metonymical strategies noted in the previous sections, and more thematically, the way it mutes the pastoral country/city binary by primarily focusing on the former and representing the latter as a virtually benign term in the guise of a "kind appealing" hunter. These merely allusive maneuvers suggest less a transumption of American precursor pastoral texts than what Harold Bloom would term a *kenosis*, the veritable reduction of these prior texts as models affecting the story's "shy little" and "secret" assertion of literary uniqueness.[15] Jewett's story, that is, internalizes and revises elements from male American pastoral writing not to deny but to become a part of an American pastoral tradition which thus, within itself, constitutes a timeless continuum rather than a series of discontinuous precedents antithetical to Jewett's writing this story in a pastoral mode. We could discuss, for example, the way Jewett recovers a pastoral relation to certain regionalist topoi, as in her sense that "New England towns have changed . . . in the last twenty years, since the manufactories have come in."[16] In alluding to the American pastoral continuity implied by Rip Van Winkle's twenty-year sleep, Jewett converts a potentially "mournful" situation of loss into happy recollections from her childhood: her grandmother's "front yard," even her grandmother's funeral that "gave me vast entertainment; it was the first grand public occasion in which I had taken any share."[17] At the same time, her sketch effectively reaffirms even as it revises in less fantastic terms the continuity between Irving's American pastoral vision and her own childlike, i.e., pastoral, scene of writing.

Jewett thus includes allusions to the American pastoral tradition in order to repeat the imagined continuity between pastoral signifier and signified, the sine qua non of American pastoral writing. To do this she must erase premonitions of these earlier works' historical obsolescence which could also point to the more pressing historical situation of her story's scene of writing. In this sense, her story evokes their precedent but proceeds to misread it. For example, where both Crèvecoeur and Cooper write about the decimation of trees or the American wilderness as signs of the destruction of the American pastoral mythos,[18] Jewett will only cite in passing "a great pine-tree . . . the last of its generation . . . felled . . . long ago" by woodchoppers. The narrative then goes on to tell us that "a whole forest of sturdy trees, pines and oaks and maples, had grown again" (xix), a fact that suggests the survivability not only of nature but also of pastoral signifying practices and the American pastoral mythos which grounds them. Moreover, as a male-personified tree which comes to accept "his new dependent," the pine tree here stands as an overdetermined synecdochical allusion to an American pastoral tradition that at once can endure beyond the intrusions of American history or social progress, and as a still-privileged tradition provides a context in which a female writer and feminized story can proceed to trace their own literary self-identities.

In short, "A White Heron," itself occurring in a belated historical and literary-historical situation, affiliates itself with an already diminished or reality-recessive American genre and literary ideology. Even Emerson, whose transcendentalist vision of nature defines Sylvia's privileged moment with the heron, had written his transpastoral American essays in the optative or subjunctive mode; in "Nature," for example, he could assert, "So shall we come to look at the world with new eyes," only with the simultaneous awareness of a contrary American tendency.[19] On the one hand, Jewett affiliates her story with the American pastoral tradition in order to mitigate if not deny the temporality associated with the writing as well as reading of pastoral literature. But insofar as even this tradition, albeit diminished, signifies a "great enterprise," a "project" that could "be of . . . use" (xx) to American society, the possibility arises that the story's latter-day reformation of its pastoral precedents will bring up the seriousness of its own enterprise. Like "the rare bird" of its title, a bird "never . . . found in this district at all," "A White Heron" also tends to identify itself as a unique pastoral project—to differentiate itself from the American pastoral "district."

It is in this context that Jewett's story works to disassociate itself from its coterminous act of affiliation with its American tradition. Subliminally identifying itself as but a "harmless housebreaker" (xx) into this ideologically diminished but "great" literary tradition, indeed alluding to this tradition through a *pre*-adolescent hero-*ine* as opposed to the male "psychological adolescent" of American pastoral literature, the story does more — or rather less — than repress the temporality invoked by the mere existence of literary precedents. For one thing it attempts to locate its pastoral praxis as if *before* such "great" precedents; at least it attempts to misrecognize its therefore *provisional* pastoral identity. Such an attempt we can now see constitutes the thematic allusion of the keynoting scene where Sylvia and cow, i.e., Jewett and her story, walk "into the dark woods" thanks to a "familiar . . . path"—the pasture path as figure of pastoral writing itself—which they never see, for "it was no matter whether their eyes could see it or not." Jewett thus deploys her allusions to the American pastoral tradition to determine her story's minor mode of pastoral writing. Even in a sketch where she refers to the culture shock of suddenly perceiving decimated trees, she removes her persona from the immediacy of the scene and its intimations, like those of the "great pine-tree" above, of the conflictual motifs of "great" American pastorals:

The noise of the lumbermen in the woods must be very annoying to the trees. . . . The scattered trees that were left standing had a shocked and fearful look, as if some fatal epidemic had slain their neighbors. Just at the edge of the clearing [my horse and I] crossed a little brook, busy under the ice and snow, and coming out to scurry and splash around a lichened rock with great unconcern, as if it were a child playing with its toys in the next room to a funeral.[20]

The scene shifts abruptly from an implicit genocide of trees already abstracted from human cause ("as if some fatal epidemic had slain . . . ") to a brook in a way clearly reminiscent of Jewett's childhood "unconcern" at the funeral of her grandmother. On one level, this shift from a "shocked" or traumatic perception to one more childlike and carefree (the brook's "coming out to scurry and splash around") asserts the continuity of a pastoral vision as well as the possibility of expressing "the virgin land" in the face of American society's intruding "lumbermen." But this shift also indicates a point at which the narrative turns away from an already allusive allusion to an Emersonian declaration of pastoral transcendence to an allusion optionally suggesting the sketch's comparatively determined minor pastoral topos: ". . . a *little* brook, busy under the ice and snow . . ." Jewett's sketch in effect settles here for a more concealed and "little" relation to a more major binary theme of American pastoral tradition that would, for example, attempt to displace the shock of civilization by means of a sublime or "transparent eyeball" experience of nature.

This "little" pastoral focus helps us identify the motivation behind Jewett's depiction of the "shy little girl" along with the "elusive" white heron as minor and virtually unperceivable figures of the story's own "rare" literary-pastoral identity. Indeed, the white heron's "green marsh," the story's as well as the heron's secret location, also balks at becoming a metaphor of the American pastoral garden. After all, it remains off limits to the hunter and Sylvia's grandmother who has warned her that she "might sink in the soft black mud underneath and never be heard of more" (xviii). Hidden from adults, this potential metaphor of "the virgin land" is "soft," that is, a malleable figure capable of offering a provisional guarantee that no one but the writer will recognize its major literary implications, implications that she herself passes over, no less than the girl, to focus on the more unrecognizable metaphor of pastoral tradition itself, the pine tree. Jewett's pastoral relation, then, to this American pastoral tradition hinges on the probability that it will slip by her own internalized censors demanding a major pastoral enterprise; or at most, that it will be considered only a "harmless housebreaker" into this tradition.

But this probability remains just that, a provisional guarantee that

"A White Heron" will elude making major pastoral claims for itself. It calls to mind another probable guarantee, the fact that to a woman writer, Jewett's work within this male-dominated literary tradition becomes minor ahead of time. Thus, she can write "A White Heron" apart from the contemporary and male-dominated competitive literary marketplace, in other words, as not "a very good magazine story." More important, she can write "her" as if immune to the mainstream textual dialectics or "anxiety of influence"which defines male modes of literary pastoral production.[21] But insofar as these guarantees remain probable, the process of determining the story's minor literary identity requires further self-referential maneuvers such as subliminally assigning the hunter himself with representing a major as well as male-identified American pastoral precedent, a precursor text to which "she" is undoubtedly attracted from beginning to end. One such text would be John Audubon's collected written sketches in his *Ornithological Biography*. In fact, at the time Jewett was writing "A White Heron," naturalists and genteel women from Boston unofficially established the first Audubon society in an attempt to preserve herons and egrets from extinction because of the then-rampant plume trade.[22] In this sense, her story could here be considered a protest directed against female consumers as well as male producers. But not only does "A White Heron" fail to dramatize this issue as such (the heron is "rare" even among the more common blue herons of New England), by having the girl experience her meeting with the hunter as an "accident" it presents this issue as secondary to its more explicit pastoral thematic.

Referred to as a "stranger" throughout the story, the hunter is an allusion to the "mysterious stranger" mythos of American literature. But as ornithologist too, he recalls Audubon himself, the most popular and romanticized ornithologist of nineteenth-century America. Audubon not only made huge pictorial sketches of American birds, among them several white herons,[23] but wrote sketches of his experiences with people he met on the frontier. As Kolodny maintains, these sketches reveal both his male "sexual" ambivalence toward nature (reminding us of the hunter who kills the birds "he seemed to like so much"), and his feeling out of place—indeed a stranger—among the people he occasionally stayed with: "[Audubon] finds no permanent or legitimate role in such scenes and remains . . . the 'stranger,' as much an intruder inside the cabin as . . . in the landscape without, where . . . he kills the 'beautiful birds' . . . that nature had provided for his admiration."[24] As the palimpsest text of "A White Heron," by a major and popular de facto American pastoral writer, Audubon's written sketches willy-nilly situate "A White Heron" in the same highly esteemed literary-nationalistic context. But even as it invites it, the story projects outside itself this specific if unconscious textual allusion. Thanks to Sylvia's grandmother, the hunter does not himself experience any estrangement in the place he spends the night. Sylvia herself, not the hunter, comes to experience an Audubon-like ambivalence toward the heron: "must she thrust aside [her chance to enter the great world] for a bird's sake?" (xxii). And since her ambivalence results from a cause outside her control—the hunter's *un*-ambivalent desire for the heron—it constitutes no more than a tenuous displacement of its male pastoral precursor, whether or not it could still be read as a muted declaration of Jewett's own literary ambition. Sylvia's final choice, in fact, effectively absolves Jewett from having to represent either the *hunter's* need to choose—and thus to signify the Audubon textual precedent—or his never feeling compelled to choose between preserving and violating nature.

Jewett's story therefore retreats not only from its conservationist, Audubon-like tenor, but also from Audubon's more dramatic mode of pastoral narration. He can openly record his anxiety over how changes in American society have destroyed his pastoral métier: "When I remember that extraordinary changes have all taken place in the short period of twenty years, I pause, wonder, and . . . can scarcely believe its reality."[25] But like her early sketch's mediation of twenty-year changes in New England, Jewett's story does not manifest anxiety over the imminent extinction of the *species* white heron *or* the pastoral topos it signifies, that is, over the extinction of the very possibility of writing this pastoral text in late-nineteenth-century America. Indeed, juxtaposing the two texts (taking Audubon's actual verbal sketches or simply their availability through hearsay) exposes "A White Heron" as being in the process of subtracting such anxiety. And this act of subtraction does not so much deny or reduce Audubon's textual influence as admit following it—like the little girl "who only followed [the hunter], and there was no such thing as speaking first"—the better to express the text's self-referential, nonaggressive, or "silent" abstention from the anxiety associated with major pastoral writing.

But the hunter also comprises an overdetermined composite allusion to such writing. On one level, he resembles Dan, Sylvia's uncle, another hunter or "great hand to go gunning." But if even Sylvia "takes after him" in the way he too could tame birds (xvii), he also differs from her in the way he has gone west to California and so has witnessed the American frontier firsthand. Suggesting an internalized image of the ambivalence and instability of male American pastoral experience (does California here connote the quest for fame and gold, hence what Smith terms the "American continental empire"?), Dan's migration also suggests the inaccessibility of major pastoral materials to American women and of course especially to the little girl who represents the story's pastoral identity. Given Mrs. Tilley's desire to have gone west as well, *she* perhaps represents the belated woman writer's "anxious" exclusion from such experience. But given Sylvia's partial duplication of her uncle's youthful relation to nature, she could represent not so much the possibility of an untainted pastoral American vision as a "minor" dispensation from having to sustain it in the face of its attendant literary as well as historical anxieties.

The story's "young man," however, stands as a modified figure of the male pastoral experience as represented by Dan. Hunting in the "New England wilderness" is his "vacation" (xviii); his quest is thus already a reduced version of this experience. These qualifications suggest less an Audubon ornithological explorer or Dan-like male adventurer than a New England naturalist more closely associated with the setting of "A White Heron." The hunter, in short, is an allusion to Thoreau, specifically the Thoreau of *The Maine Woods,* published in 1864 after his death, and of his major American pastoral work, *Walden.* Like the hunter who teaches Sylvia "many things about the birds," Thoreau in *The Maine Woods,* the very locale of the story, records his 1857 observations of birds and trees and speaks of his admiration for the Indian hunters who use guns; in general, he maintains a studious, almost taxonomic concern with the animals he sees and those which the Indians shoot: "Using a tape, I found that the moose measured just six feet from the shoulder to the tip of the hoof. . . . Some portions of the body . . . were almost covered with flies, apparently the common fly of our woods, with a dark spot on the wing."[26]

But the Thoreau to which the hunter and, in a textual sense, Jewett's story allude also emanates from the "Higher Laws" section of *Walden* where this New England precursor recalls his younger killing of birds as an amateurish but not pejorative method of practicing ornithology:

> As for fowling, during the last years that I carried a gun my excuse was that I was studying ornithology, and *sought only new or rare birds.* But I confess that I am now inclined to think that there is a finer way of studying ornithology than this. It requires so much closer attention to the habits of the birds, that, *if for that reason only,* I have been willing to omit the gun. (my italics)[27]

Thoreau objects more to the impracticality of the gun for his study of "rare birds" than to its ostensible violation of nature. The hunter in "A White Heron," then, alludes to this unreformed Thoreau, for he still uses his gun to pursue "two or three very rare [birds]" to complete his ornithological "collection" (xvii). Through Sylvia, the story objects to this *young* Thoreau, "the sharp report of [the hunter's] gun" here synonymous with the Thanatos motif of male American pastoral writing; but the story also in effect modifies this objection by recognizing that he *is* but a "young sportsman" (xviii), the latter designation serving to deflect the aggressive connotations of his hunting. Moreover, this textual allusion to a specific passage from *Walden* provides the story with a way to forget the young hunter's association with killing and with the Thoreau of this passage. Not only does Sylvia come to forget the hunter's sharp report, but this passage from "Higher Laws" goes on to make an analogy between actual hunting and symbolic hunting. If the young sportsman pursues actual hunting, it will lead directly to what Kolodny calls "the pastoral compromise," that is, the male pastoral writer's symbolic transcendence of his ambivalence toward nature: "*Make* them hunters, though sportsmen only at first, if possible, mighty hunters at last, so that they shall not find game large enough for them in this or any vegetable wilderness" (Thoreau's italics).[28]

In her inability to "understand why [the hunter] killed the very birds he seemed to like so much," Sylvia signifies not the story's rejection, but its decided or at least desired adoption, of an ephebe relation to the Thoreauvian symbolic-pastoral vision as expressed in *Walden.* Thoreau regains a relation to nature *as* nature only after this symbolic processing. In this sense, the story's "elusive" white heron, for example, remains presymbolic, a bird never seen in the story by the also ephebelike Thoreauvian hunter. Itself "crested" or royal in appearance, it clearly alludes to the "stately bird" in *Walden,* the elusive loon with "white breast" that, "confident of his own resources," escapes Thoreau's "effort" to observe it directly;[29] but combined with the bird's sounds which he does experience, the loon's elusive presence leads Thoreau to convert it into a symbol of nature's sheer thereness, its pastoral virginity. Similarly, when Sylvia sees that "the heron has perched on a pine bough not far beyond [hers] . . . and plumes his feathers for the new day" (xxi), this scene has a Thoreauvian metaphorical edge. In *Walden,* Thoreau similarly observes a bird — here an owl — growing "uneasy . . . on his perch"; but he, not the bird as in Jewett's story, closes the distance between them by converting this (also) male bird into a muted or latent symbol of human self-realization:

> He launched himself off and flapped through the pines, spreading his wings to unexpected breadth. . . . guided amid the pine boughs rather by a delicate sense of their neighborhood than by sight, feeling his twilight way, as it were, with his sensitive pinions, he found a new perch, where he might in peace await the dawning of his day.

The collatability of the two scenes seems obvious. Occurring at literal dawn, the "new day" in Jewett's story also remains literal, that is, a presymbolic referent when compared with the potentially symbolic place ("where he *might* . . . await") and time ("the dawning of his day") that identifies Thoreau's precursor text. Indeed, before "he" can assume such symbolic attributes, Jewett's heron "goes back like an arrow . . . to his home in the green world beneath" (xxii), in other words seeks refuge in a purely referential grounding.

Nurtured on Thoreau's symbolic recuperation of American pastoral vision, we may argue that the heron and story here symbolically return to a recuperated "virgin land" and pastoral vision. But no less than Sylvia with the hunter, the story leaves us pastorally expectant readers "disappointed" by a presymbolic "silence." Its locus is rather the sheer potentiality of pastoral significance. This silence could just as easily signify the story's abstention from pastoral symbolizations, particularly in relation to the Thoreauvian text it internalizes perhaps for this very reason. In *The Main Woods,* Thoreau actually comes to ask "about herons"; and though he hears only about "blue heron's [*sic*] nests in the hard-wood trees," he eventually sees "a light-colored object move along the opposite or northern shore" which his guide cannot identify, "unless it were a moose, though he had never seen a white one."[31] If only in an unconscious way, Jewett's white heron (and "A White Heron") may thus function as a trope of *metalepsis* or transumption, that is, a pastoral Maine writer's response to a narrative absence in a major pastoral writer's text dealing with the same but to her also more familiar Maine woods. This absence, in short, could provide a means for Jewett's text to declare its pastoral priority over this more imminently influential New England precursor. Such a response could also signify her attempt to fit her text into—in order to determine its minor relation to—these invoked traces of "Thoreau" or his texts' major recuperation of American pastoral literature. It is in this sense that Sylvia retains the heron's secret from the hunter, an incomparably "charming and delightful" figure to her who, in becoming a textual allusion to "Thoreau," reflects at least the possibility of transcending through language traditionally ambivalent American pastoral relations to nature. Jewett's text traces and reaffirms its reserve before even the "kindly" pastoral narrative project of Thoreau's texts which themselves, most particularly in *The Maine Woods,* "need a friend very much" (xv) for their timeless, i.e., as if on "vacation," pastoral project—their need to reflect nature totally, as in a "collection," to become successful at all.

As we have seen before, even this reserve itself must be held in reserve. Any but an unconscious allegorical inscription of this minor mode of literary pastoral production (writing on nature as if with the jackknife the hunter gives to the girl as a gift) would reintroduce serious pastoral themes (writing on nature as if with the hunter's gun);

it would induce a nonpastoral self-consciousness (the effect the hunter's gun has on Sylvia) that would point to the necessity of Thoreauvian transcendence and serious pastoral symbolicity, which is to say an anxious mode of literary production. Thus, the story's self-determined "minor" engagement with internalized versions of the American pastoral tradition is projected as an accident: "It did not appear to be her fault" (xv). And insofar as the story itself comes to feel that it "could have served and followed him and loved him as a dog loves" (xxii–xxiii), that is, could have accepted its minor place within the tradition of an albeit exaggerated "great world" of American pastoral literature, this possibility too derives less from conscious choice than from the way this world persistently if "kindly" imposes criteria or defines the terms by which it can make judgments on literary performance. In the case of Jewett's story, these criteria, as we saw, include the importance of addressing the possible demise of American pastoral literature itself and/or its Thoreauvian resurrections.

The story's self-exemptions from internalized norms of major pastoral performance clearly require an overdetermined differential praxis. There does not seem to be any one way to banish once and for all the binary oppositions which cross pastoral writing. To evade "real" American history, the story must engage the temporality of pastoral writing within literary history. To evade the latter, it must engage the anxiety of influence or American texts like Thoreau's which transume such history. To evade this locus of influence, "A White Heron" must adopt a minor relation to these self internalized precursors, but also project them outside itself in a way akin to Freud's notion of the uncanny. Indeed, this nexus of frustrations endemic to Jewett's desire to produce a minor pastoral story reappears in the autobiographical tenor of her-through-"her" textual allusion to Thoreau's *The Maine Woods*. Jewett—but is this an accident, too?—would have been approximately the age of Sylvia when Thoreau made his 1857 trip, which his work records. The hunter's accidental meeting of Sylvia, then, allegorically doubles "Thoreau's" accidental meeting of Jewett in the process of writing "A White Heron."

But Jewett has at least one strategy left to reduce the imminent resurfacing of "Thoreau" and the pastoral tradition he signifies here so as to maintain her story's minor pastoral literary identity. Born in 1847, Mary, Jewett's two-year-older sister, would have approximated Sylvia's age more closely. Jewett, in fact, dedicates *A White Heron and Other Stories,* the collection in which "A White Heron" first appeared, *to* this older sister. If we substitute Mary for Sarah in Sylvia's meeting of the hunter and its possible allegorical double as the story's very scene of writing, we could argue that in this way Jewett again distances herself from "her" textual allusion to "Thoreau." Indeed, by placing Mary "in" the story and displacing her own possible self-representation through Sylvia, Jewett can adopt an even more child-like positional relation to the production of her story precisely in comparison with her *older* sister. And what kind of pastoral story could a child write except one that all along has been excused from its potentially serious historical and literary historical ramifications?

3   Certain aspects of "A White Heron" clearly help identify "her" as the preadult form of pastoral literature which we designate as the fairy tale, a story written primarily for children. With one generic thrust, does Jewett realize her desire to write pre-pastoral or "minor" literature? Like many late-nineteenth-century woman regionalist writers, she in fact wrote stories for children, some of which she collected in an 1878 volume entitled *Play Days;* and as late as 1869, she would admit her avid consumption of such stories: "I'm not a bit grown up if I am twenty and I like my children's books just as ever I did, and I read them just the same."[32] But to write as well as read them "just the same" would require her to repress repetition per se, the discrepancy between writing and reading these stories *as* a child and as an adult wishing to adopt the imaginative position of a child. This problem confronting the adult writer and reader of children's literature was anything but an a posteriori critical problem. Margaret Fuller had earlier argued that the "excellent writer for children . . . [should be] a child herself, *as she writes,* nursed anew by her own genius. It is not by imitating, *but by reproducing childhood,* that the writer becomes [the child's] companion."[33]

Given the story's active demotion of its affiliation to the American pastoral tradition, then, the fairy tale elements of "A White Heron" here can be regarded as a further means to produce a quite literal minor pastoral text "as she writes." As a muted or displaced fairy tale—doubly so insofar as it adheres to the conventions of versimilitude or resists being read *as* a fairy tale—Jewett's story effectively determines its own "childhood" locus of production precisely in relation to its adult textual possibilities. A coterminous aspect of the story's writing, these possibilities self-censor the acknowledgement of its therefore "secret" locus; in other words, they suspend any extratextual sense of a discrepancy between an actual and an imagined childhood apprehension of the story's pastoral appearance by making this discrepancy a textual issue which in turn serves to reproduce a sense of childhood in the purely literary terms of Jewett's act of writing. In short, Jewett's deployment of faintly traced elements of the fairy tale genre positions her as the only "minor" who could read "A White Heron" as a textual mode of "reproducing childhood."

The story's invocation of this genre seems all but self-evident, what with its animistic investments of a nature magically on the verge of discourse which the child heroine and her narrator alone can understand: the cow whose "pranks" suggest "an intelligent attempt to play hide and seek" (xiii); the tree, we now reemphasize, that "must have loved" (xxi); nature at large called upon to "remember" (xxiii); a child whom "the wild creatur's counts [as] one o' themselves" and who tames them (xvii).[34] Suggesting the animistic naturalism populating children's stories, these elements that signify the fairy tale genre per se, along with the prosopopoeias discussed in the previous chapter, could also align the story with "major" concerns of Romantic literature as discernible in early German "novels," or in the contemporary interests of those like Longfellow in myth and/or "folk" literature. Indeed, we could consider Sylvia's fairy tale status as here again a sign of serious pastoral literature, "the child as swain" like the fairy tale Alice in William Empson's analysis of Lewis Carroll's tale, a tale Jewett herself had most likely read.[35]

Yet whereas in Carroll's *Alice,* the heroine's "dream cuts out the real world" (Empson), in Jewett's "A White Heron" the embryonic pastoral shepherdess continues to hear "the echo of [the hunter's] whistle haunting the pasture path" (xxiii), that is, cannot secure a definitive fairy tale or solipsistic version of pastoral. Similarly, we can emphasize that the animistic "fairy tale" imagery of Jewett's story occurs only in an allusive manner further undercut by the story's "realistic" adoption of a child's point of view: the tree, after all, only "*must* have loved"; and the cow's "intelligent" behavior results only from this nine-year-old girl's having "lent herself to this *amusement*." Thus, these fairy tale elements, and perhaps most expecially the way, as Bruno Bettelheim would note, this narrative makes "no demands . . . on the listener," point less to its desire to assume a major Romantic charge *or* explicit fairy tale status than to its wish to maintain a minor relation to both.[36] On the one hand, they show Jewett's intimate acquaintance with the fairy tale genre. Appearing in the seventeenth-century court tales of Charles Perrault (inventor of "Mother Goose") such tales became popular and were translated into English during the eighteenth century. Anyone liking children's literature like Jewett would doubtless know of their existence. Indeed, in a letter to Horace Scudder, she displays envy over the fact that he owns a copy of "dear old Hans Andersen."[37] And by a reference in one of her favorite sketches, she also shows she has read either the Grimms' rendition of the Sleeping Beauty tale called "Little Briar-rose" or Perrault's version called "La belle au bois dormant": "I remembered the Enchanted Palace and the Sleeping Beauty in the Wood, and it seemed as if I were on the way to it."[38]

On the other hand, we could argue that "*A White Heron*" is "as if on the way to" affiliating itself with the fairy tale genre and particularly this Sleeping Beauty tale. The Princess "au bois" and the Prince Charming found in most popular versions of this tale clearly resemble Sylvia, that "woods-girl" (xv), and "the handsome stranger" who not only addresses her "gallantly" (xv) but seems "so *charming and delightful*" (xviii). In Perrault's version, indeed, we find a "*petite princesse*," or a heroine synonymous with Jewett's "shy *little* girl." Moreover, other versions give the heroine a specific name, Princess Aurora, a name that Perrault assigns to one of Sleeping Beauty's two children in his cannibalistic addition to how the story usually ends, namely with the Prince kissing the Princess awake and their subsequent bethrothal.[39] In Jewett's story, the woodsy girl with her woodsy name sees the heron precisely at the auroral time of day in the story's climactic scene. Not only does she decide to look for the heron *at* dawn, but her later recollection of this "golden" moment contributes to her final silence before the hunter and in this way internalizes the dawn as part of her very identity. In this "fairy tale" context if not in the Thoreauvian pastoral precedent, the dawn comes to signify the transition from Sylvia's childhood innocence to moral awakening, a transition in line with her preadolescent age. According to Bettelheim, in fact, the psychoanalytic significance of such fairy tales turns on the heroine's passage from a "deathlike passivity at the end of child-hood," symbolized by her having been cast under a spell of sleep, to "a time of quiet growth and preparation, from which the person will awaken mature" thanks to the mediation of a princelike figure.[40] If the narrator plays down the "sexual" aspect of this maturation in "A White Heron," she still leaves Sylvia at the point "of quiet growth" in that final apostrophe to nature: "Bring your gifts and graces and tell your secrets to this lonely country child!"

Along these same lines, the "young" hunter, as he is described throughout Jewett's story, resembles Perrault's "*jeune* Prince" or the Grimms' "youth." Never attributed a name, he also resembles the nameless woodsy princes of these two versions. More, one could cite the parallel between the hunter who comes upon a "hermitage" in the woods and feels "surprise [at] so clean and comfortable a little dwelling," and Perrault's prince who, also in the process of hunting, accidentally discovers an unexpected "palace" in the woods, an es-tate whose former royal function has long since been forgotten and in which the Sleeping Princess lies under a spell. The hunter in Jew-ett's story also encounters a girl who seems to be under some spell, for when he addresses her she virtually cannot reply: "The sound of her own unquestioned voice would have terrified her,—it was hard enough to answer yes or no when there was need of that" (xix). And if only ironically, through his "charming" manner if deleterious in-tention, he metaphorically awakens this silent girl to the necessity of making a mature moral decision.

But this irony also constitutes a distancing from the story's Sleep-ing Beauty "fairy tale" identity. In citing the girl's "vaguely thrilled . . . dream of love" for the hunter (xviii), the story alludes to the fairy tale thematic of a heroine's transition from presexual childhood narcissism to a state of sexual or at least adult maturity. But Jewett's Sleeping Beauty clearly fails to respond to Prince Charming; instead, she remains silent, as if still under the spell of childhood. Bettelheim's interpretation of the fairy tale's "adult" function or telos exposes the regressive locus that here defines the story's relation to the fairy tale genre, that is, insofar as Jewett's heroine encounters the pressure of adolescence and in the end retreats from it. He argues that such pressure overdetermines the significance of "sleeping," changing it from a univocally benign indication of the heroine's sexual latency to an ambivalent image of regression: "Narcissistic withdrawal is a tempting reaction to the stresses of adolescence, but, the [Sleeping Beauty] story warns, it leads to a dangerous, deathlike existence when it is embraced as an escape from the vagaries of life."[41] Sylvia's silence or "sleeping" indicates both her withdrawal from "the stresses of adolescence" posed by the hunter and the story's own withdrawal from the mature implications of this fairy tale to which it alludes. Indeed, her final silence, her supposedly mature decision, results from Sylvia's privileging a nature that suggests the chthonic world of the fairy tale, i.e., a world of mythical animals like "evil" dragons, or as here, "good" herons.

The same regressive or pre-"fairy tale" tendencies also apply to the story's depiction of the hunter. In the Grimms' version of Sleeping Beauty, for example, many princes before the final "youth" try to enter the Enchanted Palace to waken the famed "beautiful sleeping 'Briarrose'" whom a member of the kingdom, one of its "Wise Women" (in Perrault called "fairies"), has cast under a spell for a hundred years. All these early princes fail; they get trapped within the briars surrounding the Palace and die "miserable deaths" (Grimms). But if the last prince succeeds where these early princes fail, he does so not through his "charm" but because the hundred-years magical spell has simply run its course. Might not Jewett's hunter, who himself fails in the end to make Sylvia respond to his "charming" and "kind appealing" pleas, represent one of these premature princes? Has he come to this "hermitage" while the fairy tale heroine's spell is still in progress? In any case, given that he initially comes to an already palace-reduced "hermitage" seeking a white heron (or at most, a verbally displaced "pale" heroine); that except ironically he himself fails to awaken Sylvia to a sense of adulthood (with even this ironic awakening in question); and that he suffers nothing more than disappointment at the girl's silence and his failure to capture the heron, this hunter remains but a provisional allusion to the Prince Charming and pre-Prince Charming figures of the Sleeping Beauty fairy tale.

An adolescent figure who presents Sylvia with a vision of death, "the piteous sight of thrushes and sparrows dropping silent to the ground, their songs hushed" (xxiii), on the one hand Jewett's hunter personifies for the heroine "the stresses of adolescence" and for her story the generic locus of the fairy tale per se. On the other hand, the story's equivocal depiction of him ("Were the birds better friends than their hunter might have been,—who can tell?"), along with his provisional allusion to a kind of Prince Charming *manqué*, places both him and the story prior to the "adolescence" thematic synonymous with the fairy tale. Indeed, in Bettelheim's view, princes in fairy tales, as their royal status suggests, symbolize for the child "absolute power, such as the parent seems to hold over his child"; and given the fact that they tend to appear in the guise of a "hunter figure," they also symbolize for the child "a suitable image of a strong and protective father figure."[42] But clearly the "young man" in Jewett's story requires hospitality and needs help in finding the elusive heron: "I have lost my way, and need a friend very much." Not only does *he* lack "absolute power," but the story, as we have seen in the previous chapter, inserts a *non pareil* "father figure" in those parentally disguised prosopopoeias, the "stately" pine tree and the heron with "crested head." At the very least, the tree's "sharp dry twigs [that] caught and held her and scratched her like angry talons" (xx) suggest the briars that protect as well as entrap Sleeping Beauty in her Enchanted Palace. And from this tree that eventually "held away the winds" (xxi) for a Briar-rose "Sylvia"— her very name etymologically alludes to yet conceals this "briar" association—Jewett's Sleeping Beauty comes to see "a vast and awesome world" (xxi). This paternalized figure of nature thus allows Sylvia to grow up in other than human terms; "he" absolves both her and the story from the topos of "adolescence" and therefore from the teleological function of fairy tales, as Bettelheim describes it, namely to give child readers a preliminary model for arriving at social and sexual maturity.

In effect, Jewett's already preadolescent heroine here becomes *pre-adolescent*, that is, in relation to a pre-mature Prince Charming but also in the context of a pre-pastoral fairy tale which itself is in the process of being postponed as a literary fait accompli. With regard to the Sleeping Beauty tale, a tale always already known by Jewett as she writes "A White Heron," Sylvia has yet to proceed to the stage when Perrault's "petite princesse" and the Grimms' Briar-rose were children in their fathers' courts. She remains far from the age (around fifteen in the two versions) when "adolescence" would require a Prince Charming to help her negotiate that passage from presexual or asocial childhood to "the great world" of sexual and social adulthood. Indeed, positioned against the background of Perrault's addition to this tale, Sylvia could stand as the auroral *daughter* of Sleeping Beauty, i.e., Jewett's story can imagine itself as a *potential* repetition of this already prior and privileged fairy tale. In these senses, then, "A White Heron" does not even represent a child's regression before the crisis posed by a world for which the fairy tale functionally prepares its child reader. Rather, "her" *pre*-visional rewriting of the Sleeping Beauty fairy tale, a rewriting that situates Sylvia before the time when her silence or the story's trope for childhood discourse must needs give way to the discourse of adulthood as it does at the end of many fairy tales, allows "her" in fact to become "la belle au bois dormant" —a perpetually dormant child's fairy tale as well as adult literary-pastoral text.

We can only surmise that Jewett herself, her own first name signifying princess as we saw earlier, here adopts the position of a "sleeping princess" in the act of producing a story as elusively silent to its implicit child reader as the silence that ultimately disappoints the "charming and delightful" hunter. If only to elude her own adult sensibility in writing this story for children, Jewett converts "A White Heron" into a minor Sleeping Beauty fairy tale by removing "her" from the locus of even the relatively serious childhood thematic proposed by the fairy tale genre. Unlike Perrault's Prince who himself listens and becomes "charmé de [les] paroles" of the suddenly awoken Princess,[43] no reader of this prepastoral pre-fairy tale story will likely disturb "her" minor dreaming of becoming minor literature. But the pressures for producing major literature continue beyond this story's procrastinated affiliations with minor literary genres. Sooner or later, even the excluded Thoreauvian or Prince Charming reader will remind "her" of or awaken "her" to the major implications, the serious intentionality, involved in leaving such a reader "disappointed." In this internalized semiotic sense, the story ends at the point where "she" hears "the echo of his whistle" and experiences a feeling of loss, all as if the story's "lonely" choice to remain a minor literary text were still haunted by major literary criteria: "Whatever [literary] treasures were lost to her, woodlands and summer-time, remember!" (xxiii). This appeal to a pastoral muse to provide compensation for the story's loss of its major literary possibilities points only to its desire of becoming a self-determined or self-certain minor literary text — not the realization of that desire.

Minor writing is indeed like a dream: at first easy to effect; more difficult once it registers troubling "major" associations; virtually impossible to sustain when, like the knowledge that one is dreaming within one's dream, the nature of its project threatens to surface, as it does when the writer imagines reading it in its published form. Only by forgetting readers, that is, their reminder that she is in the process of producing *a* text, can Jewett write a story invulnerable to the return of the repressed criteria of major literature.

CHAPTER FOUR   "A WHITE HERON"

AS A PRE/TEXT

I do know several literary people quite well, but whenever they read anything of mine I know they look down from their pinnacles in a benignant way and think it very well done "for her" as the country people say. And all this is not what I want. — Sarah Orne Jewett

I   In defining "a distinctive American tradition," Richard Poirier notes that American writers express "an eccentricity of defiance" through their textual "styles" as opposed to their historical references or themes per se:

> [These writers] both resemble and serve their heroes by trying to create an environment of "freedom" . . . wholly in language. American books are often written as if historical forces cannot possibly provide such an environment, as if history can give no life to "freedom" and as if only language can create the liberated place.[1]

If not showing explicit signs of "defiance," the tropological, generic, as well as thematic evasions we have seen in "A White Heron" certainly qualify as signs of such "freedom." The story's lateral procrastinations—its status as a synchronic and diachronic crossing of diminishing ideological and/or textual codes which could make *it,* as opposed to its probable conventional nineteenth-century reading, seem responsible for a closed or at least coherent interpretation—ultimately suggest that we should regard it more as a sketch than as a fully conceived story. Jewett herself clearly preferred writing sketches and sketchy stories throughout her career. As late as 1894, she advises a would-be writer to begin by writing sketches or semiplotted stories; and some years later when he sends her a story she reiterates, in effect, her preference for sketchlike writings: "Don't write a 'story' but just *tell the thing*" (Jewett's italics).[2]

But for us, Jewett's desire to write sketches also signifies her desire to procrastinate the production of an honorifically understood "Literature." Unlike the palimpsest genres of pastoral and fairy tale literature which comprise the overdetermined scenes of writing "A White Heron" and which carry with them a teleological thematic, the sketch genre lacks such a thematic and at first glance, at least, promises to neutralize the *literary* ambition willy-nilly associated with writing this story. Yet as with its American pastoral affiliations, the story's allusive self-definition as a sketch cannot by itself cancel such ambition. Though the story tends to conceal its "defiance" of traditional narrative criteria, criteria associated in the nineteenth century with European cultural authority, the sketch orientation of "A White Heron" allies it to America's ideological birthright and a literary tradition which adopts a quasi-minor or still "revolutionary" position toward this Old World and particularly English authority. The American sketch, in short, self-consciously reproduces the "minor" identity of nineteenth-century American writing in general in the face of a still-authoritarian English culture. That is, it constitutes a literary "deterritorialization" of this culture—a benign or nonviolent declaration of American independence.[3]

To be sure, Jewett herself seems anything but "revolutionary" in her literary tastes. She calls on Flaubert, an Old World writer, for a motto defining *her* ideal as a writer: "Écrire la vie ordinaire comme on écrit l'histoire."[4] She suggests that an impoverished American cultural code leads American writers to produce impoverished works: "In France there is such a code, such recognition, such richness of allusions; but here we confuse our scaffoldings with our buildings."[5] Like many other genteel American literati, she considers Tennyson the major writer of her time, a writer who like Flaubert is on a par with Shakespeare, and who when she visited him with Annie Fields seemed "like a king in captivity, one of the kings of old."[6] She prefers anglified poets like Longfellow, whose work "stands like a great cathedral,"[7] and Whittier with whom she frequently corresponded;[8] she also adopts an "English" cultural stance toward American writers. Thus, she finds "delicious" or tasteful Carlyle's depiction of Margaret Fuller as "that strange lilting, lean old maid!"; and after reading Carlyle's biography of Washington Irving, she finds this famous American *Sketch Book* writer "less great than I expected, but very moving, a creature of brilliant natural gifts, especially of speech. Carlyle says he was not a reader. Men of his impulsive nature ride off on strange ideas when they fail in what Matthew Arnold tried to teach in 'Literature and Dogma.'"[9] In short, long before she writes her one historical romance, *The Tory Lover* (1901), a novel that, significantly enough, concerns the American Revolution, one could argue that Jewett is a "Tory lover," at least with regard to literary ideology.

Yet her avowed privileging of Old World cultural codes, codes which make American works seem "less great" or like mere "scaffoldings" instead of rich, accomplished literary "buildings," could also be seen as a means not only to deny the more imminent influence of these works on her own, an influence that we have argued permeates her writing "A White Heron," but also to reduce the literary ideological significance of her own American "scaffoldings" or sketchlike works. This literarily self-diminishing strategy to make her sketches seem even "less great" than they are entitled to be if writing American sketches is an act of "freedom" becomes more apparent in the manner in which Jewett situates herself in relation to Hawthorne's literary precedent. A "daughter of Hawthorne's style," Jewett writes stories that clearly bear the impress of Hawthorne's as well as Poe's tales.[10] Sometime between 1886 and 1890, Thomas Bailey Aldrich, the genteel, anglified editor of the *Atlantic Monthly*, unwittingly gives credence to this connection in remarking to Jewett "that Hawthorne's pallid allegories will have faded away long before these two little Dulham ladies," a reference to Jewett's other oft-anthologized story which also had been first published in the 1886 *A White Heron and Other Stories*.[11]

Late in her career she would inform Charles Miner Thompson and Bliss Perry, both of whom had inquired about the affiliation of her writings to Hawthorne's, that "I never was a Hawthorne lover in early life!"[12] But Jewett clearly had read Hawthorne rather carefully, as she all but admits to Annie Fields, her closest friend who herself wrote a biography of Hawthorne. Thus, in an 1890 letter to Fields, Jewett says she has just "read part of one of Hawthorne's American Journal volumes but didn't care for it *as much as I used to*" (my italics).[13] Focusing specifically on his "suggestions for sketches," she effectively denies their seminal effect on her own work, for they "lack any reality or imagination, rootless little things that could never open seed in their turn, or make much of any soil they were put into, so 'delicate' in their fancy as to be far-fetched and oddly feeble and sophomorish. You will find it hard to believe this without the pages before you as I have just had them."[14] Any anxiety of influence Jewett may have felt toward Hawthorne here becomes itself "feeble and sophomorish." Yet we could argue that it appears in the way she tries to imagine Annie Fields as just having read Hawthorne's "suggestions" ("the pages before you as I have just had them") in order to corroborate Jewett's own judgment—which thus *demands* further confirmation or remains incomplete ("You will find it hard to believe without the pages . . ."). For the same reason, perhaps, she reduces the value of Hawthorne by focusing on his "*American* Journal" and on his "*suggestions* for sketches," that is, on prima facie nonliterary works which conveniently deny the locus of his major literary reputation: his published sketches, tales, and novels.

Yet we could also use this last piece of evidence of Jewett's literary anxiety over Hawthorne's precedent to emphasize her unconscious identification with and misprision of the more subtle ideological significance of his "American" works. Not yet sketches, these "suggestions" themselves suggest a nonideological mode of American writing. And as regards Jewett's own literary status in comparison with Hawthorne's, she willingly assumes that it is lesser, as when she responds to Aldrich's preference for her story over Hawthorne's "pallid allegories": "But Mr. Aldrich insists that I don't know the best work I can do when I see it, and never has ceased to speak of my undervaluing 'The Dulham Ladies'!"[15] Thus, while we could regard her criticism of Hawthorne's notes for sketches as a sign of her desire to deflect his literary influence, we could also consider it a sign precisely of her literary concerns as a writer, namely to produce works which will suspend the issue of literary evaluation altogether—a manifestation of "the best work I can do" sensibility. In this sense, writing in an informal genre (the letter) and addressing a close friend sympathetic to Hawthorne's literary reputation, Jewett herself produces a minor work even as she unconsciously projects the possibility of a canonized American writer's writing minor works, works that literally come to nothing but also, as pre-fictional works, do nothing to deny his established reputation as a major American writer of sketches as well as tales.

Even were we to consider her focus on such works as a kind of repression of Hawthorne's major fictional works, however, we could still argue that these putative major works themselves strive to become nothing more than "suggestions" or pre-fictional tales. They too tend to defer direct rapprochements with their surrounding literary-ideological codes of reading. Hawthorne, in short, writes prefaces and prefatory tales perhaps to avoid closed readings which would bring up the issue of textual evaluation. As with his famous preface to "The Old Manse," his prefaces to his major novels function to delay, as it were, the reader's reading of the ensuing "major" narratives. For example his preface to *The House of the Seven Gables* denominates the work the reader will soon read as a "Romance," a classification that allows him as writer "to claim a certain latitude, both as to [this work's] fashion and materials, which [I] would not have felt entitled to assume had [I] professed to writing a Novel."[16] Yet the pressures of closure are such that even writing Romance entails a moral determination; it too "as a work of art . . . sins unpardonably so far as it may swerve aside from the truth of the human heart," so that Hawthorne goes on to claim that he will make "very moderate use of the privilege," yet should not be judged guilty of committing "a literary crime even if [I] disregard this caution" in the ensuing work.

Itself nonfictional, this preface at least momentarily serves to suspend his imagination of the reader's reading what through this very preface is to him an already Romance-suspended novel. In a more telling sense, Hawthorne's 1846 preface to "The Old Manse" inserts a space between its conventionally determined nonfictional generic identity and the fictional tales it introduces. Not only does this difference foreclose the likelihood that his readers will determine a contextual connection between the two, but such prefatory remarks also serve to situate this preface as the generically unrecognizable past text from which the (to the reader) future primary tales derive. In this way, Hawthorne virtually retains a privileged reading of these ensuing tales; or at the very least, projects them as only potentially readable by others, thus distancing the historical, moral, and/or esthetic determinations that his readers will bring to bear on his fiction, which is to say the site of *its* potential literary evaluation.[17] In short, this preface functions to delay his imagination of his tale's readers, readers which it invokes in terms of restrictively realistic *or* allegorical codes: "It was the very spot in which to utter the extremist nonsense or the profoundest wisdom, or that ethereal product of the mind which partakes of both, and may become one or the other, in correspondence with the faith and insight of the auditor."[18] Referentially, this "spot" denotes a woodland place Hawthorne along with Ellery Channing discovers on a "fishing excursion" on the Assabeth River. Metaphorically, it connotes the less socially communicable place of his imagination when he wrote his "Old Manse" tales, or "that ethereal product of the mind." Metareferentially, however, this "spot" points to this preface itself where he is effectively returning to the original, imaginative ambience in terms of which he wrote his tales privately or apart from their ostensibly public accessibility, i.e., "fishing" with Ellery Channing. In this sense, the "Old Manse" preface provides less a context than a new intertextual (non-)locus for *Mosses,* one which makes *only possible* the reader's "correspondence with" these ensuing tales.

Yet Hawthorne's prefatory wish, as it were, to blindfold his reader, a blindfolding to which even so astute a reader as Poe had fallen prey in his determinate reading of "The Minister's Black Veil,"[19] itself leads to the need for a morally determinate response. He cannot present his reader with an impossible either/or textual situation, cannot prepare his reader to decide whether his tales might here be expressing "the extremist nonsense *or* the profoundest wisdom," without at the same time projecting this reader in bad faith. By projecting his desire to exclude the reader from his fiction, Hawthorne's prefatory custom risks sinning unpardonably and thus comes to double or becomes a self-referential part of his otherwise more impersonal "literary" tales. We see this "literary" fate of the preface dramatized in "The Minister's Black Veil," a "twice-told tale" whose second retelling, as it were, occurs in the way it submerges *its* putative story or the reason why Minister Hooper wears a black veil in the first place. Like Hawthorne's persona in the 1846 preface to "The Old Manse" ("So far as I am a man of really individual attributes I veil my face"),[20] Hooper wears his veil so as to generate multiple explanations among the characters in the story. In the same way, the tale veils itself and generates determinate responses from its readers. It is as if the veil the minister wears in this story, a veil which signifies a pre-*face,* were an emblematic preface *to* the story, both of them functioning on different levels to defer *by provoking* the reader's determinate response to narrative ambiguities.

Yet if the minister indeed risks sinning unpardonably by refusing at all to lift his veil ("On earth, never!"), in dramatizing this refusal the story telegraphs its own awareness of this extreme possibility. "The Minister's Black Veil" thus displaces the significance of the minister's black veil into an esthetic context; at most, in relation to a nineteenth-century non-Puritan audience, the story's veiled ambiguities risk committing a "literary crime." In his 1846 preface, Hawthorne not only observes literary propriety by wearing an autobiographical "veil" but extends an invitation to his reader to "imagine himself my guest."[21] Just as the minister's black veil would teach Hooper's parishioners to abandon their conventional codes of religious understanding, just as "The Minister's Black Veil" would teach its readers to abandon their conventional demands for literary closure—with this same rhetorical intention, Hawthorne in his prefaces can treat his reader as a "guest" to his fiction even as he considers his "preliminary talk about his external habits, his casual associates, and other matters entirely . . . surface. These things hide the man, instead of displaying him."[22]

At the same time, however, combined with the reserved authorial space provided by his prefaces, the esthetic freedom which his tales not only invite but, as in the case of "The Minister's Black Veil," also self-referentially dramatize effectively precludes for him their "twice-told" nature both as to their historical and literary-historical precedents and their anticipated responses by readers. That is, Hawthorne's prefatory writing cannot escape engaging the ideological issue of American "freedom." Thus, in the famous "Custom-House" preface to *The Scarlet Letter*, Hawthorne declares his "American" independence as a writer precisely from the commercial aspects of American society: "[My native town] ceases to be a reality of my life. I am a citizen of somewhere else. My good townspeople will not much regret me."[23] More, this a posteriori preface to *The Scarlet Letter* frames what will become his major literary work as some "pointless and inefficacious" effort,[24] a text from which he also declares his American independence. For from this moment he intends to immerse himself in "the genial atmosphere which a literary man requires" and to write "amongst other faces" or in terms of readers that will "ripen the best harvest of [his] mind" by freeing him from "familiar ones."[25] In however ironic a manner, Hawthorne's preface works to produce his freedom or reserve the possibility of producing a major literary work which his novel, not yet "the best harvest of [his] mind," leaves in its wake, and for which his preface serves as a declaration of future intentions.

Thus, despite the prefatory mode of Hawthorne's writing, a mode that would forestall various forms of literary-ideological closure and their insertion of his fictional works into the context of major literary evaluation, this mode incessantly verges on becoming a discourse beholden to a specific nineteenth-century American ideological issue. These prefictional prefaces, these ostensibly minor "suggestions" about his subsequent fiction, become a means for Hawthorne to imagine the production of virtually endless *once*-told tales, i.e., major literature. It is this "Hawthorne," the failed producer of a *minor* literature that could elude codes of literary evaluation (codes which make his "suggestions" for minor literary works seem "feeble and sophomorish"), with whom Jewett unconsciously identifies and whom she misreads. Even when, like the hunter in "A White Heron," he seems to take a "vacation" from serious literary activity by writing prefatory tales, sketches, and "suggestions for sketches," Hawthorne embarks on a no less serious literary enterprise. We need not turn Sylvia into an overdetermined metaphor of Jewett's own ephebelike shyness before a similarly shy and retiring New England precursor—thus turning ourselves into egregious pursuers of "A White Heron," like the hunter—to argue that Jewett's own misprision of Hawthorne's prefatory semiotic customs is related to her desire to produce a semiotically decisive minor literature. For example, where his prefatory works "bare the device" or "defamiliarize" his supposed referential materials (an "actual" scarlet letter and text, an "actual" minister that wore a veil), Jewett's sketchlike works take pains to *re*-familiarize such materials in a conventional literary manner. In this relational field, she can situate herself as a minor prefatory writer; in fact, we could argue that precisely in relation to "The Minister's Black Veil," the very setting of her sketchlike works becomes no more than a virtual footnote to or the as yet unfictionalized suggestion of his story. For in the Hawthorne tale we find an actual footnote which refers to a New England clergyman, "Mr. Joseph Moody, of York, Maine," as a partial model for Minister Hooper. A township very close to Jewett's South Berwick home, York, Maine, was the actual setting of her *Deephaven* fictional sketches.[26]

One further glance at Jewett's letter of 1890, the year in which she republishes "A White Heron," will show us how she positions her texts and particularly this story as a minor or less "literary" mode of writing in relation to Hawthorne's prefatory precedent. His "suggestions for sketches" seem "oddly feeble and sophomorish" when compared with a work which she prefers over his "much more famous book." Taken up on another day, this same letter records Jewett's "new admiration" for Dana's *Two Years before the Mast*,[27] an American work whose nonfictional genre further defines her nonliterary proclivities vis-à-vis Hawthorne's protofictional "American Journal." But on the same night that she has read Hawthorne's work, she remarks on feeling a "keener pleasure" at reading a work whose "one page flashes into my mind now as 'live as Kipling and as full of fresh air.'"[28] This allusion to Kipling, though it suggests Jewett's preference for English as opposed to American works—and thus her reactionary "literary" taste, sense of American cultural impoverishment, and/or anxiety as a belated American "Hawthorne"—involves a writer whose popular sketchlike works constitute less serious literary efforts than Hawthorne's.[29] As it happens, the work in question is not only an American work, but one concerned with a New England locale also in close proximity to South Berwick and the topical settings of Jewett's writings: Charles Warren Brewster's *Rambles about Portsmouth* (New Hampshire). A popular work of the time, Brewster's "Rambles" generically resemble sketches, and the passage she cites in this letter "of the marketwomen coming down the [Piscataqua] river" doubtless refers to "Ramble CXXII" in the 1869 volume.[30]

But the comparison Jewett makes between Brewster's "Rambles" and Hawthorne's "suggestions for sketches" is motivated by more than the fact of her having associated their sketches or their New England background or even the fact that Brewster like Hawthorne seemed, as his biographer describes him, "naturally retiring—unwilling to be before the public."[31] Nor does her citation of Brewster constitute a roundabout way to transume Hawthorne's literary priority by affiliating herself with a New England writer whose family, which settled in Massachusetts in 1620, was at least as originally American as Hawthorne's. Rather, compared with Hawthorne's, Brewster's sketches seem decisively nonfictional, that is, not at all intended to be read in terms of an honorific "literary" code. Moreover, given the fact that C. W. Brewster had died in 1868, Jewett's preference for his sketches over Hawthorne's at least subliminally refers to another well-known contemporary member of the esteemed Brewster family who just so happens to have been a writer of nonfictional works that bear directly on the topos of "A White Heron." William Brewster was a highly esteemed American ornithologist who not only became the president of the Audubon Society in Massachusetts but wrote works on "the live" and "dead" birds before, during, and after this 1886 story; and virtually all of his written work derived from his bird observations in New England, including Maine and Concord, Massachusetts, the home of Thoreau, the writer he most revered.[32] William Brewster was also a neighbor of Longfellow whose daughter, it turns out, just happens to have been one of Jewett's close acquaintances around the time she wrote "A White Heron."[33] Brewster "became a skilful taxidermist," owning "several cases of mounted birds and . . . the finest collection of North American birds in existence"; at the same time, much like the hunter's ambivalent ornithological interests and practices in Jewett's story, his "outstanding publications . . . dealt with the live bird rather than the dead one."[34]

Not Audubon, then, and not Thoreau but William Brewster here becomes the prototype or referential model for the hunter Sylvia leaves "disappointed" at the end of the story. Self-evidently privileging "the live bird" over "the dead one," Jewett's sketchlike story effectively disappoints, or complies with only one part of, the criteria of Brewster's major nonfictional ornithological works, works that exerted immeasurable "influence upon the development of American Ornithology."[35] If in her preference for C. W. Brewster's "Rambles" Jewett desires to define her literary interests as minor and nonliterary in comparison with Hawthorne's pre-fictional "suggestions," she also desires to define them as even more minor than William Brewster's nonfictional "publications." And insofar as William Brewster remains a subliminal allusion both in this 1890 letter and her imagination of the hunter in her story, such self-determinate "minor" comparisons occur as if altogether outside the production of "A White Heron." In this way, even four years after she has actually written the story but when its republication provides the occasion for reevaluating her desires as a writer, Jewett hopes to have written an incomparably minor sketchlike story.

2   Jewett's "minor" misreading of "A White Heron" also extends to how she desires to apprehend its appearance as a text for public consumption. Literary success, after all, especially in a postbellum commercial America, involves more than a work's engagement with an honorific code of "Literature." Thus, after Jewett has written this story, she mitigates its relation to successful marketplace literature by claiming, we recall, that "my 'White Heron' . . . isn't a very good magazine story, but I love her." In this way, she effectively reduces the story's semiotic range or readability. Early on, Jewett shows an awareness of two kinds of readers which serve as tropes that deny any great popularity to which her sketches and sketchlike stories might pretend. To her, such readers comprise "small audiences," whether "highly critical friends in Boston" or other friends, "mostly people who like to be entertained rather than puzzled."[36]

But even this "small" if friendly readership must fail in representing an internalized postponement of her story's fate, its public exteriority and the honorific or marketplace literary codes to which it will become liable. For example, in 1890 she expresses concern to a supportive editor, Horace Scudder, about his idea of publishing a companion volume of stories to *Tales of New England,* the collection in which "A White Heron" was to be republished; she feels that all these collected stories "might get into each other's way and 'trip up!' You see, I betray a sad lack of confidence in my children."[37] In relation to a "highly critical" readership, that is, she imagines the tenuous esthetic integrity her stories will have. The question thus becomes how can she *not* imagine such a reading. One way to double the reduction of her texts to sketches or mere literary "children" is to perform her own "minor" reading of works that ostensibly have larger literary pretensions, in this way projecting a general semiotic possibility regarding her own works. Thus, Jewett "sketchifies" one of her favorite regionalist novels written by a popular and serious American woman writer:

> A poor writer is at the mercy of much unconscious opposition. You must throw everything and everybody aside at times, but a woman made like Mrs. Stowe [in her *The Pearl of Orr's Island*] cannot bring herself to that cold selfishness of the moment for one's work's sake, and the recompense for her loss is a divine touch here and there in an incomplete piece of work. I felt at [her] funeral that none of us could really know and feel the greatness of the moment.[38]

In her novel, Stowe succumbs to her "unconscious opposition" and produces "an incomplete piece of work," a minor work rather than one embodying the "cold" standards of esthetic integrity. Yet Stowe's death also works to remind Jewett of Stowe's "greatness." At the same time, Jewett's personalization of the criteria of "greatness" removes its significance as a *textual* correlative, a removal literally signified by Stowe's death and the sense that "none of us could really know and feel" this greatness.

Jewett as reader thus revises Stowe's work—a work which exists as a potential model for her own literary work and "greatness,"—as escaping formal literary criteria which would insert this work into the arena of public literary evaluation. For similar reasons, we could argue, Jewett herself writes "A White Heron" with "pathetic" intrusions rather than maintaining a "cold" narrative distance. And representing an "incomplete" or a child protagonist who makes an "incomplete" decision, the story quite literally concludes with an "incomplete" or "who can tell?" coda. Reading this story, then, we are always reading Jewett's already "minor" reading of it. Obversely, her story entails a "sketchy" repression of even its "highly critical friends" or readers—sketchy because it can elude such a readership only by Jewett's figurative adoption of a post factum relation to it *as* she writes. We can imagine that, however displaced, the issue of literary "greatness" haunts Jewett's writing and tends to reappear virtually in the spaces from sentence to sentence. As in *A Marsh Island* where Dick Dale, an ephebe artist who produces sketches in spite of his initial ambition to do oil paintings, returns to town "fired by an ambition" to show "some sufficient evidence of his skill and perception," Jewett cannot write a sketchy story except as a momentary reprieve from the socioartistic system that comes to dominate or define this activity.[39] Her problem thus becomes one of sustaining the difference between her writing per se and its textual result in the face of repeated reminders that a "minor" reading of her story as she writes it will fail to sustain this very difference.

In a sense, then, Jewett must also blind herself to the medium which incurs such semiotic dualism. Her "minor" reading of a text must as such focus on the informal pictorial metaphor of sketch writing as an end in itself, unlike Dick Dale's sketching, as a way to foreclose "critical" readings. As a fictive pictorial sketch, her writing can elude the teleology of textual publication, its "popular" as well as "literary" appearance before others. From the very beginning of her career, Jewett in fact depicts her writing as a random, informal act, "until very lately . . . done merely for the pleasure of it," as she informs Horace Scudder: "If the editors will take the sketchy kind [of stories] and people like to read them, is not it as well to do that and do it successfully as to make hopeless efforts to achieve something in another line which runs much higher?"[40] Even her sense of writing "sketchy" stories according to successful marketplace as opposed to "higher" artistic standards is grounded on her purely unintentional realization of the former since, as she claims in an earlier section of this letter, "I always write impulsively—very fast and without much plan."[41] More important, she employs an example from her actual pictorial sketches to emphasize how her "impulsive" literary practice resulted in success: "Strange to say, this same fault shows itself in my painting, for the more I worked over pictures the stiffer and more hopeless they grew. I have one or two little marine views I scratched off to use up paint and they are bright and real and have an individuality —just as [my story]."

For the younger Jewett, to write is to sketch in relation to the pictorial sketch, in other words "without much plan" and for her own private "pleasure" and possession ("I *have* one or two marine views . . ."). The sketch's success occurs accidentally, that is, when the pressure to produce is absent, and when its very medium and subject do not at all connote "higher" artistic activity; sketches become no more than "views I scratched off to use up paint." Even this putative metaphorical connection between her verbal and pictorial sketching comes down to an unintentional metonymy or unselfconscious poetic theory. At best, verbal sketching for Jewett entails a reduced, otherwise major poetic principle of *ut pictura poesis,* its function here to self-conceal the "higher" parameters of publication which surround her act of writing. Sketching, in short, transforms narratives into "views," the act of reading them into virtually nonverbal immediate apprehensions. It also converts the pressure to construe writing as serious artistic work into the desire to preserve it as "pleasure." She later will make a similar point in a letter apparently written around the time of "A White Heron":

> Sometimes, the business part of writing grows very noxious to me, and I wonder if in heaven our best thoughts—poet's thoughts, especially—will not be flowers, somehow, or some sort of beautiful live things that stand about and grow, and don't have to be chaffered over . . . bought and sold. It seems as bad as selling our fellow beings, but being in this world everything must have a body, and a material part, so covers and leaves and publishing come under that head, and is another thing to make us wish to fly away and be at rest.[42]

With clear echoes from Poe's "The Power of Words"—albeit without his implicit aggressive expression of frustrated literary ambition, of desire for recognition in a "material" world defined by honorific literati—Jewett's letter expresses her desire to produce "flowers," to write without such ambition or for pleasure alone, as if writing were an ideal project that could be separated from its textual residue—"covers and leaves and publishing." But this desire remains just that. Since writing ultimately cannot escape its "body," it gives rise to "another thing to make us wish to fly away"; it leads to the thought of poetic "thoughts" which, unlike the future appreciation for unappreciated literary activity promised by Poe's "power of words," allow for a permanently immaterial, i.e., nonpublic, mode of writing that thus escapes even the "business" definition of major and minor literature.

From this perspective, we can catch glimpses of how Jewett inscribes her nonpublishing or purely pleasure-sketching ideal of writing in "A White Heron." As a trope of the story itself, Sylvia almost becomes a broken image of Jewett's ideal "flowers" (the traditional trope of poetic figures) when first confronted by the hunter's inquiry after her name—in other words the public's inquiry after "her" generic identity: "She hung her head as if the stem of it were broken, but managed to answer 'Sylvy,' with much effort" (xv). And when this informally self-named "Sylvy" climbs the tree in private, sees two hawks, and feels "as if she too could go flying away among the clouds," the informally generic or sketchy story itself momentarily envisions poetic "thoughts" whose traditional trope also happens to be birds. Similarly, both the white heron and "A White Heron" return "like an arrow . . . to [their] home in the green world beneath," the place, as we have seen, of pre-pastoral existence, as soon as they encounter "a company of shouting cat-birds" and become "vexed by their fluttering and lawlessness" (xxi–xxii). The catbirds' "fluttering and lawlessness" allude to the marketplace, Jewett's "noxious" sense of "the business part of writing" and specifically, perhaps, the demand for texts like historical romances which defined the most popular literary genre of her time.[43] Like "the solemn heron" that "goes away," "A White Heron" withdraws itself from the marketplace of "magazine" consumerism which, like the hunter with both Sylvia and the heron, would demand that the story publish or at least make public its "secret" literary location according to privileged standards of literary behavior. Indeed, the ten dollars the hunter offers Sylvia to help him capture the white heron happens to have been the going price for poetry in the *Atlantic Monthly* and *Harper's* magazine, with fifty or more dollars being the remuneration for stories and sketches.[44] His offer thus stands as a figure for both Jewett's ideal nonpublic poetic "thoughts" and her de facto socioeconomic devaluation of the story within the "business" marketplace.

But in another sense, Jewett could write her sketchy stories without their being "a bread and butter affair" for her.[45] Her economic freedom, displaced in the story as economic "thrift," allows her to imagine writing this story without the need to publish it. Like Sylvia, she can play at it without "playmates," can regard the story as a "dilatory" as well as "provoking creature" (xiii), and its pranks as an "intelligent attempt to play hide and seek" with her as well as with its potential marketplace readership. And we can even argue that her elliptical inscription and rejection in her story of the socioeconomic code of literary production and consumption, of its "popular" marketplace appeal, become one more proleptic strategy, like writing this story as a pictorial sketch, to displace its inevitable reception as a text subject to "highly critical" literary codes. But perhaps her most important strategy entails imagining not just friendly but also personally familiar readers for her stories, as when she judges the value of "An October Ride" by an audience to whom she has read it "in Portsmouth, which dear old town is not distinguished as being literary!"[46] A far cry from those "literary people" from the city who "look down" on her writing "from their pinnacles in a benignant way," these familiar and even familial readers effectively remove her texts from the precincts of both "literary" and "popular" modes of reception.

But as the example of Mrs. Tilley in "A White Heron" shows, such familiar or "regionalist" readers, whose literary tastes have nothing to do with "the great world," also require works to tell *stories,* like one of Jewett's neighbors who prefers "good books of stories, *detective ones,* none of your lovesick kind."[47] As a trope of a regionalist reading of "A White Heron," Mrs. Tilley, whose common cultural situation suggests she ought to support its non-"literary" values or "silent" commitment to a literary "life" on its own terms in the face of both monetary and "romance" temptations, in the end also demands that the story's "shy little" trope result in a conventional story. As Mrs.

Tilley shows through her immediate hospitality toward the "stranger" and predetermination of Sylvia as "afraid of folks," such a reading clearly exhibits less xenophobia toward than general agreement with its more critically sophisticated urban counterpart, that "enemy" reading which "had discovered her," albeit with a "cheerful and persuasive tone" (xv). Only the narrator would seem to condone the story's desire to exclude "stranger" readings and to project "her" nonreadability paradoxically by means of their (and our) decidable readings. Differentiated from the stranger and Mrs. Tilley, the narrator with her "pathetic" intrusions and relative omniscience concerning Sylvia seems to outline a reading far more sympathetic to the story's cow-like "dilatory" behavior and capacity to stand "still" (xiii) in order not to signal its determinable literary location or how it could otherwise be read.

More important, as a conventionally anonymous overvoice to the story as it is told, the narrator combines the attributes of a surrogate writer as well as ideal reader. In this sense, the narrator accords with the self-image of the writer as semiproducer of her sketchlike stories. To produce such a story, that is, Jewett imagines an intimate reader whose reading serves as the interchangeable double of her own. Without this intimate (and not merely culturally proximate) reader, she writes Sarah Whitman, another close friend, her "story would go very lame"; a friend like Whitman will immediately recognize and thus coproduce "those unwritable things that the story holds in its heart," things "that . . . must be understood, and yet how many a story goes lame for lack of that understanding."[48] If from early in her career Jewett senses she is "always forgetting that anyone reads [my stories] except the people I know, and it is always a delight and surprise to find a new friend,"[49] these people tend to comprise intimate friends who function as tropes identifying her published stories and reducing their vulnerability to a "cold" anonymous public reading. Writing in terms of such "friends," *structured* in turn on friends with whom she frequently corresponds, she can write literature as if it were letterature, i.e., as if it were exempt from the "highly critical" codes of literary evaluation.

In her sketch "The Confessions of a House-Breaker," for example, her otherwise anonymously directed writing suddenly comes to depend on a particular friend who alone will be able to grasp "those unwritable things." Walking alone in her New England village before others have awoken, "suddenly I became conscious that one of my friends was awake, and an understanding between us sprang up quickly. . . . I thought of one and another remote acquaintance after this, but only the first was awake and watching [with me]."⁵⁰ Likely Annie Fields, the "friend" to whom Jewett dedicates *The Mate of Daylight and Friends Ashore* in which this heretofore-unpublished work appeared,⁵¹ this friend becomes the exclusive addressee of a text that at this precise point is also transformed into a virtual letter. And because this sketch refers to a "strange hour" before others will mediate Jewett's experience of the village, its signified aspect doubles as a signifier of its private scene both of writing and of reading. Indeed, one of her favorite activities with Fields was reading literary works together, much in the way *A Country Doctor* represents Nan Prince reading with the older Mrs. Graham.⁵²

At the same time, just as we previously argued that Fields could represent to Jewett the literary priority of Hawthorne, so we could argue that even Fields, no less than the familial Mrs. Tilley with Sylvia, here becomes inadequate as a trope for a privileged, internalized reading that would unequivocally permit Jewett to imagine her sketch's inaccessibility to anonymous readings and to readings made by relatively "remote" if also intimate acquaintants. Just like the regionalist trope of reading, this exclusive-"friend" semiotic trope, this "suddenly" endowed image of co-productive "understanding," can connote, in the end, the demand for literary activity of a "higher" kind. On the one hand, a friend like Annie Fields allays Jewett's sense of her literary work *as* work; reacting to a favorable criticism of her sketches, she maintains "that it was due to many suggestions and much helpfulness that my sketches have a great deal of their (possible) value."⁵³ On the other, even Annie Fields on occasion fails to prevent Jewett from considering writing as work instead of the "pleasure" we have seen her associate with doing pictorial sketches:

> Yes, dear, I will bring the last sketch and give it its last touches if you think I had better spend any more time on it. I am tired of writing things. I want now to paint things, and drive things,

and *kiss* things . . . yet I have been thinking all day what a lovely sketch it would be to tell the story of the day we went to Morwenstow. (Jewett's italics)[54]

If Fields suggests for Jewett the intersubjective space of nonverbal, intimate, even physically immediate activity (painting, driving, kissing), precisely in contrast to the self-conscious activity of writing, she also reminds Jewett of her "literary" duties ("if you think I had better spend any more time on it").

But Jewett's here abrupt transformation of Fields from a reminder of self-conscious literary labor into a pretext for imagining a different kind of writing ("a lovely sketch") that concerns pleasure rather than work ("the day we went to Morwenstow") if nothing else reveals her constant determination to imagine an ideal private reading of her sketchy stories. In "A White Heron," the narrator who also serves in the role of intimate reader as well as (literal) co-producer of the story becomes this same pretext for a "secret" reading of its narrative. The narrator, after all, assumes the median position between her narrative and its implied reading by others. She no less than an intimate friend like Fields sooner or later comes to endorse the story's public literary existence and the modes of evaluation such an existence signifies. She too must become erased as a specific if sympathetic "friend" reading, a simultaneous inclusion and erasure which serve to conceal Jewett's authorial identity from herself and recuperate her act of writing as simple "amusement" like Sylvia's "hide and seek" game with the cow. In this sense, that unique "open place where the sunshine always seemed strangely yellow and hot" and to which only Sylvia has access (xviii) allegorically alludes more to the story's private scene of writing and reading than to Mrs. Tilley's rural farm or the narrator's mobile perspective. Here, the girl alone climbs the pine tree and, in witnessing the heron firsthand, is enabled to resist the ornithologist's desire to share this secret. Here, Jewett alone can "fly away" from serious literary demands; tempted by, yet thanks to this asocial or pre-textual space also exempt from, the pressures of publication, Jewett can imagine she writes "A White Heron" in a way which preserves its "secret," its semiotic "life," from "critical" or evaluative readings.

In short, Jewett here adopts a childlike relation to writing this story, a relation that would elude those "highly critical" codes which require a "cold selfishness" or which mean "business." If she strives to determine herself as neither the serious author nor the serious reader of her story even as she writes it, then some other notion of "writing" must constitute the author and reader of "A White Heron." In effect, Jewett merely transcribes a "writing" and "reading" which both precede her and absolve her from performing them herself. But this parentalized notion of semiosis still allows for a definitive identification on her part, namely with her father who indeed gave her "many suggestions and helpfulness" in writing her sketches by advising her to "write the things themselves," the very advice she continues to give later to an ephebe writer. Dedicating her 1881 collection of sketches, *Country By-Ways,* to him, Jewett, for example, refers to her father as if he alone defines her intimate friend: "TO T.H.J. MY DEAR FATHER; MY DEAR FRIEND; THE BEST AND WISEST MAN I EVER KNEW; WHO TAUGHT ME MANY LESSONS AND SHOWED ME MANY THINGS AS WE WENT TOGETHER ALONG THE COUNTRY BY-WAYS." Yet as a departed because dead "Dear Friend" reader and "Wisest" authorial source of these sketches, he can appear, as it were, only as an indefinite and literally absent presence identifying their semiosis. And the fact that her remarks appear in the virtually nonexistent literary genre of the "dedication" already amounts to a post factum simplification of his indeterminate relation to the writing and reading of these works, a relation concealed in their representational effects rather than revealed as their representable cause.

Even more indefinitely allegorized in "A White Heron," as we have seen, this absent paternal semiosis, no less than the "regionalist" and privileged female "friend" readings, appears on a spectrum of anticipated but erased moments of the story's apprehension by "the great world." It too serves to make Jewett's scene of writing and reading "A White Heron" as "secret" to herself as to the hunter, Mrs. Tilley, and the general reader's surrogate representative in the story, the narrator. It too serves to reduce Sarah Orne Jewett's authorial role in producing "her" insofar as it defines the story as a pre-text over and beyond its generic affiliation with the literary sketch, a genre practiced with serious literary intentions by W. D. Howells and other contemporaries. On the one hand, her story procrastinates all possible definite readings which phenomenologically would situate it as a public text. On the other, "A White Heron" gets written as if it were already in the process of being written before Jewett writes it. In short, "she" seeks to induce a state of amnesia over "her" very readability and writability, to forget that "she" will ever be read or that Jewett ever wrote the story with such a "minor" desire—the desire to produce a minor literature outside the context of the public and "publishing" world.

And so we find her writing "A White Heron" in the mode of sketching, "impulsively," all as if it were writing *itself*. Even as late as *Pointed Firs,* Jewett suggests that her relation to writing is passive more than active: "Story-writing is always experimental, just as a water-color sketch is, and *that something which does itself* is the vitality of it" (Jewett's italics).[55] Writing for her "is always experimental," a writing *in potentia,* an erasure to "white" of its very textuality, a pre-text whose "(possible) value" preserves it, as here, in a state of suspended parenthesis. This "blank page" esthetic or erasure of writing through writing may again suggest the feminist ideological aspect and strategies of Jewett's beloved story.[56] But were we to adopt or emphasize such a reading, we would still have to account for the ways the story appears to suspend it and instead desires to become a quiescent instance of a nonideological as well as non-"literary" minor literature.

3   Jewett began her career with the usual sense of artistic uncertainty. As she informs Horace Scudder, she feels she cannot "write a long story as [W. D. Howells and Scudder himself had] suggested," for "I have no dramatic talent. The story would have no plot. . . . I could write you entertaining letters perhaps . . . but I couldn't make a story about [their subjects]. . . . And what shall be done with such a girl? For I wish to keep writing."[57] Seven years later, she will still prefer to have her favorite sketch, "An October Ride," printed, simply because she likes it whether or not it enhances her literary reputation: "I don't believe I have the usual authorly feeling about what I write. I think about my sketches very much as I do about other people's."[58] My thesis has been that Jewett's minor literary ambitions,

her proclivity to produce sketches and plotless or sketchlike stories, become a supererogatory aspect of her writing "A White Heron." This story both traces and seeks to withdraw from the marketplace and honorific literary codes of success subtending its production. Even to a critic writing about Jewett's story a few years after her death, it appears to be not so much a story as "a delicate little sketch."[59]

As a story projected as having no "magazine" value, as a sketchy and to Jewett an absent datum of reading, and as an "experimental," endlessly self-determining preliminary or pre-text to serious literary activity, "A White Heron" thus carries to an extreme Jewett's earlier and more anxious sense of producing minor literature. The story, for example, retraces the allusive analogical outlines of minor writing as expressed in her "An October Ride." There, like Sylvia with the cow later, Jewett herself rides a horse named Sheila but pronounced "Shy-la"—not unlike the "shy little" heroine and story—through "the shadowy, twilighted woods, and I can hardly see my way." Jewett's own "twilighted" or suppressed recognition of the analogue between riding Shy-la and writing a shy sketch becomes apparent in the way her horse (and later, her 1886 story) provides her with the possibility of symbolic "flying," i.e., serious acts of imagination:

> I feel as if I had suddenly grown a pair of wings when she fairly flies over the ground and the wind whistles in my ears. There never was a time when she could not go a little faster, but she is willing to go step by step through the close woods . . . stopping considerately when a bough that will not bend tries to pull me off the saddle.[60]

In writing this sketch, Jewett touches on images rife with "higher" literary significance; but in riding this horse, the "vehicle" of this narrative and protoimage of "her" (Jewett's later story), she can also proceed "step by step through the close woods," that is, avoid the immediate serious "literary" pressures called up by such unplanned-for images —images like that "bough that will not bend" which could halt her writing altogether. Similarly, just as Sylvia experiences anxiety over "the great red-faced boy who used to chase and frighten her," so Shy-la "shies" when some "boys . . . come and throw a stone. . . . I think Sheila would like to bite a boy, though sometimes she goes through her best paces when she hears them hooting, as if she thought they were admiring her, which I never allow myself to doubt."[61]

Innocuous and merely referential, this allusion to boys could easily stand for the patriarchal resistance Jewett experiences even in writing a simple sketch. But as she also suggests and as we have seen to be the case in "A White Heron," Jewett's *sketch* not only shies at such pressures but can accept the admiration, the literary appreciation, *they* also suggest. Jewett herself recognizes the serious potential of her writing, the way "she could . . . go a little faster" and experience a "suddenly grown . . . pair of wings when" such writing "fairly flies over the ground" or literal reference. This metareferential reading, however, clearly violates the nonfictional modus operandi of "An October Ride." The nonfictional sketch allows for a certain authorial control which obviates the problem of writing minor literature in a less-subject-to-closure fictional sketch. Jewett can evince her desire for producing minor literature here only by our own over-determination of the sketch's decidedly nonsymbolic images. Toward the end of the sketch, for example, Jewett tells of Sheila's leading her to a now-abandoned "parsonage" during a rainstorm where she discovers "high" writing over a fireplace, a literal reference *kept* literal or symbolically quiescent, despite the fact that the former parson can now suggest to us a representative of the major New England literary as well as religious tradition—a Hawthorne, perhaps, in the Old Manse: "he must have been a tall man to have written so high."[62] A house playfully alluded to as "haunted," the parsonage serves as a mere practical refuge for Jewett; there she builds a fire "and though . . . very well contented there alone I wished for some friend to keep me company, it was very selfish to have so much pleasure with no one to share it."[63]

This scene, too, makes "minor" allegorical sense only after our preceding discussion of "A White Heron." Except for after the fact when the sketch will have appeared in public, Jewett's scene of writing this nonliterary "fire" remains private or unshared even by "some" close "friend," an indefinitely imagined intimate reader. And as she leaves this parsonage, which is to say ends this sketch, she expresses a "hope the ghosts who live [there] watched me with friendly eyes."[64] Her sketch has temporarily come to rest in what for her constitutes an abandoned literary-patriarchal tradition, a tradition reduced to "friendly" influence. So too, Jewett projects an image of how her writing this sketch or modest "fire" will appear to others, for as she leaves, in the last words of the sketch, "I looked back myself, to see a thin blue whiff of smoke still coming from the great chimney. I wondered who it was that made the first fire there,—but I think I shall have made the last." Jewett here imagines her sketch's insubstantiality, its smokelike appearance to others in relation to a putatively abandoned tradition. Where such smoke appears in Jewett's sketches, an imaginative "fire" is always about to go out, her "pleasure" in lighting it unshared. And because of its insubstantial or smokelike residual appearance, her sketch, she can assume, will never attract future public attention. At least she would like to "think" that she alone "shall have made the last" writing and reading of this noncompetitive—because virtually unwritten—minor pre-text.

But this "I think" also betrays the tentativeness with which Jewett conceives her "thin" literary productions. Writing in terms of a self-determinately minor literary genre and a putatively obsolete literary tradition can at best forestall but not cancel the major literary pressures surrounding the act of writing her sketches. She cannot defend against such pressures by nonliterary projections of fences, say, to maintain "the reserve, the separateness, the sanctity of the front yard of [our] grandmothers." Even the fact that "Americans are too fond of being stared at," as she suggests in "From a Mournful Villager," argues for an expected invasion of privacy, the sense of others forcing her to "writ[e] down the family secrets for any one to read" or "having everybody call you by your first name."[65] Sketches, like fences, cannot sustain the "reserve" required to avoid public exposure and scrutiny, at least not without an imminent anxious awareness of the improbability that they will succeed in doing so. Through her non-fictional sketches, then, Jewett allegorically expresses or, as Leslie Brisman persuasively argues about another would-be minor writer, George Darley, cultivates "the myth of the small poet."[66] She does this by appealing to a reactionary bourgeois value system that privileges privacy, especially privacy associated with literary activity here symbolized by token Americana fences and which, despite its minor aspect, still suggests her anxious concern with an impinging literary world bound to regard her strategic preference for the sketch or literary "fence" in the context of more dominant literary genres and codes of evaluation.

In short, Jewett's American sketching propagates but fails to realize her "freedom" to become a minor writer. But in "A White Heron," she attempts to gain a more convincing vision of minor literature. Here she differentiates her "little" text from public notions of major and minor literature precisely by tracing her text's inevitable engagement with such notions, engagements which "she" strives to regard as being as accidental as Sylvia's encounter with the hunter: "But who could have foreseen such an accident as this?" The explicitly fictional sketch, after all, not only engages the possibilities of major literary production in more immediate terms, but also permits the "who can tell?" ambiguity of its textual surface, that aspect of the text which will be perceived by others. Even as Jewett adopts this post factum perspective on the story *as* she writes it, a perspective which includes that indefinite "something which does itself" as its primary author, she, like Sylvia with her experience of the white heron, can only remember how "A White Heron" traced a transitory symbolic event—a major literary possibility—that "came flying through the golden air." Even as it "floats and wavers" in this major literary ambience, however, it encounters the "shouting cat-birds" of the public literary marketplace, quickly disappears from this possibility, and "goes back like an arrow presently to [its] home in the green world beneath." Much like Sylvia's climbing back down from the pine tree immediately after this event, this descent suggests the story's own descension from major or "higher" to a lower or minor literary status.

In the year Jewett republished "A White Heron," she half-humorously depicts the changing literal size of her publications. Other writers in *The Atlantic* and *Harper's* write "good big" stories;

> so does not S. O. J., whose French ancestry comes to the fore, and makes her nibble all round her stories like a mouse. They used to be as long as yardsticks, they are now as long as spools, and they will soon be the size of old-fashioned peppermints, and have neither beginning or end, but shape and flavor may still be left them, and a kind of public may still accept [them] when there is nothing else.[67]

Yardsticks to spools to peppermints: in a nonserious, nonhonorifically critical manner, Jewett here records a diachronic diminution in her works that virtually outlines her hidden agenda for producing minor literature, an agenda that gets inscribed in "A White Heron" in unconscious semiotic terms. She records the literal change of her works from larger to smaller stories; she regards them in the context of a literary evaluative code, the criterion of "good big" stories. Yet she also outlines a nondialectical category of minor literature, one that cannot be measured since it has "neither beginning or end" but instead the "shape and flavor," the form and value, of "old-fashioned peppermints." And who but a child or a *minor* could hope to appreciate such written "peppermints"?

By means of the internalized or unconsciously allegorized signifiers of its own nonliterary ambition, its own figurative self-reductions, its neither decisive nor indecisive but rather nondecisive "literary" and "popular" allusions to "the great" literary "world" as it gets written, Jewett's "A White Heron" dreams the possibility of a nondialectical species of minor literature. By means of these unconscious fictional media, she here produces a text which she can never quite read because she has never quite written it—and which she can never quite write because it promises to disappear like a small piece of candy in the hands of a child. Doubtless, minor literature originates in the comparative binary context of major and minor literature. But for Jewett, if only in the act of writing this story and if only as a desire that attempts to return to a permanent "home . . . beneath," minor literature here becomes released, like the white heron itself, into a category which she determines as being radically afield from its hierarchical origins. Even as a fiction of writing per se, so long as she effectively induces a potential semiotic relation to it, that is, as the writing and reading of a woman "always nine years old," "A White Heron" continues to exist as some "rare bird" of minor literature accidentally located in the "district" of regionalist, feminist, pastoral, and sketchy modes of literary production.

Of course, American literary history, with variant criteria that revise but institutionalize examples of minor literature in the contexts of a by-definition privileged major literature, has itself, like the hunter, "stuffed and preserved" "A White Heron" in *its* "collection," particularly in anthologies of American literature. No matter their good intentions, the same holds true for the story's numerous critiques. Even this present criticism, a criticism that purports to uncover the story's marginal "minor" echoes, cannot help but use them to deconstruct the canonical unconscious of such criteria and critiques. In the end, this criticism must also remain a "disappointed" hunter or Ornethologist. It too must leave behind no more than—but also no less than—"this lonely country child!"

EPILOGUE

Ten years later, in 1896, Jewett will write *The Country of the Pointed Firs,* a work most critics agree possesses qualities that raise her literary importance above other local color contemporaries. This work clearly seems to express rather than erase the major issues I have tried to argue "A White Heron" strives to elude: the relative independence of regionalist culture; the capacity of women to be self-dependent; the survivability of the American pastoral ideal; the interdependence —or relative literary "freedom"—of American sketch writing. Not unlike *Deephaven* (1877), Jewett's earliest collection of fictional sketches, the narrative of *Pointed Firs* comprises a series of topically related sketches. But in this later work the sketches seem more cogently unified in style and theme by a narrator who on her summer vacation from a large city visits Dunnet Landing, a fictionalized New England village. There she meets the work's "strangely self-possessed" protagonist, Mrs. Todd, an older woman, who comes to represent the almost sacred mystique as well as neglected history of this rural culture, "a world in which women are alone but not tragic" (Pryse), also an "ageless pastoral world" that ironically (Berthoff), ambivalently (Martin), or synthetically exists in tandem with "the movement of history" represented by the narrator's urban world (Donovan).[1] Through meeting other villagers and listening to their and especially Mrs. Todd's stories about past and present inhabitants, the narrator, we could argue, becomes freed from her urban biases and initiated into the unique human ways of this largely feminine rural subculture.

To be sure, such critical depictions of *Pointed Firs* usually carry the implication that it is an exception in a minor writer's career—it stands as a major work "for her," as Jewett might have remarked.[2] Indeed, literary critics often define minor writers by their having produced at least one semimajor work, a work to which their preceding works seem embryonic prologues, i.e., minor according to the minor writer's own self-produced criterion. But these depictions also show how *Pointed Firs* transcends or questions the "minor" donneé of its regionalist topos, that is, how it manages to avoid the limitations of a literary-historical passé school of writing that stressed "the verisimilitude of detail without being concerned often enough about truth to the larger aspects of life or human nature."[3] *Pointed Firs,* in fact, seems literarily ambitious over and beyond the way it suggests the narrator's gradual cultural education. Jewett endows Mrs. Todd, for example, a person whose very name (Death) represents her tragic cast, with clear symbolic attributes. The "novel" depicts her as a feminized version of a "strangely self-possessed" Ancient Mariner who tells her stories to some initially naive Wedding Guest.[4] Similarly, Jewett explicitly situates the plight of Joanna Todd, the dead cousin of Mrs. Todd's also dead husband, against the background of Hawthorne's "unpardonable sin" theme. Moreover, Joanna Todd's self-imposed exile after her lover leaves her, her exile from Dunnet Landing and its communal sense of self-identity, could be said to represent the tension-ridden literary identity of *Pointed Firs* itself, its ambivalent (but therefore esthetically innovative) allegiance to being a unified narrative comprising near-autonomous parts or sketches like its very regionalist topos.

Yet like "A White Heron" though with a more explicit acknowledgment of pressures to become major literature, *Pointed Firs,* we could argue, also seeks to elude such pressures. Already a "feminization" of the Coleridgean Ancient Mariner, for example, Mrs. Todd recounts her stories no more compulsively than the narrator, at best a minor wedding guest in this context, is *compelled* to listen to them and so leave Dunnet Landing a *radically* changed person. Indeed *Pointed Firs* literally displaces this Mariner allusion from Mrs. Todd to a "strange and unrelated person" named Captain Littlepage (13). But even here, Mrs. Todd casts doubt on the authenticity of the tales (and tales within tales) he tells the narrator by noting his having "been a great reader all his seafarin' days" (29). In either case, Mrs. Todd as Mariner alludes to Coleridge's major poem without challenging or diminishing its originality, its power to have established the criterion by which this latter-day version represents "wisdom-giving strolls" (6) rather than vatic trances. *Pointed Firs* does not so much revise as revive Coleridge's major Romantic poem as a protoytpe which serves to expose the less sensational, less imaginatively ambitious if more realistic narrative topos of this later work. Even such realism, however much one could argue it seeks to make credible Coleridge's *super*-natural topos to a late-nineteenth-century audience, also sacrifices the text's perhaps unconscious claims and revisionary exemplification of Romantic "genius," the honorific signifier of major literature throughout this century. On the one hand, then, Captain Littlepage's co-presence in the narrative as Mariner figure serves to diminish our recognition of Mrs. Todd in this role. On the other, his idiosyncratic character as well as his tall tales represents a Romantic poetics which cannot make its way into *Pointed Firs* without making the text itself seem a "strange and unrelated" mode of fiction—but a "little page" in comparison with the Coleridgean precedent it invokes.

Such self-reductions, such sketched and hence virtually withdrawn allusions, thus identify Jewett's practice even in her putatively major work. The same practice also occurs more explicitly and perhaps with greater "anxiety" in her allusion to Hawthorne's "unpardonable sin." Mrs. Fosdick, yet another female narrator encased in *Pointed Firs*, informs the narrator about Joanna Todd's sense of her unpardonable sin, her separation from society and its consolations, in a way that distances its immediate affective relevance as an operative moral code for the inhabitants (and readers) of this Dunnet Landing world: "Yes, she was one o' them poor things that talked about the great sin; we don't hear nothing about the unpardonable sin now, but you may say't was not uncommon then" (77). In the already distanced manner of a narrative within a narrative, *Pointed Firs*, no less than Jewett's "A White Heron," affiliates itself with only to neutralize an issue clearly associated with a major American literary precedent. By analogy, this "*great* sin," a sin that lacks force in her present-day New England, also signifies a *major* literary subject made to seem "unrelated" to the present narrative's thematic concerns. Undoubtedly, one could cite this analogy as a more sophisticated confirmation of Matthiessen's judgment that Jewett's writings never dealt with "blinding hates and jealousies," let alone "the fever of lust and the thirst of avarice."[5] But one could cite it also to show how her writing takes place on the cutting edge of these romantic and modernist shibboleths, these evaluative touchstones that minimally condition our recognition of "major" literary efforts; and that the motive for such displacement is to secure a literarily untrammeled space, so to speak, wherein she can produce texts somehow excused from the question of their literary value.

Even the latent self-referentiality of *Pointed Firs*—its temptation, like Joanna Todd's, to become a series of fetishized or autonomous parts, and yet avoidance of this temptation by unifying them through a narrator—shows signs of becoming repressed. Jewett here makes this narrator abdicate responsibility for her text, allowing us to interpret its structural ambiguity as a sign of its evasiveness rather than "innovation."[6] In a chapter entitled "William's Wedding," which Jewett was writing at the time of her death but which has been included in received editions of *Pointed Firs*, the narrator calls attention to the translatability of her narrative by readers not directly familiar with the region's customs and their significance for its inhabitants. In one sense, the wedding—and here indeed the narrator becomes a wedding guest not inhibited by the strange and estranging "genius" of Imagination—serves as a symbolic culmination of the narrator's experience at Dunnet Landing. The elderly William, brother of Mrs. Todd, represents a potential isolate or regionalist casualty who takes care of his mother on an island near the village. His marriage to Esther Hight, who also takes care of an octogenarian mother, symbolizes for the narrator the transcendence of isolation and death, the transcendence of death by Dunnet Landing itself. We are thus not surprised to read the narrator's words upon hearing of this wedding from Mrs. Todd:

> It is difficult to report the great events of New England; expression is so slight, and those few words which escape us in moments of deep feeling look but meagre on the printed page. One has to assume too much of the dramatic fervor as one reads;

but . . . when [Mrs. Todd] said to me, "This weather'll bring
William in after her; 'tis their happy day!" I felt something take
possession of me which ought to communicate itself to the least
sympathetic reader of this cold page. It is written for those who
have a Dunnet Landing of their own: who either kindly share
this with the writer or possess another. (217)

Despite her initial sense of the particularity of this "New England"
experience, the narrator quickly comes to feel that the social and esthetic significance of this situation "ought to communicate itself" to
any reader who has read the narrative up to this point or can virtually take her position. In this sense, the scene's significance seems immediately or symbolically transmissible. It easily transcends the possible mediations of its particular or contingent referential base which
would otherwise limit the communicability of its significance. The
narrator's explicit acknowledgment of and yet movement away from
this possible limitation seem to corroborate Richard Cary's view that
Jewett "carefully preserved [the] dichotomy of separateness and empathy" in the narrator's relation to Dunnet Landing society; thus the
narrator "does not merely perform a necessary chore" or serve simply as transparent reporter of the other narratives which indeed comprise much of her own narrative, but also "emerges with a strong integrity of her own."[7] That is, we can argue that the narrator actually
achieves independent character status even in her role as amanuensis
within *Pointed Firs*. This role, after all, could function as a narrative
trompe l'oeil which both highlights the narratives and/or events she
does merely "report," and reinvests her, in her apparent passivity, with
the status of a surrogate reader who consolidates our own esthetic
relation to these particular narratives and/or events. In short, the narrator in this passage appears to identify herself as a literal, symbolic,
and even semiotic "Wedding Guest."

But one could also argue that the narrator's movement away from
the possibly nonuniversal significance of this scene betrays a wish for
narrative unselfconsciousness, a desire not to perceive the possibility
that these Dunnet Landing materials might become a "cold page."
The narrator, after all, is a surrogate literary artist who has come to
Dunnet Landing to write. She even remains plagued by what we recall
Jewett terming "the business part of writing" (p. 155 above), a voca-

tion that at first makes her view Mrs. Todd's "wisdom-giving" walks with her as a distraction to "a long piece of writing, sadly belated now, which I was bound to do": "Literary employments are so vexed with uncertainties at best, and it was not until the voice of conscience sounded louder in my ears . . . that I said unkind words of withdrawal to Mrs. Todd" (6–7). Thus, pointing to the ubiquitous metaphoricity of these references to "the great events of New England" manifests both the narrator's concession of her "vexed" sense of writing to the spontaneous if (to her literary audience) minor story-telling figures of Dunnet Landing, and her anxiety over the inadequacy of her present narration of these "events." She desires to forget their "literary" significance. But her movement here to an imagined symbolic reading of William's wedding also confesses the vulnerability of both her Dunnet Landing materials and her relation to them, namely that they *could* become "this cold page"— an allusion reminiscent of "that cold selfishness" that Jewett finds necessary "for one's work's sake" (pp. 153 ff. above).

In short, such "great events of New England" could result in a text whose semiotic effect she senses she cannot fully control or predict. Resembling a classic rhetorical aporia, this passage never communicates the narrator's reaction to the scene, only the substitutive claim that it "ought to communicate itself to the least sympathetic reader." The movement from the possibility of this scene's contingency (conditionally communicable) to the assumption of its universality (unconditionally communicable) itself entails a movement from a self-certain to uncertain "ought," from a declarative to a subjunctive mode of expression, regardless of whether the scene's supposed significance pertains to an imagined esthetic or social apprehension. From either register of reading, the narrator's latent awareness of her text's materiality, that anything expressed in her narrative might "look but meagre on the printed page," suffices to disrupt the very illusion which in fact conditions the possible relevance or metaphoricity of what she here tries to "report" to the general reader.

In order to sustain her narrative's signifying power and ultimate significance, then, the narrator appeals to readers distanced from the immediate occasion of her present narrative: to "those who have a Dunnet Landing of their own." But even here, she cannot quite believe in her text's being, as it were, metaphorically apprehended as she writes it; instead, she resorts to a series of qualifications that far from ensuring this apprehension tend to expose her separation from such a reader and, since she necessarily recognizes how this reader affects the text she is presently writing, from her own narrative activity. Thus, she first addresses readers relatively unfamiliar with this New England event but who still "share this with the writer," that is, have firsthand experience with similar if not identical regional events. But then she shifts her attention from *this* reader, apt to make an analogical translation of this referentially specific scene on the basis of kindred social experience, to readers that will apprehend it *only* as metaphor—readers who "possess another" *kind* of *Dunnet Landing."* We could argue that this sequence from a relatively personal or social to a relatively anonymous or esthetic validation of her "report" betrays her awareness of her narrative's possible failure to communicate what she wants to *assume* she communicates here. We could also argue that she here simply repeats on another level her initial anxiety over her narrative's "cold" exterior, its own "meagre [appearance] on the printed page," precisely at the moment she attempts to envisage its probable transmission to others. In this sense, she invokes the first kind of reader to buffer her from the perception of her narrative's fate, its less certain significance in the hands of some urban reader, say, who has no familiarity at all with regional events or the feelings they "ought" to evoke.

The passage thus remains a more un-decisive aporia than it rhetorically intends. On the one hand, it concedes the possibility of its contingency while raising the ante of its metaphoricity to foreclose the possible consequence of this contingency—failure to become a narrative with universally apprehensible significance. On the other, it exposes the narrator's lack of author-ity as a "writer" over and beyond her amanuensis role here and elsewhere in *Pointed Firs*; that is, the passage reveals her dependence on an ever more abstract or absent reader to testify to the scene's self-evident transparent significance *for her.* But ironically, her very lack of narrative conviction or control over its imagined reception may function as a strategy to delay its (imagined) immediate reading—and therefore the external evaluation both of the "great" event it refers to and, what must occur later, its already modest denomination as a textual *report.* If we read the passage in this manner, we can see how it effectively requires the so-called second imagined reader to perform an abstract act to appreciate the metaphorical tenor of a represented scene which in fact never gets to be fully represented. This reader must supply his or her own Dunnet Landing, but in doing so, he or she will virtually be reading a different narrative or, quite literally, "[another] Dunnet Landing."

Jewett's no doubt unconscious undermining of her narrator's author-ity and yet intimation of this narrator's strategy for recuperating her authority result in this passage's self-identity as a palimpsest text or substitute mode of writing. As in "A White Heron," this passage from *Pointed Firs* propagates an image of writing which *preexists* writing or which simultaneously "represents" an authorial nostalgia for the representational presence of a reference "too difficult to report" and its paradoxical transcription — a writing to which the narrator/writer alone will remain privy. We can only surmise, of course, to what extent this semiotic pattern applies to Jewett's production of *Pointed Firs* as a whole. Given its "unconscious" occurrence, this sentimental notion of writing, this strategy of authorial recuperation, does not necessarily redound to, say, the ironic substantiality of the narrator's "character." This after all nameless narrator could just as easily represent the absence or at best "cold" residuum of Jewett's own desire either to maintain a privileged self-present relation with the regionalist materials of *Pointed Firs*, or to delay her text's reception in the public domain by imagining its nonreadability and therefore its evasions of social as well as esthetic judgments.

The passage thus self-referentially outlines a nondecisive if not at all undecidable writing which likely reflects the fantasized epistemology behind *Pointed Firs'* narrative operations. This nondecisiveness appears in the ways the passage itself resorts to indefinite references and auxiliary verbal constructions: "It is difficult," "One has to assume," "I felt something," "It is written," "those . . . who . . . share this . . . or possess another." Or again, it appears in other passages through the use of verbal-conventional reflexes to close disruptions that might expose the contingency of the passage's material references to public gaze and thus short-circuit the strategy of the aforementioned epistemological fantasy. Each reader will find the "counter-parts" to characters like Mrs. Todd and William "in every village in the world, thank heaven, and the gift to one's life is only in its discernment" (218). Coupled with the ensuing maxim about life in general, this "thank heaven" excuses the narrative as well as narrator from reflection on the possibly atypical nature of its materials by resorting to the supposedly self-evident universalism of a sublated Christian ethos and/or an idealistic organic view of nature and society.

Jewett's critical apologists and future revisionists doubtless have reasons to regard *Pointed Firs* as itself one of "the great events of New England," as either a fine-tuned esthetic and/or social unity of parts or a text rich with ideological and literary subcodes of the kind we discerned in "A White Heron," but here more in force. Yet they must do so in the face of this text's self-repressive mode of narration to disguise its appearance *as* a text in the field of potential ideological and literary evaluations; its retiring allusions to literary precedents to determine as well as neutralize its own minor literary ambitions as a "little page" within literary history; and its reliance on established ideologies, discourses, or unexamined truisms to induce the illusion of an unproblematic unity or "book of parts." Owing to her own modest literary success, Jewett was unable to forget the possibility of producing major literature, a "long piece of writing, sadly belated," by the time she came to write *Pointed Firs*. Nonetheless, the very fact that she kept adding other sketches to this work after its publication (and that her editors could add the posthumous sketch from which we have drawn the passage discussed above) tends to confirm her nondecisive "minor" intention with regard to its identity. In the "little" self-effacing language that she often employed in letter writing, she herself expresses surprise at the success and apparent unity of *Pointed Firs*: "How little I thought of the Pointed Firs being eminent and turning into a book of parts when I began."[8]

Jewett's reticent and "little" literary ambition in fact becomes inscribed in this work. *Pointed Firs* represents not so much nostalgia for a communal, feminine, or pastoral America existing in critical tension with megalopolitan, patriarchal, or literary-historical realities, as nostalgia for a now superseded minor mode of writing such as she dreamed of in "A White Heron." In 1885, one year before she

published this story, she virtually had declared this "minor" consciousness of writing as an ideal:

> I often think that the literary work which takes the least promi-
> nent place nowadays is that belonging to the middle ground.
> Scholars and so-called intellectual persons have a wealth of lit-
> erature in the splendid accumulation of books that belong to
> all times, and now and then a new volume is added to the great
> list. Then there is the lowest level of literature, the trashy news-
> papers and sensational novels, but how seldom a book comes
> that stirs the minds and hearts of the good men and women
> of such a village as this.[9]

More ambivalent but no less an aspect of its production are *Pointed
Firs*' struggles to return to this "middle ground," to remain some distance from "the main road" as defined in the more imaginary terms
of "A White Heron." If both works occasionally find themselves praised
in conventional or revisionary American literary histories, they do so
with the caveat of their disaffection from "intellectual" and "sensational" criteria that continually reproduce the demand for major literature and thus the ideology of literary canonicity. At the very least,
these works raise the question of what it can mean for a literary text
to desire to become a "middle," anomalous, or canonically free minor literature emblematically appearing as a "shy little girl," a "rare"
white heron, and a "great pine-tree" that "was left for a boundary
mark, or for what reason, no one could say . . ."

NOTES

INDEX

NOTES

Prologue

1 Charles Altieri, "An Idea and Ideal of a Literary Canon," *Critical Inquiry* 10, no. 1 (September 1983): 53. The entire volume of this *Critical Inquiry* is devoted to essays on the theoretical and practical significance of literary canons.

2 Barbara Herrnstein Smith, "Contingencies of Value," *Critical Inquiry* 10, no. 1 (September 1983): 10. Seemingly at odds with Altieri's position about canonical texts, not only does Smith regard the latter as beholden to the "subject's 'needs,' 'interests,' and 'purposes' . . . always changing — as well as to the way such texts "also produce the needs and interests they satisfy and evoke the purposes they implement" (12–13) — she notes that such "[e]valuations are among the most fundamental forms of social communication and probably among the most primitive benefits of social interaction" (20). Whether we regard canons as ideal or contingent formations, as transcendent cultural idealizations or politically (or even personally) motivated cultural fictions, Altieri's and Smith's arguments lead us to the difficulty if not impossibility of developing a "noncanonical theory of value and evaluation" (Smith, 7). In any case, my discussion of "A White Heron" and minor literature in general in this work occurs in medias res: in a sociohistorical milieu where canonical pressures operatively influence the construction of texts and even the choice of critical topics.

3 Charles Miner Thompson, "The Art of Miss Jewett," *Atlantic Monthly* 94 (October 1904), collected in Richard Cary, ed., *Appreciation of Sarah Orne Jewett* (Waterville: Colby College Press, 1973), 48; F. O. Matthiessen, *Sarah Orne Jewett* (Boston: Houghton Mifflin, 1929), 145–46. Matthiessen has little to say about "A White Heron" specifically. He merely paraphrases the story's theme, maintaining that Sylvia's preservation of

the heron's secret shows she "is truer to nature than to the potential lover she is dimly conscious of in the young hunter" (83).

4 Warner Berthoff, "The Art of Jewett's *Pointed Firs," Fictions and Events: Essays in Criticism and Literary History* (New York: E. P. Dutton, 1971), 247, and Jay Martin, *Harvests of Change: American Literature, 1865–1914* (Englewood Cliffs: Prentice-Hall, 1967), 145. Berthoff reads the significance of the story according to his notion of regionalist ideology which attempts to postpone its "inevitable dissolution" by orienting itself toward "the past" and privileging "intercourse with nature" (as the protagonist in the story, "*only* a little girl," does) over the postbellum urban-centered, industrialized "grossness" of American society (250). He also argues that Jewett failed to master narrative technique until late in her career with *Pointed Firs* (246–47).

5 Josephine Donovan, *Sarah Orne Jewett* (New York: Frederick Ungar, 1980), 71 and 70. Donovan maintains that this conflict was Jewett's "central dilemma" both in her "life and in her fiction during the early 1880's" when she was living partly in her South Berwick, Maine, home and partly with her friend, Annie Fields, in Boston (13). Donovan elsewhere tries to value Jewett's work as "great literature" (15).

6 Richard Cary, *Sarah Orne Jewett* (New York: Twayne Publishers, 1962), 102–3.

7 Annis Pratt, "Women and Nature in Modern Fiction," *Contemporary Literature* 13, no. 4 (Autumn 1972): 477, 479.

8 Jane Morrison has made a fine movie of this story, though she entitles it "The White Heron" and misdates its writing as 1896—the publication date of Jewett's "major" work, *Pointed Firs*. Matthiessen uses the definite article in *Sarah Orne Jewett*, 82, 91, and 102, as does Martha Hale Shackford, "Sarah Orne Jewett," in David Bonnell Green, ed., *The World of Dunnet Landing: A Sarah Orne Jewett Collection* (Lincoln: University of Nebraska Press, 1962), 363, and more recently, Alfred Habegger, *Gender, Fantasy, and Realism in American Literature* (New York: Columbia University Press, 1982), 104–5 and 372.

Introduction

1 T. S. Eliot, "What Is Minor Poetry?" *On Poetry and Poets* (New York: Noonday Press, 1963), 46.

2 Stephen E. Tabachnick, "The Problem of Neglected Literature," *College English* 43, no. 1 (January 1981): 35 and 42. Eliot also associates "minor poetry" with "the kind . . . we only read in anthologies" ("What Is Minor Poetry?" 35).

3 Leslie Fiedler, *What Was Literature? Class Culture and Mass Society* (New York: Simon and Schuster, 1982), 140.

4 Ibid., p. 129. Cf. Raymond Chandler who sought to do "delicate things" in a "mass language . . . within the grasp of superficially educated people." *Raymond Chandler Speaks,* ed. Dorothy Gardiner and Kathrine Sorley Walker (Boston: Houghton Mifflin, 1977), 80; also see 83, 91, and esp. 94–95.
5 Denis Donoghue, "Does America Have a Major Poet?" *New York Times Book Review,* December 3, 1978, 9.
6 Ibid.
7 T. S. Eliot, "Tradition and the Individual Talent," *The Sacred Wood,* rpt. ed. (London: Methuen, 1967), 50; my italics. I regard his use of "really" here as synonymous with "major."
8 Maria Corti, *An Introduction to Literary Semiotics,* trans. Margherita Bogat and Allen Mandelbaum (Bloomington: Indiana University Press, 1978), 132.
9 Northrop Frye, *Anatomy of Criticism* (Princeton: Princeton University Press, 1957), 5, 18, 97, 107–8; See also p. 104.
10 Frank Lentricchia places Frye in this context in *After the New Criticism* (Chicago: University of Chicago Press, 1980), esp. 3, 5, 7, 9, and 16–22. Paul A. Bové also associates Frye's criticism with the New Criticism in *Destructive Poetics: Heidegger and Modern American Poetry* (New York: Columbia University Press, 1980), esp. 93 and 109–10. Cf. Helen Vendler's remarks in "Poet's Gallery," *New York Review of Books* 27 (February 7, 1980), 12: "It was never claimed by the founders of the so-called "New Criticism" that any text, no matter how trivial, could be usefully considered in painstaking detail. Only texts of a certain sort can bear that sort of inquiry; for others, 'twere to consider too curiously so to consider them. There are authors—even great authors—in whose work one simply cannot find the freighted detail, polyphony of voices, ambiguity of intent, and so on."
11 Northrop Frye, "The Archetypes of Literature," *Fables of Identity* (New York: Harcourt, Brace & World, 1963), 12–13. Lentricchia, *After the New Criticism,* 18 et passim, coins the term "New Critical shibboleth"; he also refers to Frye's "literary universe" as a kind of structuralist *langue* (107), as I will have occasion to do at the bottom of this paragraph.
12 Frye, "Archetypes of Literature," 9, 10.
13 Lentricchia, *After the New Criticism,* 18.
14 Frye, "Archetypes of Literature," 10.
15 Frye, *Anatomy of Criticism,* 87.
16 Frye, "Archetypes of Literature," 12–13.
17 Ibid., p. 9.
18 Murray Krieger best expresses this "secondary" situation of the New Critic before the literary work in his "The Existential Basis of Contextualist Criticism," Hazard Adams, ed., *Critical Theory since Plato* (New York: Harcourt Brace Jovanovich, 1971), 1224–31. Somewhat in the man-

ner of a Platonic rhapsode, the critic, in Krieger's words, "*from his lesser place,* follows the poet in the free—yet imitative—play that makes his activity creative as well" (1231; my italics).

19 Frye, *Anatomy of Criticism,* 310 et passim.

20 Geoffrey H. Hartman discusses this "democratic" aspect of Frye's criticism in "Ghostlier Demarcations: The Sweet Science of Northrop Frye," *Beyond Formalism: Literary Essays, 1958–1970* (New Haven: Yale University Press, 1970), 25. Also cf. Lentricchia, *After the New Criticism,* 7.

21 Ibid., p. 40.

22 Samuel Taylor Coleridge, *Biographia Literaria,* chap. 13, in *Critical Theory since Plato,* 470–71; Coleridge's italics.

23 Lentricchia, *After the New Criticism,* 21–22, 24–26.

24 Chandler, *Raymond Chandler Speaks,* 82.

25 Harold Bloom, *The Anxiety of Influence: A Theory of Poetry* (New York: Oxford University Press, 1973), 5, 12, 30.

26 Leslie Brisman, *Romantic Origins* (Ithaca: Cornell University Press, 1978), 184, 192, 193; cf. p. 196.

27 Ibid., pp. 199, 207, 222.

28 Ibid., pp. 187, 223.

29 Bloom, *Anxiety of Influence,* 14–15.

30 Brisman, *Romantic Origins,* p. 211.

31 Bloom, *Anxiety of Influence,* p. 120.

32 Ibid., p. 13.

33 Ibid., p. 95.

34 Harold Bloom, *Agon: Towards a Theory of Revisionism* (New York: Oxford University Press, 1982), 45.

35 Both Lentricchia, *After the New Criticism,* 320, 321, 326, and esp. 338, and Bové, 25, stress the relation between Bloom's criticism and that of his formalist precursors.

36 T. S. Eliot, "The Metaphysical Poet," *Critiques and Essays in Criticism: 1920–1948,* ed. R. W. Stallman (New York: Ronald Press, 1949), 54 and 47. Bloom's canonical reduction of Eliot is implicitly expressed in many of his "influence" essays, but see his *The Breaking of the Vessels* (Chicago: University of Chicago Press, 1982), 8 and 17–21. After I completed this work, an excellent essay appeared by John Guillory, "The Ideology of Canon-Formation: T. S. Eliot and Cleanth Brooks," in *Critical Inquiry* 10, no. 1 (September 1983), which also asserts the "motivated" nature of Eliot's critical revisions of "the minor stance"; Guillory maintains, esp. 178–181, that in his essays on minor poets Eliot is attempting to construct a "not competitive" canon "alongside the already finished house of literature," and that "the figure of the minor poet," for Eliot, "cannot be detached from the problematics of influence."

37 Bloom, *Breaking of the Vessels,* 13.

38 Bloom views criticism and indeed literature itself as a kind of "plagia-

rism" performed for the sake of achieving an impossible originality. See his contribution to "Plagiarism—A Symposium," *TLS*, April 9, 1982, 413. Frye defines his criticism as a "bricolage" activity in his study of the Bible as a paradigmatic Western text, *The Great Code: The Bible and Literature* (New York: Harcourt Brace Jovanovich, 1982), xxi.

39 Hartman, "Ghostlier Demarcations," 33.

40 Lentricchia, *After the New Criticism*, 343–45.

41 Bové, *Destructive Poetics*, 13, 15, 19.

42 Ibid., p. 23.

43 Terry Eagleton, *Walter Benjamin or Towards a Revolutionary Criticism* (London: Verso Editions, 1981), 47.

44 Bloom, *Anxiety of Influence*, 78.

45 Donoghue, "Does America Have a Major Poet?" 9.

46 Fredric R. Jameson, "The Symbolic Inference; or, Kenneth Burke and Ideological Analysis," *Critical Inquiry* 4 (Spring 1978): 519.

47 Donoghue, "Does America Have a Major Poet?" 9.

48 Lentricchia, *After the New Criticism*, 345; cf. p. 136.

49 Bové, *Destructive Politics*, 29, 30.

50 For a discussion of the historical association between art and a labor theory of value, see Kurt Heinzelman, *The Economics of the Imagination* (Amherst: University of Massachusetts Press, 1980), esp. 140–65.

51 Thus, Geoffrey H. Hartman, *Criticism in the Wilderness: The Study of Literature Today* (New Haven: Yale University Press, 1980), argues that as the quantity of writing increases, so should the "quality of reading to preserve the great or exceptional work as something still possible" (165). For a discussion of the political aspect of "literary studies," their "incorporation and subsequent neutralization of dissent (also known as pluralism), and networks of . . . [critical] experts" concerned less "about society" than "about masterpieces in need of periodic adulation and appreciation," see Edward Said, "Opponents, Audiences, Constituencies, and Community," *Critical Inquiry* 9, no. 1 (September 1982): 22 et passim.

52 In the 1980 *MLA Bibliography*, for example, fifteen or more articles are devoted explicitly to Woolf's nonfictional or other minor works where no single article (among five Jewett entries) addresses *Pointed Firs*.

53 Eliot, "What Is Minor Poetry?" 46.

54 I use the terms "exchange value" and "use value" in the sense described by Bertell Ollman, *Alienation: Marx's Conception of Man in Capitalist Society*, 2d ed. (Cambridge: Cambridge University Press, 1976), 177–86 et passim. Ideally, all commodities should be produced for their use value or "the power to satisfy some human need" (182); but especially in capitalist society, such a mode of production is impossible since the value of one's labor has been "alienated" or abstracted by the putative "free market" which forces the worker to put his "own products under the control of others," as in making "articles whose qualities are intended to at-

tract customers rather than give satisfaction [to their producer]" (183). Recent Marxist critics, especially deriving from Louis Althusser, maintain that literary and other (formerly termed) "superstructural" activities entail "material" practices; they constitute "commodities" which become repressed as such in capitalist society. See Rosalind Coward and John Ellis, *Language and Materialism* (London: Routledge & Kegan Paul, 1977), 36, 47, 58, 60–92 et passim. For the Marxist emphasis on the work of art as a "commodity," see Hayden White, "Literature and Social Action: Reflections on the Reflection Theory of Literary Art," *New Literary History* 11 (Winter 1980): 376–78. On Marx's own notion of the difference between "productive" and "nonproductive" labor, see S. S. Prawer, *Karl Marx and World Literature* (New York: Oxford University Press, 1978), 308 ff.

55 Fredric R. Jameson, "Marxism and Historicism," *New Literary History* 11 (Autumn 1979):56.

56 Fredric R. Jameson, "The Ideology of the Text," *Salmagundi* (Fall 1975 / Winter 1976), 242.

57 Ibid.

58 Ibid., p. 243.

59 White, "Literature and Social Action," 379.

60 Jean-Paul Sartre, *What Is Literature?* trans. Bernard Frechtman (New York: Harper Colophon Books, 1965), 17.

61 Cf. Coward and Ellis, *Language and Materialism,* 72: "Ideology is the practice in which individuals are produced and produce their orientation to the social structures so that they can act within those structures in various ways." Thus, any social revolution or call for it must be "accompanied by a revolution in ideology," since by itself such revolution could mark "a return to the structures that have been overthrown, brought about by the way people habitually and unconsciously act and relate."

62 Eagleton, *Walter Benjamin,* 98.

63 Such freedom can also constitute a perceived weakness in Marxist literary criticism to account for the esthetic value of literary works, as Terry Eagleton notes in his *Criticism and Ideology: A Study in Marxist Literary Theory* (London: Verse Editions, 1978), 162.

64 Eagleton, *Criticism and Ideology,* 162–63.

65 Jameson, "Marxism and Historicism," 58.

66 Eagleton, *Criticism and Ideology,* 166–67, 73.

67 Walter Benjamin, "The Author as Producer," *Reflections,* trans. Edmund Jephcott, ed. Peter Demetz (New York: Harcourt Brace Jovanovich, 1978), 223.

68 Ibid., p. 233.

69 White, "Literature and Social Action," 379.

70 Jameson, "Symbolic Inference," 519.

71 Jameson, "Ideology of the Text," 223.

72 Eagleton, *Walter Benjamin,* 98.

73 Coward and Ellis, *Language and Materialism,* 67 et passim.

74 Terry Eagleton, "Text, Ideology, Realism," *Literature and Society: Selected Papers from the English Institute* (Baltimore: Johns Hopkins University Press, 1978), 161. Also cf. his *Criticism and Ideology,* 95.

75 Eagleton, "Text, Ideology, Realism," 161, 160.

76 Eagleton, *Criticism and Ideology,* 92.

77 Eagleton, "Text, Ideology, Realism," 161.

78 Ibid., p. 152.

79 Eagleton, *Walter Benjamin,* 113.

80 Eagleton, "Text, Ideology, Realism," 153.

81 With Brecht as his source, Eagleton argues that one "cannot determine the realism of a text merely by inspecting its intrinsic properties. On the contrary, you can never know whether a text is realist or not until you have established its effects—and since those effects belong to a particular conjuncture, a text may be realist in June and antirealist in December." "'Aesthetics and Politics,'" *New Left Review* (January–February 1978), 28. Also cf. Jameson, "Ideology of the Text," 233, and Eagleton's differentiation of the Marxist view of realism from that of the *Tel Quel* critics in his "Text, Ideology, Realism," 157–58.

82 Eagleton, "Text, Ideology, Realism," 153. Jameson, "Marxism, and Historicism," similarly urges that we should read past texts not with the idea of reducing them to a necessarily privileged (even Marxist) point of present reference, but to establish a dialectical relation to them: "We must try to accustom ourselves to a perspective in which every act of reading, every local interpretive practice, is grasped as the privileged vehicle through which two distinct modes of production confront and interrogate one another. Our individual reading thus becomes an allegorical figure for this essentially collective confrontation of two social forms" (70).

83 Tillie Olsen, *Silences* (New York: Delta/Seymour Lawrence, 1978), 38.

84 Nina Baym, "Melodramas of Beset Manhood: How Theories of American Fiction Exclude Women Authors," *American Quarterly* 33 (Summer 1981); 136 et passim.

85 Eagleton, *Criticism and Ideology,* 185.

86 Jameson, "Marxism, and Historicism," suggests that Marxism can conceive without at the same time fetishizing a utopian, nonalienated artistic activity that will transcend and not necessarily obliterate still-possible bourgeois modes of (alienated) literary production. On the one hand, bourgeois criticism (the *Tel Quel* group included) fetishizes the notion of art as play in the process of trying "to think away the unthinkable reality of alienated labor" (57). On the other, Jameson agrees with Althusser that Marxist theoretical practice "excludes from the outset any possibility for theory to *alienate itself speculatively* in its own ideational products by either presenting them as ideal realities without a history of

their own, or as idealities that refer to a reality which would itself be non-historical" (58). In short, Marxist formulations of a utopian art recognize *their own* historical-dialectical situation; they also recognize that any utopian perspective must *remain* dialectical. Marxism's "utopian impulse," therefore, would entail only the dialectical revision of past modes of (alienated) labor—their supersession rather than annihilation or disappearance within Marxist historical consciousness. Thus, according to Jameson, "the proper articulation of any concrete mode of production structurally implies the projection of all other conceivable modes" (71). Also cf. István Mészáros, *Marx's Theory of Alienation* (New York: Harper & Row, 1972), on art in bourgeois society as one more alienated labor activity in the division of labor, hence inadequate as a utopian mode for Marxism (210–14); he also cites Marx's notion of transcending alienated labor by a continual *Aufhebung* that "implies not only the supersession of any given form of alienation but also the 'preservation' of some of its 'moments'" (242).

87 Paul de Man, "Shelley Disfigured," *Deconstruction and Criticism* (New York: Seabury Press, 1979), 66. Cf. Jean Baudrillard, *The Mirror of Production,* trans. Mark Poster (St. Louis: Telos Press, 1975), who maintains that Marxist theory depends on the very bourgeois code of production or labor, the *langue* of capitalism, whose "decipherment" Marxist theory can only repeat and "where there is properly neither finality, cipher nor value" (19); obversely, Marxist theory also repeats bourgeois culture's "reverse fascination with non-work" or "the end of exploitation by work," and thus covertly privileges an esthetic wherein art is made to express "the pure form of labor . . . in non-labor" (40, 41).

88 Eliot, "What Is Minor Poetry?" 45, 50.

89 Eagleton, *Criticism and Ideology,* 185.

90 See n. 86, above.

91 Baudrillard, *Mirror of Production,* 50.

92 Ibid., p. 46.

93 Gilles Deleuze and Félix Guattari, *Anti-Oedipus: Capitalism and Schizophrenia,* trans. Robert Hurley, Mark Seem, and Helen R. Lane (New York: Viking Press, 1977), 5, 26, 33, 19, 54, 50, 45, 8; also see pp. 36–41. For a further discussion of *Anti-Oedipus* and the views set forth in this section, especially in relation to deconstructive criticism, see Vincent B. Leitch, *Deconstructive Criticism: An Advanced Introduction* (New York: Columbia University Press, 1983), 211–223.

94 Ibid., p. 31.

95 Ibid., p. 42.

96 Gilles Deleuze and Félix Guattari, *Kafka: Pour une littérature mineure* (Paris: Editions de Minuit, 1975), 29; my translation with the help of Bruce Lewis.

97 Ibid., pp. 34, 46–47.

98 Ibid., pp. 29–30.
99 Ibid., p. 30.
100 Ibid., pp. 31, 34, 35, 38, 39.
101 Deleuze and Guattari, *Anti-Oedipus,* 40.
102 Ibid., pp. 40, 41.
103 Deleuze and Guattari, *Kafka,* 49.
104 Ibid., pp. 40, 41, 42.
105 Ibid., pp. 35–37.
106 *Collected Works of Edgar Allan Poe,* Vol. 2, ed. Thomas O. Mabbott (Cambridge: Belknap Press, 1978), 219.
107 Deleuze and Guattari, *Kafka,* 49.
108 Ibid., pp. 44–45, 35, 48, 50, 33, 35.
109 Edward Said discusses the "power relationship" implicit in discursive acts in "The Text, the World, the Critic," in Josué V. Harari, ed., *Textual Strategies: Perspectives in Post-Structuralist Criticism* (Ithaca: Cornell University Press, 1979), 181–84.
110 Jacques Derrida, *Positions,* trans. Alan Bass (Chicago: University of Chicago Press, 1981), 41.
111 Roland Barthes, *The Pleasure of the Text,* trans. Richard Miller (New York: Hill and Wang, 1975), 13.
112 Roland Barthes, "From *Roland Barthes by Roland Barthes,*" *A Barthes Reader,* ed. Susan Sontag (New York: Hill and Wang, 1982), 419.
113 See Roland Barthes, "From Work to Text," *Textual Strategies,* 73–81. Though Barthes says here that he can read (read: enjoy or consume) "works" but "cannot *rewrite* them" (as one in effect does with "texts") (80), he doubtless would agree that there exist marginal "works"/"texts" that one can attempt to re-"write." See Barbara Johnson, *The Critical Difference: Essays in the Contemporary Rhetoric of Reading* (Baltimore: Johns Hopkins University Press, 1980), 11, and Vincent B. Leitch, *Deconstructive Criticism: An Advanced Introduction* (New York: Columbia University Press, 1983), 198–204, for arguments maintaining that Barthes transforms Balzac's "Sarrasine" into a "writerly" text and that *S/Z* can be considered a poststructuralist rather than structuralist critical activity. For another example of Barthes's semiotic practice in this vein, see his "Textual Analysis of a Tale by Edgar Poe," trans. Donald G. Marshall, *Poe Studies* 10, no. 1 (June 1977):1–12.
114 Coward and Ellis, *Language and Materialism,* 58.
115 Cf. Roland Barthes, "Criticism as Language, in David Lodge, ed., *20th-Century Literary Criticism* (London: Longman Group, 1972), 650: "Critical writing . . . can never be other than tautology. . . . If there is such a thing as a critical proof, it lies not in the ability to *discover* the work under consideration but, on the contrary, to *cover* it as completely as possible with one's own language." Paul de Man also argues for criticism's "literary" status through tracing the latter's operations in *Blind-*

ness and Insight: Essays in the Rhetoric of Contemporary Criticism (New York: Oxford University Press, 1971), esp. 49, 76, and 107.

116 Edward Said, "The Problem of Textuality: Two Exemplary Positions," *Critical Inquiry* (Summer 1978), 683.

117 Paul de Man, of course, would argue that *all* literature by definition deconstructs both itself and the criticism that purports to perform this deconstruction. See *Blindness and Insight,* esp. 16–19 and 31. But in his critique of de Man, Paul Bové, *Destructive Poetics,* 31–48, extrapolates from de Man's own analyses of "the possibility that certain poets, influenced by predecessors who of course themselves understood fiction and the void, misinterpret their predecessors and are thus mystified and in need of deconstruction. In such situations, the interpreters' job is to demystify these later writers in the tradition to reveal what their acquiescence to the hardened tradition obscures, namely, the insight of their great predecessors" (47). In the preface to his *Allegories of Reading: Figural Language in Rousseau, Nietzsche, Rilke, and Proust* (New Haven: Yale University Press, 1979), ix, de Man himself seems to suggest that certain texts deconstruct themselves with greater authority or more exemplary force than others; for this reason, his critical choice of these writers "is partly due to chance, but since the ostensible pathos of their tone and depth of their statement make them particularly resistant to a reading that is no longer entirely thematic, one could argue that if *their* work yields to such a rhetorical scheme, the same would necessarily be true for writers whose rhetorical strategies are less hidden behind the seductive powers of identification." J. Hillis Miller also acknowledges the hierarchical assumptions behind such criticism, *Critical Inquiry* 6 (Summer 1980):612: "Deconstruction . . . sees the notion of a determining material base as one element in the traditional metaphysical system it wants to put into question. Insofar as the authors of the traditional canon both express that system and reveal what is problematic about it, and do this more completely than other writers, deconstructive critics will continue to find Plato or Hegel, George Eliot or Balzac, more worthy of close attention than, say, the works of popular culture." This recanonifying aspect of deconstructive criticism may be considered an aberration of Derrida's position as practiced by the so-called "Yale critics." See Leitch's discussion of Joseph Riddel in *Deconstructive Criticism,* esp. 93–100, who argues for the elimination of such hierarchical privilegings (even of "literature" over nonliterary texts) by means of an egalitarian notion of "writing." Still, a "common operation" of deconstructionist practice, as Jonathan Culler argues, "is that which takes a minor, unknown text and grafts it onto the main body of the tradition, or else takes an apparently marginal element of a text, such as a footnote, and transplants it to a vital spot" (*On Deconstruction: Theory and Criticism after Structuralism* [Ithaca: Cornell University Press, 1982], 139).

Such grafting inevitably entails a "major" recuperation of the otherwise (conventionally determined) "minor" text.

118 Eagleton, *Walter Benjamin,* 46.

Chapter One

1 John Eldridge Frost, *Sarah Orne Jewett* (Kittery Point: Gundalow Club, 1960), 154.

2 Jewett's *Country By-Ways* (Boston: Houghton Mifflin, 1881) contains sketches to which I will refer throughout this work: "River Driftwood," "From a Mournful Villager," "An October Ride," and "A Winter Drive."

3 *Sarah Orne Jewett Letters,* ed. Richard Cary (Waterville: Colby College Press, 1967), 52.

4 Berthoff, *Fictions and Events,* 263.

5 Umberto Eco, *The Role of the Reader: Explorations in the Semiotics of Texts* (Bloomington: Indiana University Press, 1979), 22.

6 Parrington discusses Jewett in this diminished political context in *Main Currents in American Thought: An Interpretation of American Literature from the Beginnings to 1920,* 3 vols. (New York: Harcourt, Brace, 1930), 238 et passim. Berthoff suggests Parrington's perspective on Jewett when he remarks about her major work: *"Pointed Firs* is a small work but an unimprovable one, with a secure and unrivaled place *in the main line of American literary expression"* (*Fictions and Events,* 263; my italics).

7 Berthoff, *Fictions and Events,* 263.

8 Cary, *Sarah Orne Jewett,* 32.

9 Donovan, *Sarah Orne Jewett,* 100; also see n. 5, pp. 000–00, above.

10 Martin, *Harvests of Change,* 145–46.

11 Fredric Jameson, *The Political Unconscious: Narrative as a Socially Symbolic Act* (Ithaca: Cornell University Press, 1981), 87.

12 Quoted in the introduction to *A Bibliography of the Published Writings of Sarah Orne Jewett,* compiled by Clara Carter Weber and Carl J. Weber (Waterville: Colby College Press, 1949), viii–ix. In 1893, Jewett would again allude to this problem but as if it were *no longer* a problem; still, one could argue that it was part of her "political *unconscious"*: "When I was writing the Deephaven sketches [before 1877] . . . it was just the time when people were beginning to come into the country for the summer in such great numbers. It has certainly been a great means of broadening both townsfolk and country folk. I think nothing has done so much for New England in the last decade; it accounts for most of the enlargement and great gain that New England has certainly made. . . . But twenty years ago city-people and country-people were a little suspicious of each other . . . the only New Englander generally recognized in literature was the caricatured Yankee" (*Letters,* Cary, 84).

13 Donovan, *Sarah Orne Jewett*, 49.
14 *Letters of Sarah Orne Jewett*, ed. Annie Fields (Boston: Houghton Mifflin, 1911), 90.
15 In his introduction to *Deephaven and Other Stories* (New Haven: College and University Press, 1966), Richard Cary argues that the "choice [Sylvia] makes between the values of city and country is the one her creator invariably advocates. The relative worth of primitivism and sophistication is never in question in Miss Jewett's mind" (21). Also cf. Paul John Eakin, "Sarah Orne Jewett and the Meaning of Country Life," in *Appreciation of Sarah Orne Jewett*, who argues that in "A White Heron" as contrasted to *Pointed Firs*, Jewett brings the outsider-insider or native-visitor theme "into open conflict" (218).
16 Martin, *Harvests of Change*, 2–24.
17 Jerold Wikoff discusses "the passing of the self-sufficient [New England] farm" due to these and other reasons even before the Civil War in an article, "The Early Decline of Farming," from the *Valley News*, April 20, 1982. The *Valley News* is a local newspaper covering the central Vermont and New Hampshire region. On the severe decline of population in New England after the Civil War, see Martin, *Harvests of Change*, 135.
18 Donovan, *Sarah Orne Jewett*, 71–72.
19 Jewett manifests uneasiness with the "electric car" and "wireless telephones . . . if you love people enough you can be your own battery," in *Letters*, Fields, 138 and 242, as well as the railroad (*Letters*, Cary, 77). In *Civilizing the Machine: Technology and Republican Values in America, 1776–1900* (New York: Penguin Books, 1977), John F. Kasson discusses how "technological growth reached a crisis" in the United States in the latter part of the nineteenth century (183 ff.), and quotes Jewett as a technological reactionary dedicated to preserving "the lost youth and vanished way of life of a generation effaced, in . . . Jewett's phrase, by 'the destroying left hand of progress'" (188).
20 *Letters*, Cary, 83–84. Cf. quoted letter, n. 12, above, in this present context.
21 Anthony Wallace gives a studied sociological account of the triumph of early American industrial capitalism over the Jeffersonian and/or general Enlightenment ideology of craft-oriented, agrarian, as well as communitarian visions of American society, and the effect of this triumph on particular people from the respective new classes, in *Rockdale: The Growth of an American village in the Early Industrial Revolution* (New York: Alfred A. Knopf, 1978), 243–45, esp. 261, et passim. The resistance of New England villages to such change existed but was always imminent. Ironically, this situation pertains a hundred years later, as we can see from an article by Kay Longcope, "Big Industry in Small Town has Fans, Detractors," *Boston Globe*, January 21, 1979, which depicts the sense of social conflict the villagers near Jewett's home experience over the coming of a Pratt & Whitney plant: "Some people say North Berwick (pop.

2,800 [double what it was in 1831]) is in danger of losing its small town character on a spurt of growth young people welcome and older residents deplore."

22 Matthiessen, *Sarah Orne Jewett*, 20.

23 For example, in her sketch "The Confessions of a House-Breaker," collected in *The Mate of Daylight and Friends Ashore* (Boston: Houghton Mifflin, 1885), Jewett depicts a predawn scene in her village that made it seem "most wonderful to be awake while everybody slept, and to have the machinery of life apparently set in motion for my benefit alone" (241). Here, of course, "machinery" has to do with a quasi-theatrical setting used as a figure for the village's infrastructure seen from an unfamiliar perspective — much as Wordsworth perceives the city in early morning in his sonnet composed on Westminster Bridge — rather than expresses a sub rosa ideological allusion to industrialism. "Machinery" here becomes a benign, virtually empty referent. Note the coincidence between the temporal perspectives of Jewett in this sketch, a "housebreaker" *out* of her house at predawn, and Sylvia in "A White Heron," another "housebreaker" embarked on a predawn escapade.

24 Berthoff, *Fictions and Events*, 262.

25 Jewett, "From a Mournful Villager," 127.

26 Jewett, "River Driftwood," 4–5.

27 Ibid., p. 6.

28 Ibid.

29 Interestingly, the usual coupling in anthologies and literary histories of Jewett and Freeman, namely as contemporary (and relatively successful) local color writers, albeit with obvious contrastable views of the New England (usually female) character, is here ironically justified by Freeman's avowed appreciation for "A White Heron." Indeed, in her 1894 novel *Pembroke*, a major character appears with the name "Sylvia Crane," a double allusion to Jewett's story.

30 Jewett, "River Driftwood," 8.

31 See Annis Pratt's interpretation of the story, p. xxvii, above.

32 The probability of Jewett's awareness of this debate stems from her high esteem for Arnold as an intellectual authority, as some of her letters show. See *Letters*, Cary, 34 (fn. 4), 51, and 80; she later visited Mrs. Arnold on one of her European trips with Annie Fields. Jewett also owned his work in her personal library. Theodore Jewett Eastman, *A List of the Books from the Bequest of Theodore Jewett Eastman That Bear the Marks of Ownership of Sarah Orne Jewett* (Harvard Library, 1933), 2.

33 One could argue for this "ignorance" from another perspective. All three characters react to each other in terms of restricted fantasies: Mrs. Tilley, because of her loss or "family sorrows," sees both the hunter and Sylvia (who "takes after him" [8]) as substitutes for Dan, her son; Sylvia sees the hunter and heron "as if she were a desert-islander," that is, in terms

of a child's fantasy that isolates her from others; and the hunter, of course, sees both the two women and the heron exclusively in terms of his single-minded "dream" (xxii).
34 See n. 8, p. 182, above.
35 *Letters,* Fields, 59–60.

Chapter Two

1 Shulamith Firestone has emphasized this issue in her *The Dialectic of Sex,* a relevant version of which appears in her "On American Feminism" collected in Vivian Gornick and Barbara Moran, eds., *Woman in Sexist Society: Studies in Power and Powerlessness* (New York: Basic Books, 1971), esp. 486. Many feminist critics have discussed the woman writer's ambivalent situation in nineteenth-century patriarchal society wherein she could effectively produce *only* "minor literature," that is, literature conforming to male stereotypes about women's "proper place" or "nature." See, for example, Elizabeth Winston, "The Autobiographer and Her Readers," in Estelle C. Jelinek, ed., *Women's Autobiography: Essays in Criticism* (Bloomington: Indiana University Press, 1980), 95. I am also indebted to Mary Kelley for her work on "literary domestics," American woman novelists of the nineteenth century, which situates this issue in a specifically American cultural context. See her *Private Woman, Public Stage: Literary Domesticity in the Nineteenth Century* (New York: Oxford University Press, 1984).
2 Eleanor Flexner, *Century of Struggle: The Woman's Rights Movement in the United States,* rev. ed. (Cambridge: Belknap Press, 1975), 65. Flexner also argues that by "1848 [one year before Jewett was born], it was possible for women who rebelled against the circumstances of their lives to know that they were not alone" (77). Sheila M. Rothman also discusses the changing social milieu after the Civil War of women and the woman's movement in her *Woman's Proper Place: A History of Changing Ideals and Practices, 1870 to the Present* (New York: Basic Books, 1978).
3 Donovan, *Sarah Orne Jewett,* claims that "Eliot . . . was never a favorite, though Jewett's library included all Eliot's major works" (4). Jewett's objections to Eliot were likely on literary rather than ideological grounds (see Donovan, 24).
4 *Letters,* Cary, 17, fn. 3. Cary suggests that Jewett may have chosen this pseudonym "from George Eliot, whose life and works she wrote about."
5 Elaine Showalter, "Women Writers and the Double Standard," in *Woman in Sexist Society,* 325–27. Also see her *A Literature of Their Own: British Women Novelists from Brontë to Lessing* (Princeton: Princeton University Press, 1977), esp. 19 ff. and 36 et passim.
6 Quotation from "River Driftwood" occurs on p. 60, above. "From a

Mournful Villager," 120–21; my italics. The issue of "suffrage" for women was complicated and even displaced—hence made more difficult for women—by the issue of abolition. Ellen Carol Du Bois, *Feminism and Suffrage: The Emergence of an Independent Women's Movement in America, 1848–1869* (Ithaca: Cornell University Press, 1978), discusses how the postbellum problem "for feminists was how to make progress for women suffrage in the face of abolitionists' reluctance to support them" (77).

7 Sarah Orne Jewett, *A Country Doctor* (Boston: Houghton Mifflin, 1884). Jewett's preference for this novel is noted in the Webers' *Bibliography,* 10.

8 Matthiessen quotes Jewett's own connection with this novel's father figure in *Sarah Orne Jewett,* 75–76.

9 Jewett, *A Country Doctor,* 282–83.

10 Annette Kolodny, "Some Notes on Defining a 'Feminist Literary Criticism,'" *Critical Inquiry* 2 (Autumn 1975):76. Flexner, *Century of Struggle,* discusses the somewhat tenuous political or practical influence of Fuller's *Woman in the Nineteenth Century* on the century's woman's movement (66). I am here more concerned with its literary-ideological influence on Jewett's production of "A White Heron."

11 Margaret Fuller, *Woman in the Nineteenth Century and Kindred Papers,* ed. Arthur Fuller (Boson: John P. Jewett, 1855), 63, 72, et passim.

12 Jewett, *A Country Doctor,* 52–54.

13 Fuller, *Woman in the Nineteenth Century,* 37 and 40; see pp. 120–21 for Fuller's example of a "bad" father who cares only to restrict his daughter's education. Fuller's enlightened friend Miranda and her relation to the "good" father are usually considered to represent Fuller's own early upbringing by *her* father. Paula Blanchard agrees with but also expresses some reservations about this connection in her *Margaret Fuller: From Transcendentalism to Revolution* (New York: Delacorte Press / Seymour Lawrence, 1978), 215–18.

14 Fuller, *Woman in the Nineteenth Century,* 96.

15 For a discussion of female friendships in the nineteenth century, see Carroll Smith-Rosenberg, "The Female World of Love and Ritual: Relations between Women in Nineteenth-Century America," *Signs* 1 (1975):9, 11, 14, et passim. Smith-Rosenberg notes that "homosocial" relations between women were encouraged by men; on the surface, that is, they posed no homosexual or gender-separatist threat to the patriarchy. Donovan, *Sarah Orne Jewett,* 13, briefly discusses Jewett's "life-long monogamous partnership" with Annie Fields. Showalter, "Women Writers and the Double Standard," 331 and 329, discusses how male critics and writers denigrated Victorian women writers by referring to them as "old maids" or "spinsters," women who did not confirm and conform to the patriarchal image of women as guardians of an idealized domestic life.

16 Jewett, *A Country Doctor,* 307.

17 Ibid., p. 295.
18 Fuller, *Woman in the Nineteenth Century,* 176, 129, 158.
19 Ibid., p. 121.
20 Elaine Showalter, "Feminist Criticism in the Wilderness," in Elizabeth Abel, ed., *Writing and Sexual Difference, Critical Inquiry* 8, no. 2 (Winter 1981):204.
21 Berthoff, *Fictions and Events,* makes an analogous if patriarchally coded point about the women represented in Jewett's later work, *Pointed Firs.* For the women left to face the "blight that has settled on the region" by themselves, "the only choice, the sacrifice required for survival, is to give up a *woman's proper life* and cover the default of the men to be guardians and preservers of a community" (250; my italics).
22 The term is Ellen Moers's from her *Literary Women* (Garden City: Doubleday, 1976), 122 ff. For a male critic like Berthoff, *Fictions and Events,* 250, Sylvia's choice entails her defensive desire to preserve the farmstead or region from the "grossness" of American society as represented by the hunter's "offering her money."
23 Martin, *Harvests of Change,* alludes to this etymology (144). For a discussion of Sylvia as a figure of nature within a patriarchal paradigm, see Chapter 3, pp. 121–22, below.
24 Moers, *Literary Women,* 250–51.
25 Mary Jacobus, "The Question of Language: Men of Maxims and *The Mill on the Floss,*" in *Writing and Sexual Difference,* 210.
26 Fuller constantly alludes throughout *Woman in the Nineteenth Century* to ideal virgin and/or "self-sufficient" women in classical literature: for example to Sappho (47–48), the Sibyl (99), Cassandra (105–6), and especially the "Muse and Minerva" (115–16) as well as "Ceres" (121). As W. K. C. Guthrie notes in his *The Greeks and Their Gods,* rpt. ed. (Boston: Beacon Press, 1955), 101, the Greek goddess Demeter (in Roman mythology, Ceres) was assumed to be the mother of and sometimes Artemis herself, "an earth goddess, associated essentially and chiefly with the wild life and growth of the fields, and with human birth." In any case, Jewett's allusive association of Sylvia with a major feminine mythic figure, albeit inscribed within a patriarchal tradition, could easily outline an exclusive feminine declaration in ways beyond my present argument. First, it appeals to the authority of this tradition, but only in the guise of its honorific, presently defunct or historically out-of-sight influence. Alluding to this inoperative literary-patriarchal tradition, the connection with Artemis effectively *dis*-associates Sylvia from a restrictive patriarchal conscription of this goddess and frees her to become an image for oppressed women of all times. Second, Jewett's use of this classical allusion, however subtle, amounts to her de facto declaration of woman's ability to know and make use of this learning, that is, her (here demonstrated) ability to conceive new and not simply reproduce "proper" meanings—

in short, like Fuller's classical allusions, it is a demonstration of woman's intellectual capacities in the face of stereotypical male assumptions and restrictions concerning them (cf. Rothman, *Woman's Proper Place*, 29 et passim).

27 Oskar Seyffert, *A Dictionary of Classical Antiquities*, rev. and ed. by Henry Nettleship and J. E. Sandys (Cleveland: World, 1961), 43.

28 On the feminist use of "metamorphosis," see Nina Auerbach, "Magi and Maidens: The Romance of the Victorian Freud," in *Writing and Sexual Difference*, 294–97. Cf. Deleuze and Guattari's view of this trope's use by the "minor" writer, pp. 33–34, above. For a conservative view of how literature displaces myths by "credible" or "realistic" if still unconscious reconstructions, see Northrop Frye, "Myth, Fiction, and Displacement," *Fables of Identity*, esp. 34–37.

29 Judith Fryer, esp. 6, purports to use this "American Eve" framework in examining certain novels by male writers, *The Faces of Eve: Women in the Nineteenth Century American Novel* (New York: Oxford University Press, 1976).

30 Annis Pratt, "Women and Nature in Modern Fiction," argues that Sylvia's quest for the heron makes her emblematic of an ontological relation to nature decisively inaccessible to and different from the teleological paradigms of patriarchal quest literature and notions of self-identity (450; see p. xxvii, above). Annette Kolodny, "Turning the Lens on 'The Panther Captivity': A Feminist Exercise in Practical Criticism," in *Writing and Sexual Difference*, 343 et passim, also touches on this issue in discussing how this captivity narrative reveals "male figures of greed and violence . . . repeatedly breach[ing], or attempt[ing] to breach, the precincts of the lady's various Dream Gardens, her romantic trysting place, her person, and . . . her wilderness abode." In the same vein but with a particular focus on criticism, cf. Baym, "Melodramas of Beset Manhood."

31 Mary Daly, *Gyn/ecology: The Metaethics of Radical Feminism* (Boston: Beacon Press, 1978), 74–89, provides a context by which we could assert that the tree is a feminist archetype and the heron a possibly counter-patriarchal image inversely analogous to patriarchal "rapes" of matriarchal orders. Fryer, *Faces of Eve*, quotes Otto Weininger to show patriarchal notions of woman's ontological naiveté: "Woman has no relation to the idea, she neither affirms nor denies it; she is neither moral nor anti-moral: mathematically speaking, she has no sign; she is purposeless, neither good nor bad . . . she is as non-moral as she is non-logical" (8). His depiction ironically turns out to be true for some feminist theorists discussed later.

32 Fuller, *Woman in the Nineteenth Century*, 102.

33 Fuller had argued that the pejorative representation of Eve in the Judeo-Christian tradition had been superseded by the transcendent representation of the Virgin Mary (47 and 56). Susan Gubar, "'The Blank Page' and the Issues of Female Creativity," in *Writing and Sexual Difference*, argues

that the Virgin Mary allusion in women's literature might be viewed as a "revisionary metaphor" reclaiming the power of creativity for women (261).

34 Fuller, *Woman in the Nineteenth Century,* 135.

35 Ibid., p. 175.

36 One could argue that this ideological privileging of childhood permeates the writings of Howells and especially Twain, notably in the latter's "Old Times on the Mississippi." Childhood as a topos is also a "regionalist" ideologeme and could reflect the way Jewett's story reflects or even exploits the late-nineteenth-century American audience's interest in nostalgic representations of simpler if past modes of American life. In this sense, it seems no coincidence, perhaps, that as Matthiessen notes (*Sarah Orne Jewett,* 60–61), Jewett published a poem in an *Atlantic Monthly* of 1875, the edition in which Twain published the fifth section of "Old Times on the Mississippi."

37 Nina Baym, *Women's Fiction: A Guide to Novels by and about Women in America, 1820–1870* (Ithaca: Cornell University Press, 1978), 196.

38 Contrary to Baym and Mary Kelley, Ann Douglas discusses and criticizes the "feminization of American culture," the cooption of women writers, reduced to "sentimental" concerns in their fiction, by the patriarchal-clerical Christian tradition: *The Feminization of American Culture* (New York: Alfred A. Knopf, 1977), esp. 254 ff. Also cf. Cheri Register, "American Feminist Criticism: A Bibliographical Introduction, in Josephine Donovan, ed., *Feminist Literary Criticism* (Lexington: University Press of Kentucky, 1961), who argues that for "women like George Eliot and the Brontës, writing something other than sentimental novels was a rebellious act, and necessarily ideological and time-bound" (10).

39 Nancy C. Miller, "Emphasis Added: Plots and Plausibilities in Women's Fiction," *PMLA* 96, no. 1 (January 1981):36 and 39.

40 Sandra M. Gilbert and Susan Gubar, *The Madwoman in the Attic: The Woman Writer and the Nineteenth-Century Literary Imagination* (New Haven: Yale University Press, 1979), 58; my italics.

41 Miller, "Emphasis Added," 41.

42 Adrienne Rich, "Vesuvius at Home: The Power of Emily Dickinson," *On Lies, Secrets, and Silence: Adrienne Rich, Selected Prose, 1966–1978* (New York: W. W. Norton, 1979), 166 and 162. Coppélia Kahn, "Excavating 'Those Dim Minoan Regions': Maternal Subtexts in Patriarchal Literature," *Diacritics* (Summer 1982), argues that contrary to male critics who assume genres to have universal significance, the "feminist reader consciously notes the gender perspective of this genre, and tries to learn from it about the working myths of patriarchal culture" (41). For a further discussion of the diminutive imagery used by women writers and its significance in their works, see Moers, *Literary Women,* 244 and 245. In this present context, it is ironic that Matthiessen, a male critic, maintains that

Jewett and Emily Dickinson were for him at the time of his critical biography of Jewett "the two principal women writers America has had" (*Sarah Orne Jewett*), 152.

43 Myra Jehlen, "Archimedes and the Paradox of Feminist Criticism," *Signs* 6, no. 4 (Summer 1981):583.

44 Fuller, *Woman in the Nineteenth Century*, 221–22, associates these vocational options available to women. Also see Rothman, *Woman's Proper Place*, 30 ff.

45 Virginia Woolf, *A Room of One's Own* (New York: Harcourt, Brace & World, 1929; rpt. 1957), 74 et passim. Showalter also addresses this issue throughout her *A Literature of Their Own,* as does Annette Kolodny, "A Map of Rereading; or, Gender and the Interpretation of Literary Texts," *New Literary History* II (Spring 1980), esp. her discussion of Susan Glaspell's "A Jury of Her Peers," 460–63. Howells himself judged literature according to how it raised broad questions about life and society without giving self-serving "romantic" answers: "What is our religion, what is our society, what is our country, what is our civilization? You cannot read [Tolstoy] without asking yourself these questions, and the result is left with you." W. D. Howells, "On Zola and Others," collected in Cleanth Brooks, R. W. B. Lewis, Robert Penn Warren, eds., *American Literature: The Makers and the Making,* Vol. 2 (New York: St. Martin's Press, 1973), 1370.

46 See n. 2, pp. 213–14, below.

47 Cf. Gilbert and Gubar's discussion of Anne Brontë's *The Tenant of Wildfell Hall* and of other women writers who inscribed their coerced but revolutionary status *as* writers within their works: "[the woman writer through her characters] produces a public art which she herself rejects as inadequate but which she secretly uses to discover a new aesthetic space for herself. In addition, she subverts her genteelly "feminine" works with personal representations which endure only in tracings, since her guilt about the impropriety of self-expression has caused her to efface her private drawings just as it has led her to efface herself" (*Madwoman in the Attic,* 81). As I will try to argue, feminist critical narratives such as Gilbert and Gubar's themselves purport to be "secretly" gender-inflected discourses. For a further discussion of this issue, namely the virtual exclusion of male readers from a feminist if not feminine text, see Kolodny, "A Map of Rereading," esp. 463–65, and her "Reply to Commentaries," 588–89, in the same volume of *New Literary History.*

48 Adrienne Rich, "Compulsory Heterosexuality and Lesbian Existence," *Signs* 5, no. 4 (Summer 1980):652 et passim. For Rich, of course, the notion of "lesbian continuum," the subliminal resistance of all women in past and present patriarchal societies, refers to "a range—through each woman's life and throughout history—of woman-identified experience; not simply the fact that a woman has had or consciously desired genital

sexual experience with another woman" (648). Not only has "heterosexuality" been imposed on women as a norm to which they must conform, so has "heterosexual romance" for the woman writer; male critics, according to Rich in *On Lies, Secrets, and Silence*, privilege such representational romances as a "key to [the woman artist's] life and work" (158).

49 Rich, *On Lies, Secrets, and Silence*, 158.
50 Kolodny, "Some Notes on Defining a 'Feminist Literary Criticism,'" 90.
51 Elizabeth Berg, "The Third Woman," *Diacritics* (Summer 1982), 19.
52 Alice Jardine, "Gynesis," *Diacritics* (Summer 1982), 58. The difference between French and American feminisms becomes apparent when we see an American feminist critic like Josephine Donovan use the concept of an "authentic" feminine identity. See her "Afterword: Critical Re-vision," in *Feminist Literary Criticism*, 77 et passim. French feminist critics, on the other hand, seeming to adopt what to radical American feminist critics resembles a neoconservative position, would basically if reservedly agree with Julia Kristeva's warning in Elaine Marks and Isabelle de Courtivron, eds., *New French Feminisms: An Anthology* (Amherst: University of Massachusetts Press, 1980), "that certain feminist demands revive a kind of naive romanticism, a belief in identity (the reverse of phallocratism), if we compare them to the experience of both poles of sexual difference as is found in the economy of Joycian or Artaudian prose. . . . I pay close attention to the particular aspect of the [avant-garde] work . . . which dissolves . . . even sexual identities" (138).
53 Jacobus, "Question of Language," 211, 210.
54 Cf. Kolodny's discussion of the relation between feminist criticism and male critical paradigms like Harold Bloom's, in "A Map of Rereading." Also cf. Gilbert and Gubar, *Madwoman in the Attic*, 73, and Mary Daly's feminist antimethod and/or self-conscious subversion of male-dominated discourses in *Gyn/ecology*, 22–29. In a different but no less revolutionary context, Deleuze and Guattari also argue for the sabotaging of the "major language" (see pp. 31–33, above).
55 See Rothman, *Woman's Proper Place*, 21–23.
56 *Letters*, Fields, 106.
57 Ibid., p. 246.
58 Cary, *Sarah Orne Jewett*, 141.
59 Sarah Orne Jewett, *A Marsh Island* (Boston: Houghton Mifflin, 1885), 181, 168. Dale explicitly notices the "patriarchal character to the [Owen] family" (109).
60 Ibid., p. 156.
61 *Letters*, Cary, 19, fn. 19. One should also note that Jewett's father practiced ornithology. Frost, *Sarah Orne Jewett* 22.
62 Jewett, *A Marsh Island*, 92.
63 Ibid.
64 Jewett, *A Country Doctor*, 270.

65 Ibid., pp. 133, 137.
66 Cf. Coppélia Kahn, "Excavating 'Those Dim Minoan Regions,'" who argues that feminist criticism should apply itself to discovering the maternal subtext of literary works, that is, should read "the text as the scene of interplay between infantile fantasy and manifest content" wherein the former "emanates from early childhood, when the child's most important relationship is with the mother" (36).
67 Frost, Sarah Orne Jewett, 22–23.
68 Jewett, A Marsh Island, 26, 64, 156, 154.
69 Cary, Sarah Orne Jewett, 138.
70 Jewett, A Country Doctor, 134.
71 For the significance of the grandmother in the girl's process of developing self-identity, see Elizabeth Abel, "(E)Merging Identities: The Dynamics of Female Friendship in Contemporary Fiction by Women," Signs 6, no. 3 (Spring 1981):427.
72 Juliet Mitchell, Psychoanalysis and Feminism (New York: Vintage Books, 1975), 96 and 57. In a way relevant to the position I will soon take, she also makes a "revised" Freudian perspective attentive to "the Minoan-Mycenean pre-Oedipal phase so crucial for femininity" (109 et passim).
73 Ibid., p. 97.
74 Nancy Chodorow, "Being and Doing: A Cross-Cultural Examination of the Socialization of Males and Females," in Woman in Sexist Society, 186.
75 Nancy Chodorow, The Reproduction of Mothering: Psychoanalysis and the Sociology of Gender (Berkeley: University of California Press, 1978), 123. Chodorow goes on to stress that the girl's turning away from the mother to the father "is at most a concentration on her father of a girl's genital, or erotic, cathexis. But a girl never gives up her mother as an internal or external love object, even if she does become heterosexual" (127). Rich, of course, disagrees with Chodorow's heterosexual orientation ("Compulsory Heterosexuality and Lesbian Existence," 636). For another clinical corroboration of the Chodorow-like position, see Irene Fast, "Developments in Gender Identity: Gender Differentiation in Girls," International Journal of Psycho-Analysis 60 (1979): esp. 451 and 457.
76 Chodorow, Reproduction of Mothering, 123.
77 Chodorow, "Being and Doing," 191, 192; Reproduction of Mothering, 127.
78 Frost discusses Jewett's especially close relation to her older sister Mary (Sarah Orne Jewett, 75–76).
79 Larzer Ziff, The American 1890s: Life and Times of a Lost Generation (New York: Viking Press, 1966), 283, discusses the negative attitudes of women toward childbearing in general.
80 Jewett, A Country Doctor, 120, 122.
81 Mitchell, Psychoanalysis and Feminism, 97.
82 Jean-Paul Sartre, What Is Literature? 16. Cf. n. 39, p. 211, below, the passage cited from Barbara Herrnstein Smith's "Contingencies of Value."

83 *Letters,* Cary, 30.
84 Jane Gallop, "The Ghost of Lacan, the Trace of Language," *Diacritics* (Winter 1975): 24, a review of Mitchell's *Psychoanalysis and Feminism.* For further discussion of Lacanian psychoanalysis from a feminist viewpoint, see Gallop's *The Daughter's Seduction: Feminism and Psychoanalysis* (Ithaca: Cornell University Press, 1982), and Anika Lemaire's feminine if not feminist consideration, *Jacques Lacan,* trans. David Macey with preface by Jacques Lacan (London: Routledge & Kegan Paul, 1977), esp. 82 ff., where she discusses Lacan's notion of "the Name of the Father" as "paternal metaphor" or "representative of the law which founds humanity, [whose] speech must be recognized by [from the child's position, the preoedipal] mother."
85 Geoffrey H. Hartman, "Psychoanalysis: The French Connection," in Geoffrey H. Hartman, ed., *Psychoanalysis and the Question of the Text* (Baltimore: Johns Hopkins University Press, 1978), 92.
86 Ibid.
87 Ibid., p. 94.
88 I use Roman Jakobson's definition of these tropes from his "The Metaphoric and Metonymic Poles," in *Critical Theory since Plato,* 1113 and esp. 1114. My discussion of "A White Heron" from p. 102 to the end of this chapter follows in spirit, at least, the critical principles used by Roland Barthes in his examination of Balzac's "Sarrasine" in *S/Z,* trans. Richard Miller (New York: Hill and Wang, 1974), especially where he claims to initiate "a process of nomination which is the essence of the reader's activity: to read is to struggle to name, to subject the sentences of the text to a semantic transformation. This transformation is erratic; it consists in hesitating among several names. . . . The connotator refers not so much to a name as to a synonymic complex whose common nucleus we sense even while the discourse is leading us toward other possibilities, toward other related signifieds: thus, reading is absorbed in a kind of metonymic skid, each synonym adding to its neighbor some new trait, some new departure" (92).
89 Jewett, "River Driftwood," 19.
90 Jewett, "A Winter Drive," 169. One could add to this list of trees as parental tropes. In "An October Ride" she notes how "old pines" stand "a little way back watching their children march in upon their inheritance, *as if they were ready to interfere and protect and defend*" (98; my italics). Or again from "A Winter Drive," "It seems as if the tree [like an internalized cathected parent] remembered what we remember; it is something more than the fact of its having been associated with our past" (167).
91 Jewett, "A Winter Drive," 178.
92 Richard A. Lanham, *A Handlist of Rhetorical Terms* (Berkeley: University of California Press, 1968), 83.
93 Cf. Joseph Campbell who argues that in primitive societies, certain birds

possess divine attributes which humans can attain by a kind of ritualistic imitation; thus, in climbing the tree, we could say, Sylvia metaphorically defines the place around it as holy ground, as a true "hermitage" or spiritual retreat consecrated as such by her vision of the heron. To quote from Campbell, *The Flight of the Wild Gander: Explorations in the Mythological Dimension* (New York: Viking Press, 1951; rpt. 1960), 167, "In many lands the soul has been pictured as a bird, and birds commonly appear as spiritual messengers: angels are modified birds. But the bird of the shaman is one of particular character and power, endowing him with an ability to fly in trance beyond all bounds of life, and yet return." Other "mythic" interpretations could be made of this after-all epiphanic moment with the white heron. Is it an allusion to the appearance of the New Testament angel — or even the Holy Ghost (Jewett was an Episcopalian), i.e., the Father's absent presence — announcing the Immaculate Conception to a Virgin Mary figure who will give birth to her own sacred innocence?

94 See Mitchell, *Psychoanalysis and Feminism*, 107: "The pre-Oedipal girl abandons her mother as love-object. . . . At the same time, she is likely to give up her clitoris too . . . her manual masturbation of it. She wants nothing to remind her of the wound to her narcissism — neither her all-responsible, 'castrated' mother, nor her own 'little penis.' The two go together. The girl realizes that she cannot possess her mother, hence the clitoris loses its active connotations, and when its sensitivity reemerges at puberty it is likely to be in a masturbatory role with passive aims . . . now either auto-erotic or as a preliminary to vaginal penetration."

95 Mary C. Rawlinson, "Psychiatric Discourse and the Feminine Voice," *Journal of Medicine and Philosophy* 8 (1982):172.

96 Jewett often alludes to South Berwick's shipbuilding past economy throughout her writings. See Jay Martin who discusses this topic in relation to an added section of *Pointed Firs*, "The Queen's Twin," (*Harvests of Change*, 143). Frost also mentions this shipbuilding patrimony in *Sarah Orne Jewett*, 1–3.

Chapter Three

1 Leo Marx, *The Machine in the Garden: Technology and the Pastoral Ideal* (New York: Oxford University Press, 1964; rpt. 1977), 23. The traditional definition of pastoral is as simple as its topos. For example, Eleanor Terry Lincoln, *Pastoral and Romance: Modern Essays in Criticism* (Englewood Cliffs: Prentice-Hall, 1969), 2, claims that the literary pastoral's "distinctions from other genres . . . ultimately rest on a view of life or a way of representing it"; it is the view of a pastoral "shepherd," who can take the form of "a hunter, a fisherman, a king, a child, or a shipwrecked mariner

. . . separated by mountain or meadow, forest or sea, from commitment to the sophisticated and active world of strife." Both this shepherd and the text's reader gain a perspective on this world that results in "a reassessment of accepted values . . . an education, sometimes so sudden as to be a revelation," which allows them to "re-emerge from the place apart to return, strengthened and enlightened, to active engagement in the imperfect world." In this chapter, I am concerned with pastoral more as a "representing" than as "a view of life," though of course the two are inextricably woven together. The sociohistorical as opposed to "literary" ramifications of a pastoral text would lead us to regard the obtrusive "machine in the garden" in "A White Heron" as pregnant with *reference*, that is, to a particular "regionalist" or cultural conflict (see n. 19, p. 192, above). But here I wish to regard this "machine" as an obstacle to Jewett's *literary imagination* of "the pastoral ideal," an imagination whose surrogate site in the story is the child heroine.

2 Marx, *Machine in the Garden,* 25.

3 Ibid., p. 31.

4 Henry Nash Smith, *Virgin Land: The American West as Symbol and Myth* (New York: Vintage Books, 1957), 138 ff.

5 Marx, *Machine in the Garden,* 91.

6 Smith, *Virgin Land,* 183.

7 Cf. pp. 63–64, above.

8 See Geoffrey H. Hartman's seminal discussion of the "westering" movement understood in poetic or textual terms in his "Poem and Ideology: A Study of Keats's 'To Autumn,'" *The Fate of Reading and Other Essays* (Chicago: University of Chicago Press, 1975), esp. 126–34.

9 Marx, *Machine in the Garden,* 177.

10 Frye, *Anatomy of Criticism,* 151–52. Also see Frye, "Myth, Fiction, and Displacement," n. 28, p. 197, above.

11 Cf. Ralph Waldo Emerson, "Nature," *Selections from Ralph Waldo Emerson,* ed. Stephen E. Whicher (Boston: Riverside Press, 1957), 23: "To speak truly, few adult persons can see nature. . . . The sun illuminates only the eye of the man, but shines into the eye and the heart of a child."

12 Annette Kolodny, *The Lay of the Land: Metaphor as Experience and History in American Life and Letters* (Chapel Hill: University of North Carolina Press, 1975), 68.

13 Fuller, *Woman in the Nineteenth Century,* 109.

14 *Kolodny, Lay of the Land,* 4, 14, 22, 60, 66, et passim. Kolodny argues, for example, that in his *Letters from an American Farmer,* Crèvecoeur's narrative shows the gradual failure to imagine "the pastoral compromise"; he comes to doubt whether Americans can sustain or "husband" an agrarian relation to the land because of their desire to exploit and civilize "her," even as they seek more ("virgin"/"mother") wilderness they find attractive in and of itself.

15 See p. 13, above.

16 Jewett, "From a Mournful Villager," 131.

17 Ibid., p. 138.

18 Kolodny, *Lay of the Land,* 60 et passim.

19 Emerson, "Nature," 55. Larzer Ziff discusses the social and political American climate in which Emerson began his career as an essayist and speaker in *Literary Democracy: The Declaration of Cultural Independence in America* (New York: Viking Press, 1981), 13–30. Emerson's influence on Jewett seems clear and affects the way she writes about nature even in her letters. In what is virtually a gloss of Emerson's "transparent eyeball" experience in "Nature," Jewett writes Annie Fields (*Letters,* Fields, 51–52): "When one goes out of doors and wanders about alone at such a time, how wonderfully one becomes part of nature, like an atom of quicksilver against a great mass. I hardly keep my separate consciousness, but go on and on until the mood has spent itself."

20 Jewett, "A Winter Drive," 182.

21 See Kolodny, "A Map of Rereading," and Gilbert and Gubar, *Madwoman in the Attic.*

22 Robert O. Paxton, "Web-Footed Gentry," *New York Review of Books* 26 (December 20, 1979):13, mentions this fact in his review of James Hancock and Hugh Elliott's *The Herons of the World.* Approximately ten years later, in 1896, Charles B. Grinnell would help found the first official Audubon society in Massachusetts.

23 John James Audubon, *The Art of Audubon: The Complete Birds and Mammals* (New York: Times Books, 1979), Plates 370 (p. 384), 368 (p. 386) and 374 (p. 391).

24 Kolodny, *Lay of the Land,* 79.

25 Quoted in ibid., 76, from Audubon's *Delineations of American Scenery and Character.*

26 Henry David Thoreau, "The Allegash and East Branch," from *The Maine Woods,* collected in *Walden and Other Writings of Henry David Thoreau,* ed. Brooks Atkinson (New York: Modern Library, 1950), 576.

27 Henry David Thoreau, *Walden,* in *Walden and Other Writings of Henry David Thoreau,* 141.

28 Ibid.

29 Ibid., pp. 156–57.

30 Ibid., pp. 176–77.

31 Thoreau, *Maine Woods,* 551.

32 *Letters,* Cary, 18. Martin, *Harvests of Change,* 142, argues that the "children's stories" written by the New England women regionalist writers "dramatize the conventional virtues of the weakened, later nineteenth-century Protestant ethic: self-reliance, individualism, honesty, thrift, hard work, and prudence. Essentially, they were idealizing the lost youth of New England in writing of the simpler virtues of childhood."

33 Margaret Fuller, "Children's Books," collected in *Woman in the Nineteenth Century,* 312; my italics.

34 Barbara Packer depicts such investments as explicitly fairy tale elements, though not with reference to Jewett's story, in *Emerson's Fall: A New Interpretation of the Major Essays* (New York: Continuum, 1982), 56.

35 William Empson, *Some Versions of Pastoral* (Norfolk: New Directions, 1960), 241 ff. In 1872, one year or so after Jewett ceased using pseudonyms, in particular "*Alice* Eliot," she writes to her aunt about how she hopes "Fannie likes 'the Alice book.'" As Cary records, Fannie, or Frances Perry Dudley, "observed that 'The first copy of *Alice in Wonderland* to arrive in town was read by young and old until its binding was broken" (*Letters,* Cary, 21 and 22 (fn. 9]).

36 Bruno Bettelheim, *The Uses of Enchantment: The Meaning and Importance of Fairy Tales* (New York: Vintage Books, 1977), 26; also see his introduction for a discussion of further fairy tale elements. Harold E. Toliver, *Pastoral Forms and Attitudes* (Berkeley: University of California Press, 1971), esp. 363–65, discusses the appearance of the trope metamorphosis, the dissolving of the boundaries between human and "natural" existence, in the genre of "pastoral romance": In the "Ovidian" tradition, the change from human into "beastly" identity—as we noted previously to be the case with Sylvia and the white heron (see pp. 79–82)—"is merely one stage in a rebirth that eventually restores harmony between the hero and nature" (Toliver, 364). For a feminist revision of this pastoral-motivated trope, also an element of the fairy tale, see n. 28, p. 197, above. Also cf. Gilbert and Gubar, *Madwoman in the Attic,* for an example of a feminist revision of the Snow White fairy tale. They argue that the woman is here split into a male-idealized "angelic" figure and a contemptuous "monster" kept transfixed before the "mirror, mirror on the wall" (36–44). In this context, Jewett's attraction to and evasion of the Sleeping Beauty tale (as I will maintain) could again be understood in a feminist ideological perspective, i.e., as a subtle means of rejecting "Prince Charming."

37 *Letters,* Cary, 18.

38 "An October Ride," 100; Charles Perrault, *Popular Tales* (Oxford: Clarendon Press, 1878), and *The Complete Grimms' Fairy Tales* (New York: Pantheon Books, 1972). Annis Pratt, "Women and Nature in Modern Fiction," alludes to Jewett's story in the context of this fairy tale: "The advent of the Prince Charming and his stirring of the heroine's latent femininity would itself be the moment of epiphany in the usual fairy tale or narrative" (478).

39 For Princess Aurora, see, for example, *The Sleeping Beauty and Other Fairy Tales,* retold in English by Sir Arthur Quiller-Couch (London: Hodder and Stroughton, 1911).

40 Bettelheim, *Uses of Enchantment,* 232. Another aspect of the story calls

for Bettelheim's analysis along these same lines. In both the Perrault and Grimm versions of this tale, Sleeping Beauty pricks her hand on a spindle, a situation that Bettelheim associates with an adolescent girl's first experience of menstruation (233). Sylvia, of course, does not prick her hand, but she does climb a tree whose "sharp dry twigs caught and held her and scratched her like angry talons" (xx); she does climb down from the tree "ready to cry . . . because her fingers ache and her lamed feet slip" (xxii); and, in a suggestion and displacement of loss of blood, she does return to the farmstead "paler than ever . . . her worn old frock . . . smeared with pine pitch" (xxii).

41 Bettelheim, *Uses of Enchantment,* 234.
42 Ibid., p. 205.
43 Perrault, *Popular Tales,* 13.

Chapter Four

1 Richard Poirier, *A World Elsewhere: The Place of Style in American Literature* (New York: Oxford University Press, 1966), 5.

2 See p. 44, above; also *Letters,* Cary, 91 and 120.

3 See pp. 31–33, above. Debate over a national American literature was, of course, a critical commonplace throughout the nineteenth century in the United States. For a discussion as well as demystification of the itself-mythic "independent" force of the American Declaration of Independence, see Gary Wills, *Inventing America: Jefferson's Declaration of Independence* (New York: Doubleday, 1978), esp. xiii–xxvi and 334–69.

4 Cary's introduction to *Letters,* 16. Cary, *Sarah Orne Jewett,* 52, suggests that Jewett "gravitated toward [Flaubert] because of mutual aims rather than . . . consciously modeled her style upon his." Josephine Donovan, on the other hand, wants to maintain that Jewett's attraction to Flaubert and his views of writing defines her as a kind of proto-French Symbolist writer (*Sarah Orne Jewett* 135).

5 *Letters,* Fields, 112.

6 *Letters,* Cary, 82; *Letters,* Fields, 102.

7 *Letters,* Fields, 15.

8 F. O. Matthiessen, *Sarah Orne Jewett,* 56 and 88 f. For further reference to Jewett's relation to Whittier, see Frost, *Sarah Orne Jewett,* 70, 78, 83, et passim.

9 *Letters,* Fields, 83, 121–22.

10 Matthiesen, *Sarah Orne Jewett,* 151; Cary, *Sarah Orne Jewett,* 84–85, 97–99, 149, et passim; Jewett also owned a four-volume set of Poe's works (*Books from the Bequest of Theodore Jewett Eastman,* 37). See Gilbert and Gubar, *Madwoman in the Attic,* and Kolodny, "A Map of Rereading," for a possible feminist interpretation of this situation. The literary

influence of male New England literary precursors like Emerson (n. 19, p. 205, above), Thoreau (pp. 129–33, above), and Hawthorne seems fairly clear. Contemporary critics were quick to register the stylistic resemblance between Jewett's writings and Hawthorne's. See Julia R. Tutwiler, "Two New England Writers—in Relation to Their Art and to Each Other" (1903), in *Appreciation of Sarah Orne Jewett,* 28, and Charles Miner Thompson, "The Art of Miss Jewett," in this same volume, who finds "in Miss Jewett's writings . . . many traces of [Hawthorne's] influence. . . . [The] likeness is plain in such stories as 'The Gray Man' and 'The Landscape Chamber'" (40).

11 Quoted in *Letters,* Cary, 65, fn. 2.

12 *Letters,* Fields, 196.

13 Ibid., 72.

14 Ibid., pp. 72–73.

15 *Letters,* Cary, 64–65.

16 Preface to *The House of the Seven Gables,* collected in *The Complete Novels and Selected Tales of Nathaniel Hawthorne,* ed. Norman Holmes Pearson (New York: Modern Library, 1937), 243; also quoted in Poirier, *A World Elsewhere,* 7. My interpretation of Hawthorne clearly runs counter to Quentin Anderson's thesis of Hawthorne's being the exception in American literary history in taking "society for granted as the ground of our humanity" and in not flirting with the antisocial vision of "the absolutism of the self." Anderson, *The Imperial Self: An Essay in American Literary and Cultural History* (New York: Random House, 1971), ix.

17 For further discussion of Hawthorne's use of prefaces as sketches and their relation to his art and readers, see James M. Cox's two essays, "Emerson and Hawthorne," *Virginia Quarterly* 45 (Winter 1969): esp. 99–107, and "The Scarlet Letter: Through the Old Manse and the Custom House," ibid., 51 (Summer 1975): 432–47.

18 Nathaniel Hawthorne, "The Old Manse: The Author Makes the Reader Acquainted with His Abode," *Hawthorne: Selected Tales and Sketches,* intro. by Hyatt H. Waggoner (New York: Holt, Rinehart and Winston, 1973), 574.

19 Edgar Allan Poe, "Review of Nathaniel Hawthorne's *Twice-Told Tales,*" *Edgar Allan Poe: Selected Prose, Poetry and Eureka,* intro. by W. H. Auden (New York: Holt, Rinehart and Winston, 1950), 452. Cf. Cox, "Emerson and Hawthorne": "The reader [of Hawthorne's *The Scarlet Letter* through the Custom House Preface] is made to read allegorically an action whose essence is always anti-allegorical" (101).

20 Hawthorne, "Old Manse," 581.

21 Ibid., p. 583.

22 Nathaniel Hawthorne, "Preface to *The Snow-Image and Other Twice-Told Tales,*" *Hawthorne: Selected Tales and Sketches,* 590.

23 Nathaniel Hawthorne, *The Scarlet Letter,* ed. Harry Levin (Boston: Houghton Mifflin, 1960), 47.
24 Ibid., p. 39.
25 Ibid., p. 47.
26 Indeed, the actual site of Jewett's *Deephaven* sketches was York, Maine, a locale she was reticent in specifying: "Since 'The Shore House' was written I have identified Deephaven with it more and more. Still I don't like to have people say that I mean York when I say Deephaven" (*Letters,* Cary, 32). We could make an even more bizarre case for the way "A White Heron" determines its literary minority vis-à-vis Hawthorne's major influence. Jewett's story, we recall, first appeared in a volume entitled *A White Heron and Other Stories.* In this collection appeared "The Gray Man," a story which not only Thompson (n. 10, above) but Cary, *Sarah Orne Jewett,* thinks bears the impress of "The Minister's Black Veil" insofar as it represents "character implied by externalities — one's looks, clothes, habitation" (53), and concerns a Minister Hooper-like unsmiling figure clearly personifying death (an unusual Jewett topos) who bursts upon a wedding party, leading the bridegroom, symbol of "mankind . . . to remove [the gray man's] shadow from present happiness, however transitory," by showing him the door (99). Focusing on this collection as itself a "text," we can note how this allusion to "The Minister's Black Veil" has already become an allusion to Hawthorne's "The Gray Champion" by its very title, a story which also possesses certain thematic affinities with "The Gray Man." Just as Hawthorne's "gray" figure abruptly appears and disappears in times of American "darkness, and adversity, and peril" ("The Gray Champion," *Hawthorne: Selected Tales and Sketches,* 148), Jewett's "gray" figure appears and "disappears summarily and is later glimpsed by a wounded farmer's boy in battle" (Cary, 99). Yet where Jewett's figure invites allegorical closure (the groom shuts "death" out of doors), Hawthorne's figure remains ambiguous, a personification *verging* on becoming, in the words of the story, a "type of New England's hereditary spirit" whenever "domestic tyranny [should] oppress us, or the invader's step pollute our soil" (148). Inviting such closure, Jewett's figure also seems universal or nonspecific; on the other hand, Hawthorne's "The Gray Champion," we could say, "champions" the "American" cause and attempts to assert the cultural continuity between Puritan theocracy and post-Revolutionary democracy—a major American thematic. Hawthorne's story, however, is also possibly ironic when one considers the narrator's possibly jingoistic political stance, his nationalistic paranoia about the "invader's step" that could "pollute our soil."
  In short, the signification of Hawthorne's story is itself "gray," in marked contrast to Jewett's story's expectancy of semiotic closure and its uncritical American thematic. Jewett's semiotically determinate and thematically evasive practice suggests her wish to avoid comparison with

Hawthorne's "gray"—not to mention his "black"—story's semiotic inde-
terminacies and critical American mythoi. More important, appearing
in a collection entitled and keynoted by "A White Heron," "The Gray Man"
could easily serve as an unconscious middle term whereby the sketchy
or quasi-determinate appearance of this "white" story escapes comparison
with Hawthorne's sketchy tales and especially their projection of an indeterminate mode of textual expectancies. *A White Heron and Other
Stories* thus becomes a means for Jewett to determine the repressed intertextual locus of "A White Heron." We could say that she here displaces
Hawthorne's "black" influence on and by her "gray" story; and insofar
as the latter invites comparison with Hawthorne's "gray" story, she makes
it more invisible, so to speak, by her "white" story which after all involves
a "gray-eyed" child heroine.

Caring to write only a simple and brief rural tale, Jewett, like the heroine of "A White Heron," encounters by "accident" the unspecified (the
hunter is nameless) but still "young" precedent of "Hawthorne," his tales
and sketches. And like the heroine before the hunter when he first asks
her name, "she"—the story—when asked about "her" literary identity or
affiliation, "hung her head as if the stem of it were broken" and answers
only "with much effort." Almost a repressed image of Hawthorne himself, a "shy" and also "pale" girl, Sylvia, figure of the story itself, is here
perhaps associated not so much with a broken flower as with a broken
"white hawthorn" shrub or little tree (connoted by her very name) *sans*
its blossom or full name (she "managed to answer 'Sylvy' "—not "Sylvia"),
that is, without its full literary self-identity's being revealed. "A White
Heron," then, is but an erased version of "A White Hawthorne."

27 *Letters,* Fields, 75.
28 Ibid., p. 73.
29 If we assume that Fields's 1890 dating of this letter is accurate, Kipling
   would not yet have moved to Vermont for the first of his three winter
   visits (1892), hence would have been for Jewett an "English" writer—if
   indeed she could ever have considered him an "American" writer on the
   basis of these visits. Jewett "met" Kipling on her third trip to Europe in
   1898 (Cary, *Sarah Orne Jewett,* 12).
30 Charles W. Brewster, *Rambles about Portsmouth: Sketches of Persons,
   Localities and Incidents of Two Centuries,* Vol. 1 (Portsmouth: C. W. Brewster & Son, 1859) and Vol. 2 (1869) "with a Biographical Sketch of the
   Author by Wm. H. Y. Hackett," 272–73. Attesting to this work's popularity, the second edition contained an index in small typeface of the persons mentioned in both volumes.
31 Ibid., 2:21.
32 *Dictionary of American Biography,* Vol. 3 (New York: Charles Scribner's
   Sons, 1929), 31.
33 Jewett became close friends with Alice Longfellow; on one of her trips

with her and other friends, "we played like a parcel of children" (letter quoted in Frost, *Sarah Orne Jewett,* 79). She also deviated from her usual reticence and gave a public reading to help raise money for a Longfellow memorial (*Letters,* Cary, 59, fn. 1). The "Alice" part of her early pseudonym, "Alice Eliot" (cf. n. 4, p. 194, above), may have originated in the child Alice that appears in Longfellow's famous poem "The Children's Hour." If so, then one could argue that Jewett de-nominates herself as a "minor" writer from the very beginning of her career.

34 *Dictionary of American Biography,* 3:30.

35 Ibid., p. 31.

36 *Letters,* Cary, 45.

37 Ibid., p. 63.

38 *Letters,* Fields, 47. Donovan, *Sarah Orne Jewett,* 124, cites this passage to show Jewett's sense of "great literature" and her "awareness of a central problem the woman writer has had to face . . . how to shed herself of the intrusions and distractions that keep her from having the time to sustain imaginative vision" (124–25). Another example of Jewett's sketchification of novels appears in a letter where she claims that even "good" novels have a virtually "soap opera" effect on her, that is, inspire an all-encompassing if transitory desire to "eat" and make them disappear rather than to "taste" them for long periods: "Novels are good as they go along. It is only when they stop that you take it in that the pretty bubble is made of soap suds. . . . what a delightful thing it is to have the mood for books on one and the chance to give up everything for it, but with me it doesn't last many days, that enchanting and desperate state of devouring cover and all" (*Letters,* Fields, 165–66).

39 Jewett, *A Marsh Island,* 8 and 111. Donovan, *Sarah Orne Jewett,* 63, argues that in this novel Jewett has "the most empathy for Dick Dale," namely, "the difficult problem of loving the rural world but realizing the limitations it imposed on his own intellectual and artistic ambitions. This clearly was Jewett's own dilemma. Dick's choice of the city and professional development parallels Jewett's own decision." As regards my argument here that Jewett writes her texts in relation to a socioartistic system of values—a canonical situation—cf. Barbara Herrnstein Smith, "Contingencies of Value," 24, where she argues that the writer's imagination of her readers effectively appends the images within the text being constructed: "For, in selecting this word, adjusting that turn of phrase . . . the author is all the while testing the local and global effectiveness of each decision by impersonating in advance his or her various presumptive audiences. . . . Every literary work . . . is thus the product of a complex evaluative feedback loop that embraces not only the ever-shifting economy of the artist's own interests and resources as they evolve during and in reaction to the process of composition, but also all the shifting economies of his or her assumed and imagined audiences, including those

who do not yet exist but whose emergent interests, variable conditions of encounter, and rival sources of gratification the artist will attempt to predict—or will intuitively surmise—and to which . . . his or her own sense of the fittingness of each decision will be responsive." Needless to say, I would maintain that these evaluational economies of writing in terms of reception occur in Jewett's case in an ideologically unconscious manner.

40 *Letters,* Cary, 30.

41 Ibid., p. 29.

42 *Letters,* Fields, 62–63.

43 See Robert E. Spiller, *The Cycle of American Literature* (New York: New American Library, 1956), 116–19. Larzer Ziff, *American 1890s,* 286 ff., discusses Jewett in relation to this consumerist literary marketplace demand. He also notes Henry James's awareness of the separation between businessmen and their cultured wives who, "with their free use of leisure, were the chief consumers of novels and therefore were increasingly becoming producers of them" (275).

44 The average payment to authors and contributors to magazines like the *Atlantic* postbellum America "was ten dollars a page, or three-quarters of a cent a word"—hence, the de facto monetary value of a poem was greater than that of a story. Frank L. Mott, *A History of American Magazines: 1885–1905,* Vol. 3 (New York: Appleton, 1930), 39. Cf. Martin, *Harvests of Change,* 2–24, concerning postbellum changes in the literary relations of production and consumption effected by the rise of popular magazines.

45 *Letters,* Cary, 30.

46 Ibid., p. 44.

47 *Letters,* Fields, 27.

48 Ibid., p. 112.

49 *Letters,* Cary, 46.

50 Jewett, "Confessions of a House-Breaker," 239.

51 Weber and Weber, *Bibliography of the Published Writings of Sarah Orne Jewett,* 10.

52 See letter cited on p. 145, above. That Jewett read together and often with Annie Fields is clear; for example, she writes Fields, "I long to read [Arnold's essays on Celtic poetry] all with you" (*Letters,* Fields, 54). Also see Jewett, *A Country Doctor,* 149.

53 *Letters,* Fields, 69.

54 Ibid., p. 17.

55 Ibid., p. 118.

56 See Susan Gubar, "'The Blank Page' and the Issues of Female Creativity." Jewett's author-disavowing sense of creativity also appears in her "atom of quick-silver" letter: "Good heavens! what a wonderful kind of chemistry it is that evolves all the details of a story and writes them presently in one flash of time!" (*Letters,* Fields, 51–52).

57 *Letters,* Cary, 29.
58 Ibid., p. 44.
59 Elias Lieberman, *The American Short Story: A Study of the Influence of Locality in Its Development* (Ridgewood: Editory, 1912; rpt. Folcroft Press, 1970), 45.
60 Jewett, "An October Ride," 93–94.
61 Ibid., p. 106.
62 Ibid., p. 110.
63 Ibid., pp. 107, 114.
64 Ibid., p. 115.
65 Jewett, "From a Mournful Villager," 127.
66 See pp. 12–13, above.
67 *Letters,* Fields, 81.

Epilogue

1 Marjorie Pryse, "Introduction to the Norton Edition," in Sarah Orne Jewett, *The Country of the Pointed Firs and Other Stories,* ed. Mary Ellen Chase (New York: W. W. Norton, 1981), xiii. All references to *Pointed Firs* will be to this edition, by page numbers in parentheses. Warner Berthoff, *Fictions and Events,* 263; Jay Martin, *Harvests of Change,* 145–47; and Josephine Donovan, *Sarah Orne Jewett,* 100 and 104.
2 We can see this reserve in operation in Henry James's unpublished eulogy of Jewett cited in Matthiessen, *Sarah Orne Jewett,* 136–37. James tries to justify his assessment of Jewett's "sober and tender . . . temperately touched . . . beautiful little quantum of achievement" by noting that her "admirable gift . . . would have deserved some more pointed commemoration than . . . her young course of production" actually revealed. James's periphrastic praise of her writing is that of a would-be major writer paying tribute to a literary peer who wrote works that were filled with promise but doubtless were "little" or "minor" for this very reason—especially when compared with but also including her own "pointed" exception. Perhaps the most outstanding example of critical praise for *Pointed Firs* remains Willa Cather's. In her later years, Jewett served as a kind of mentor for Cather who, in her 1925 edition of *Pointed Firs,* xviii–xix, praised it as one of three American classics, the other two being Hawthorne's *The Scarlet Letter* and Twain's *Huckleberry Finn.* But in *Not under Forty* (New York: Alfred A. Knopf, 1936), Cather seems to equivocate slightly on her earlier estimation by making this comparison in terms of "style" (95) and noting that Jewett "was content to be slight, if she could be true" (89). Mathiessen, with an unconscious patriarchal sleight of hand, canonizes Jewett on the basis of *Pointed Firs,* claiming she deserves this accolade only when she "is secure within her limits,"

that is, because "she achieved style" or the fusion of her materials, technique, and personality. True, "style" takes her work beyond the mere "historical value . . . the clumsiest Dreiser novels will have"; but at the same time, this "style" leaves her only a membrane away from literary nothingness: "Without style Sarah Jewett's material would be too slight to attract a second glance. With it she has created—not a world, but a township in the State of Maine" (145–46).

Critics of *Pointed Firs* since Matthiessen lapse into the same qualifications. Carlos Baker's judgment that *Pointed Firs* is "the best piece of regional fiction to have come out of nineteenth century America" (quoted in Frost, *Sarah Orne Jewett*, 140; also in Cary, *Sarah Orne Jewett*, 144) carries with it the qualification that local color writing is of more interest to the literary historian than to text-oriented critics. Warner Berthoff, for example, terms *Pointed Firs* "a masterpiece of the local color school," which he says "is not at all to talk it down" (261); yet he comes to state that this work qualifies Jewett as at best "a scrupulous minor artist" (243) and serves as a prelude to Sherwood Anderson's "more ambitious work" of American regional writing, *Winesburg, Ohio* (260). Even as a "triumph of style," as Irving Howe calls it ("The Country of the Pointed Firs," *Celebrations and Attacks* [New York: Horizon Press, 1979], 134), *Pointed Firs* exemplifies one of America's better "minor works" since the world it evokes "cannot sustain profound exegeses or symbol hunting."

3 William Flint Thrall and Addison Hibbard, *A Handbook to Literature,* rev. by C. Hugh Holman (New York: Odyssey Press, 1960), 266.

4 As the narrator leaves Dunnet Landing, "Mrs. Todd seemed able and warm-hearted and quite absorbed in her bustling industries, but her distant figure looked mateless and appealing, with something about it that was strangely self-possessed and mysterious" (131). From the very beginning, the narrator, we could say, mystifies Mrs. Todd's character, gives her a certain "literary" depth or aura of priestesslike proportions: "[Mrs. Todd] stood in the centre of a braided rug, and its rings of black and gray seemed to circle about her feet in the dim light. Her height and massiveness in the low room gave her the look of a huge sibyl, while the strange fragrance of the mysterious herb blew in from the little garden" (8). The most famous "literary" mystification of Mrs. Todd is a classical allusion to Antigone after she recounts to the narrator the story of her lost love and dead husband: "There was something lonely and solitary about her great determined shape. She might have been Antigone alone on the Theban plain. It is not often given in a noisy world to come to the places of great grief and silence. An absolute, archaic grief possessed this countrywoman; she seemed like a renewal of some historic soul, with her sorrows and the remoteness of a daily life busied with rustic simplicities and the scents of primeval herbs" (49). Such "archaic" allusions, of course, distract us from more immediate and perhaps more pressing literary prece-

dents, that of a "possessed" Coleridgean "sibyl" and a "rustic" Wordsworthian "Michael" whose simple life and "sorrows" elevate her to "historic" or poetic status. All three passages juxtapose images of Mrs. Todd's enduring life ("bustling industries," "the little garden," "rustic simplicities") with images of her deathlike separation from others (her "mateless" appearance, the "circle about her feet," her "lonely and solitary" and "absolute, archaic grief"), so that for the narrator she represents a kind of life in death—the reverse of death in life that defines Coleridge's Mariner. For a further unspecified allusion to "The Ancient Mariner" structuration of the relationship between the narrator and Mrs. Todd, see the later-added "The Foreigner," esp. 160–68, where, in relation to the topic of "ghost stories," the narrator notes how "Mrs. Todd glanced . . . at me, with a strange absent look, and I was really afraid that she was going to tell me something that would haunt my thoughts on every dark stormy night as long as I lived" (160).

5 Matthiessen, *Sarah Orne Jewett*, 144–45.
6 Donovan, *Sarah Orne Jewett*, 99.
7 Cary, *Sarah Orne Jewett*, 146.
8 Quoted in Frost, *Sarah Orne Jewett*, 105. Matthiessen, *Sarah Orne Jewett*, 144, speaks of Jewett's tendency to use "little" and "dear" adjectives in her letters.
9 *Letters*, Cary, 51; also quoted in Donovan, *Sarah Orne Jewett*, 133–34.

INDEX

Designed by Richard Hendel

Composed by Metricomp, Grundy Center, Iowa

Manufactured by Thomson-Shore, Inc., Dexter, Michigan

Text and display lines are set in Sabon

Library of Congress Cataloging in Publication Data

Renza, Louis A., 1940–
    "A White heron" and the question of minor literature.
    (The Wisconsin project on American writers)
    Includes bibliographical references and index.
        1. Jewett, Sarah Orne, 1849–1909. A white heron.
    2. Canon (Literature) I. Title.
PS2132.W53R4 1984   813'.4   84-40157
ISBN 0-299-09960-1